Visual C++ .N[...]
For Dummies

Cheat Sheet

KU-054-309

The Debug Toolbar

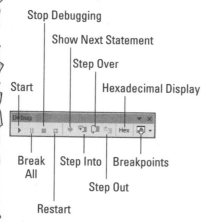

Stop Debugging
Show Next Statement
Step Over
Start
Hexadecimal Display

Break All
Step Into
Breakpoints
Step Out
Restart

The Build Toolbar

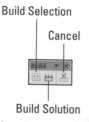

Build Selection
Cancel
Build Solution

Regular Expression-Matching Commands

.	Match any single character
*	Match any number of characters
+	Match one or more of the preceding characters
^	Match the beginning of a line
$	Match the end of a line
[ ]	Match one or more specific characters
[^]	Match anything but specific characters
[-]	Match any letter in range of characters

Keyboard Shortcuts

Indent a group of lines	Select the lines and then press Tab
Outdent a group of lines	Select the lines and then press Shift+Tab
Look for matching () {} <> or []	Press Ctrl+] to move between the opening (, { ,<, or [and the closing), }, >, or]
Set a bookmark	Move the cursor to where you want to place the bookmark and then press Ctrl+K, Ctrl+K to set it
Jump to a bookmark	Press Ctrl+K, Ctrl+N to find the next bookmark in the file. Press Ctrl+K, Ctrl+P to find the previous bookmark.
Switch editor windows	Press Ctrl+Tab or Ctrl+F6 to cycle to the next editor window. Press Shift+Ctrl+Tab or Shift+Ctrl+F6 to cycle to the preceding editor window.
Build the solution	Ctrl+Shift+B
Compile the current file	Ctrl+F7
Debug the program	F5
Stop debugging	Shift+F5
Run the program without debugging	Ctrl+F5
Insert or remove a breakpoint	Ctrl+B
Step over	F10
Step into	F11
Step out	Shift+F11
Get help on a keyword	F1
Switch to the next code window	Ctrl+Tab or Ctrl+F6
Close the current window	Ctrl+F4
Complete word with IntelliSense	Ctrl+Spacebar or Alt+right arrow

For Dummies: Bestselling Book Series for Beginners

Visual C++ .NET For Dummies®

Cheat Sheet

Creating Managed C++ Applications

1. Choose File⇨New⇨Project..

2. Under Project Types, select Visual C++ Projects.

3. Under Templates, select Managed C++ Application.

4. In the Name box, type the name of your project.

   This creates a folder with the same name as your project in the Visual Studio Projects folder in your My Documents folder. If you want the folder to be created somewhere else, type the folder's name in the Location box, or click the Browse button to bring up a folder browse window.

5. Click OK.

Class View Icons

Protected member function

Class

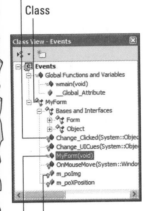

Protected data member

Public member function

Creating Unmanaged C++ Applications

1. Choose File⇨New⇨Project.

2. Under Project Types, select Visual C++ Projects.

3. Under Templates, select Win32 Project.

4. In the Name box, type the name of your project.

5. Click OK.

   The Win32 Application Wizard appears.

6. Click Application Settings.

   The Wizard displays the settings you can change.

7. Click Finish.

Data Types

Type	Description
double	Floating-point number
int	Integer
string	Text, such as "Hello World"
char	Single character
float	Floating-point number with less precision than a double
long	32-bit integer
short	16-bit integer
unsigned	Precedes int, long, and short to indicate that the number is always positive

Hungry Minds™

For Dummies: Bestselling Book Series for Beginners

...Fo
Dum

BESTSE
BOOK S

For Dummies b
aren't really dur
computing mak
a down-to-eart
fears and build
survival guide f

*"I like my cop
friends; now*

— *Irene C., Orwell, Ohio*

*"Quick, concise, nontechnical
and humorous."*
— *Jay A., Elburn, Illinois*

WITHDRAWN

*"Thanks, I needed this book. Now I
can sleep at night."*

— *Robin F., British Colum*

Already, millions of
made For Dummies
computer book seri
So, if you're looking
learn about comput
give you a helping h

ungry Minds™

1/01

Visual C++®.NET
FOR
DUMMIES®

by Michael Hyman and Bob Arnson

Hungry Minds™

Best-Selling Books • Digital Downloads • e-Books • Answer Networks • e-Newsletters • Branded Web Sites • e-Learning

New York, NY ◆ Cleveland, OH ◆ Indianapolis, IN

Visual C++® .NET For Dummies®

Published by
Hungry Minds, Inc.
909 Third Avenue
New York, NY 10022
www.hungryminds.com
www.dummies.com

Library of Congress Control Number: 2001094146

ISBN: 0-7645-0868-7

Printed in the United States of America

10 9 8 7 6 5 4 3 2 1

1B/RU/RR/QR/IN

Distributed in the United States by Hungry Minds, Inc.

Distributed by CDG Books Canada Inc. for Canada; by Transworld Publishers Limited in the United Kingdom; by IDG Norge Books for Norway; by IDG Sweden Books for Sweden; by IDG Books Australia Publishing Corporation Pty. Ltd. for Australia and New Zealand; by TransQuest Publishers Pte Ltd. for Singapore, Malaysia, Thailand, Indonesia, and Hong Kong; by Gotop Information Inc. for Taiwan; by ICG Muse, Inc. for Japan; by Intersoft for South Africa; by Eyrolles for France; by International Thomson Publishing for Germany, Austria and Switzerland; by Distribuidora Cuspide for Argentina; by LR International for Brazil; by Galileo Libros for Chile; by Ediciones ZETA S.C.R. Ltda. for Peru; by WS Computer Publishing Corporation, Inc., for the Philippines; by Contemporanea de Ediciones for Venezuela; by Express Computer Distributors for the Caribbean and West Indies; by Micronesia Media Distributor, Inc. for Micronesia; by Chips Computadoras S.A. de C.V. for Mexico; by Editorial Norma de Panama S.A. for Panama; by American Bookshops for Finland.

For general information on Hungry Minds' products and services please contact our Customer Care Department within the U.S. at 800-762-2974, outside the U.S. at 317-572-3993 or fax 317-572-4002.

For sales inquiries and reseller information, including discounts, premium and bulk quantity sales, and foreign-language translations, please contact our Customer Care Department at 800-434-3422, fax 317-572-4002, or write to Hungry Minds, Inc., Attn: Customer Care Department, 10475 Crosspoint Boulevard, Indianapolis, IN 46256.

For information on licensing foreign or domestic rights, please contact our Sub-Rights Customer Care Department at 212-884-5000.

For information on using Hungry Minds' products and services in the classroom or for ordering examination copies, please contact our Educational Sales Department at 800-434-2086 or fax 317-572-4005.

For press review copies, author interviews, or other publicity information, please contact our Public Relations Department at 317-572-3168 or fax 317-572-4168.

For authorization to photocopy items for corporate, personal, or educational use, please contact Copyright Clearance Center, 222 Rosewood Drive, Danvers, MA 01923, or fax 978-750-4470.

Hungry Minds™ is a trademark of Hungry Minds, Inc.

About the Authors

Michael Hyman is the CTO of DataChannel. He previously worked on XML, Internet, and media technology at Microsoft and has hung out at various shrink-wrap software companies up and down the West Coast. Michael has written numerous other computer books, including *Dynamic HTML For Dummies, Visual J++ For Dummies,* and *PC Roadkill.* Michael has a degree in Electrical Engineering and Computer Science from Princeton University. When not busy working, he sits on his surfboard waiting for waves, pumps iron, and changes diapers.

Bob Arnson is a software engineer at a major software and services company. Before re-joining the professional geek corps, he spent years editing and writing online as well as dead-tree publications, including *VB Tech Journal* and *VC++ Professional.* Bob has written several other books on Visual Basic, Visual C++, and Borland C++.

Dedications

To Miriam Beth and Gabrielle Mia

— Michael Hyman

To Mario

— Bob Arnson

Authors' Acknowledgments

Special thanks to my wife, Sarah, who has put up with my late night writing sessions and the accompanying bleary-eyed exhaustion from the weeks in which I get an hour of sleep a night. Of course, to my daughters for not typing or drooling on the keyboard too much while I dshkl. Thanks to the readers for being such a very special audience. (Always wanted to say that.) And thanks to the folks at IDG Books (whoops HMI) who have slaved away to make this book happen.

— Michael Hyman

To my friends in New Hampshire and Michigan, thanks for helping me deal with mild bouts of insanity during long days and nights when beta crunches and book deadlines intersected. Special thanks to my fellow Fat Club members — remember the first rule! Thanks must go to all the folks at Hungry Minds for keeping us on track and getting this book out the door looking good and reading ~~good~~ well. And to Microsoft for coming up with some cool new technology in .NET.

— Bob Arnson

Publisher's Acknowledgments

We're proud of this book; please send us your comments through our Hungry Minds Online Registration Form located at www.dummies.com.

Some of the people who helped bring this book to market include the following:

Acquisitions, Editorial, and Media Development

Project Editor: Susan Pink

Senior Acquisitions Editor: Jill Schorr

Technical Editor: Allen Wyatt, Discovery Computing Inc.

Editorial Manager: Constance Carlisle

Permissions Editor: Laura Moss

Media Development Specialist: Megan Decraene

Media Development Manager: Laura Carpenter VanWinkle

Media Development Supervisor: Richard Graves

Editorial Assistant: Amanda Foxworth

Production

Project Coordinator: Jennifer Bingham

Layout and Graphics: Brian Drumm, Kelly Hardesty, LeAndra Johnson, Jackie Nicholas, Jill Piscitelli, Jeremy Unger

Proofreaders: John Greenough, Andy Hollandbeck, Angel Perez, Dwight Ramsey, Marianne Santy, TECHBOOKS

Indexer: TECHBOOKS

Special Help
Ronald Terry

General and Administrative

Hungry Minds Technology Publishing Group: Richard Swadley, Senior Vice President and Publisher; Mary Bednarek, Vice President and Publisher, Networking; Joseph Wikert, Vice President and Publisher, Web Development Group; Mary C. Corder, Editorial Director, Dummies Technology; Andy Cummings, Publishing Director, Dummies Technology; Barry Pruett, Publishing Director, Visual/Graphic Design

Hungry Minds Manufacturing: Ivor Parker, Vice President, Manufacturing

Hungry Minds Marketing: John Helmus, Assistant Vice President, Director of Marketing

Hungry Minds Production for Branded Press: Debbie Stailey, Production Director

Hungry Minds Sales: Michael Violano, Vice President, International Sales and Sub Rights

Contents at a Glance

Cartoons at a Glance

By Rich Tennant

"OK, I think I forgot to mention this, but we now have a Web management function that automatically alerts us when there's a broken link on The Aquarium's Web site."

page 297

"I can't really explain it, but everytime I animate someone swinging a golf club, a little divot of code comes up missing on the home page."

page 126

"Excuse me — is anyone here NOT talking about Visual C++ .NET?"

page 5

page 207

"It was at this point in time that there appeared to be some sort of mass insanity."

page 69

Cartoon Information:
Fax: 978-546-7747
E-Mail: richtennant@the5thwave.com
World Wide Web: www.the5thwave.com

Table of Contents

Introduction

· ·

So, you're thinking of tackling C++ .NET. That's a great idea. In fact, there are three great reasons for doing so: power, profit, and popularity. C++ is very powerful. It's used to create products such as Excel and Access. It's used also in MIS departments and by consultants to create mission-critical applications to help run businesses. And, of course, plenty of hackers and nerds use it to create tools, utilities, games, and cool multimedia master-pieces.

The skills you acquire will help you write not only .NET applications but also applications that can run on a variety of operating systems. And C++ lets you do almost everything almost everywhere, so lots of people use it.

Besides, if you're a geek like we are, what else could you possibly want to do?

About This Book

This book is supposed to be fun. You don't have to read the entire thing chapter by chapter. Maybe you're already familiar with Visual Studio. Skip the chapters about that. If all you need to do to pass your class is figure out what pointers are, start there. Or maybe while you're reading a chapter you suddenly fall asleep. That's okay too. Naps are good.

Now, if you're completely new to the whole C++ thing, you might instead start at the beginning and find out how to use Visual Studio .NET as well as C++. Also, we're supposed to tell you that it's okay if you don't memorize every single word in this book. But that's not true. Memorize it all. Stand up in the local park and recite it. You'll get to meet some nice people in blue uniforms.

Going from 0 to 60 with C++ isn't an easy task. C++ is a complex language, with lots of rules, quirks, and confusing concepts and terms. Besides normal programming, C++ also offers object-oriented programming, which is a whole other kettle o' fish.

On top of the complexities of the C++ language, you're faced with the array of tools in Visual Studio .NET. With more than 120MB of editors, libraries, and so on, Visual C++ can be intimidating. It's hard to know where to start.

That's where this book comes in: It gives you the big picture of both C++ and Visual C++. Rather than bog you down with details, it explains the important information and concepts. And in a way a normal person can understand.

You won't find out everything there is to know about C++ in this book — that would have required a few thousand pages or very small type. But you will get an excellent foundation in C++ that you can expand by writing your own programs.

Conventions Used in This Book

We use *italics* when we're defining a new term, **bold** when we want you to type something, and `monofont` for code, code terms, and screen messages. You'll also see the hot keys for commands underlined, as in File⇨Open.

What You're Not to Read

The nasty note Michael's wife wrote because he's been working on this book too long. Anything written by a politician. E-mail with pictures of Russian tennis stars. And, if you desire, any text in this book that has a Technical Stuff icon in front, because that can get a little geeky.

Foolish Assumptions

You don't need programming experience to read and understand this book. But if you've performed some programming-like tasks before, such as creating spreadsheet macros or database programs, you'll feel much more comfortable than if you've never dealt with the concept of a program before.

If you already know BASIC, COBOL, Pascal — or even better, C — this book will have you writing C++ in no time. (If you're already a pro at writing C++, however, this book probably isn't the best choice for you.)

Regardless of your programming background, we assume that you know how to run Windows programs and have a basic understanding of files and programs. Also, we assume that if you're going to try to run any of the programs in this book, you have .NET and Visual Studio .NET. And you have them installed and operational.

How This Book Is Organized

This book has four parts. Part I provides a quick guide to Visual C++. It helps you get up and running and introduces the main features of Visual C++.

Part II is an overview of C++ programming fundamentals (note that many of the topics are applicable to C as well). You'll also find out how to create a variety of .NET programs.

Part III introduces the world of object-oriented programming and delves into more .NET stuff.

Part IV, the Part of Tens, offers tips and solutions for various problems commonly encountered by beginning C++ users. It also provides some cool Top Ten lists of handy information.

And last but not least, the appendix tells you how to install the sample programs from the CD.

Icons Used in This Book

Icons are pictures designed to grab your attention. Here's what the icons used in this book mean:

This icon alerts you to nerdy technical discussions you can skip if you want.

Heads up! This icon flags information you should try to remember. Sometimes that's just because it's a cool bit of info, but other times it's because you may be sorry if you don't remember.

Shortcuts and insights that can save you time and trouble are indicated by this icon.

And this icon is for stuff that is applicable only to unmanaged programs, which is .NET lingo for what used to be known as good old normal C++ programs.

This book comes with a lot of sample programs that illustrate important aspects of Visual C++ programming. To save you the hassle of typing lines and lines of code, all the code is included on the accompanying CD.

Where to Go from Here

Hawaii. Taiwan. Fiji. Anywhere but where Michael's wife suggested he go when he ignored the note she left him.

Part I
Visual C++ .NET in Six Easy Chapters

"Excuse me – is anyone here NOT talking about Visual C++ .NET?"

In this part . . .

*P*art I gives you a tour of Visual C++, from what's in the box to how to use the Visual C++ tools.

You begin by looking at a program and finding out about the basics of object-oriented programming. Then you use the Visual C++ wizards to create a .NET program. Plus, you find out how to use important parts of the Visual C++ environment, such as the compiler, the text editor, and the Solution Explorer.

Chapter 1

What's in the Visual C++ .NET Package?

In This Chapter

▶ Examining what's in the Visual C++ package

▶ Finding out about the various Visual C++ features

▶ The difference between managed and unmanaged programs

So you've decided to become a C++ programmer. That's a great idea. You'll be able to beef up your resume, create some cool custom applications, and meet all types of fascinating people. And, most important, you'll be able to say that you've installed one of the largest products ever created.

Visual C++ Features

Sometimes, good things come in small packages.

When you first see the Visual C++ box, you might wonder whether FedEx forgot a couple of boxes. The Visual C++ box is small and doesn't weigh much. How could it possibly contain so many megabytes of software? What happened is that Microsoft took the heaviest part of most software packages — the books — out of the box and put them on the CD-ROM instead. (The manuals are available separately, though, if you feel like sacrificing some trees.)

When you open the Visual C++ box, you find CD-ROMs containing the Visual C++ software. The CDs contain a variety of features that help you create C++ programs:

✔ Compilers

✔ Debuggers

✔ Integrated development environment

✔ Application frameworks

✔ Libraries

✔ Windows utilities

✔ General utilities

✔ Online documentation library

✔ Sample programs

The following sections of this chapter describe most of these features in a little more detail to give you a basic idea of what all this stuff does before you install it.

A compiler that launched a thousand programs

Compilers translate code from a form that programmers can understand (*source code*) to a form that computers can understand and run (a program called an *executable*). Visual C++ has two compilers:

✔ A command-line compiler

✔ An everything-wrapped-up-into-one integrated development environment

As you work through the tasks and exercises in this book, most of the time you use the integrated compiler because its user interface is easy to use.

What's a command-line compiler?

A *command-line compiler* is a compiler that doesn't have a graphical user interface. Command-line compilers are fast but not very user-friendly. You tell them what to do by giving them some rather complicated-looking instructions, as shown in this example:

```
cl /FR /WX foo.cpp
```

In the preceding line, the first item is the name of the command-line compiler that you want to use, the next two items are options that tell the compiler what to do, and the last item is the file you want to compile. (You can tell whether someone uses the command-line compiler rather than the Visual C++ environment if they

know that /FR means to generate browser info and /WX means to treat all warnings as errors. Anyone else will think these terms are just a bunch of gibberish.)

In the good old days, command-line compilers were the only compilers available. People who started programming a long time ago often continue to use the command-line compilers because they've become accustomed to them and because they've developed all sorts of nifty tools to use with them. Beginners usually prefer the Visual C++ environment because it's much easier to use.

The Venus flytrap of development: The debugger

If your program has more than a few lines in it, it's bound to have some problems when you first compile it. If it doesn't, you're a real code jockey (a hotshot programmer) or you copied your program from a book.

You'll undoubtedly run into two types of problems: syntax errors and logic errors. *Syntax errors* occur when you type something incorrectly, forget to supply information that the compiler needs, or use a command incorrectly. The compiler finds syntax errors for you and tells you what line they're on. You need to correct all the syntax errors or the compiler won't be able to create an executable.

Logic errors occur when you design or implement your program improperly. Perhaps you forgot to include an important piece of information. Or maybe you printed the wrong variable. With logic errors, the program compiles perfectly but some part of it doesn't work correctly when it runs.

For example, suppose that you write a program to manage your checking account. When you deposit money in your account, you remember to have the program add that number to your balance. But when you withdraw money, you forget to have the program subtract the money from your balance. (A sort of Freudian withdrawal slip.) This is a logic error. You forgot an important step and, as a result, your program reports that you have more money in your account than you actually do.

Logic errors can be hard to find. Tracking them down by looking at the source code is usually difficult. Instead, you track them down by using a tool called a debugger. The *debugger* lets you run a program line-by-line so that you can examine the values in the program and pinpoint the location and cause of the problem.

2-4-6-8, how do we integrate?

Visual C++ contains an *integrated development environment* (devenv.exe) that combines the various development tools into a single easy-to-use environment. If you use the Visual C++ environment, you don't need to know how to use the various stand-alone tools.

What are all those different library versions?

Many times, you'll discover that several different versions of a library exist. Each version corresponds to a different combination of options that the library supports and is represented by a letter (or letters) placed before the library name, after the library name, or both. For example, mfc70d.lib means that this MFC library is the debuggable version.

The letters are described here:

- D   Debuggable
- MT   Multithread version
- O   OLE (Object Linking and Embedding)
- S   Static
- U   Unicode

The Visual C++ environment contains the following major components:

- Editors, which let you write and modify your source code and resources without leaving the environment
- A compiler, which lets you compile your program (or find syntax errors that prevent your program from compiling)
- A debugger, which helps you find mistakes so that you can correct them
- A project manager, which lets you easily build executables (and DLLs and LIBs)
- A browser, which helps you understand the relationships of the various objects in object-oriented programs
- Visual programming tools (wizards), which enable you to easily create Windows applications
- Property sheets, which make it easy for you to control the behavior of Visual C++

You can use and control any of these components just by choosing menu items and clicking the choices in dialog boxes. This makes performing complex tasks easy because you don't need to learn (and remember) the rather arcane command-line options (called *switches*). You use the Visual C++ environment throughout the book as you find out about different programming techniques.

Libraries that never charge an overdue fine

Libraries are predefined sets of functions and classes that handle many common programming tasks. Visual C++ includes a number of libraries. Libraries make your life as a programmer easier because you can use these preexisting items rather than create your own.

The .NET Framework is basically one big library. The runtime libraries (abbreviated RTL) include the various helper functions such as math, disk, and string-manipulation commands. The RTL libraries include libc.lib, libcmt.lib, and msvcrt.lib.

Maxwell Smart utilities

Visual C++ includes a number of utilities that help you figure out what .NET and Windows programs do. Usually, only advanced programmers use these utilities, the most important of which is Spy++. Spy++ displays Windows messages and classes that are being used by a running program. Use it to track your own programs or even to spy on someone else's program.

A number of other utilities make writing programs easier. Most of these utilities are for advanced programmers and are designed to be used with the command-line tools. The most frequently used utility is NMAKE, which is used with the command-line tools to build programs.

You might find other utilities useful even if you don't use the command-line tools. WINDIFF, for example, lets you compare two files to find the differences between the two. ZOOMIN lets you magnify part of the screen, which is useful for making sure that everything's lined up perfectly.

Getting by with a little help from your friends

Everything in Visual C++ — the compilers, debuggers, IDE, frameworks, libraries, utilities — has to be documented, but Microsoft avoids bulky packages by putting the documentation online. Visual C++ has an online help system that lets you read all about a feature from within the IDE, so help is always right where you need it. You can also launch the help system in a separate window. For the ultimate geek setup, you can run multiple monitors on your system so that you'll always have a separate help window available as you track down a particularly thorny problem.

Sample programs to get you started

Visual C++ includes numerous sample programs that make it easier for you to master and write programs in C++. Some of the sample programs illustrate a particular technique; others provide full working programs, such as a multi-file text editor. A handy feature of the sample programs is that you can cut and paste code from them to use in your own programs. This can save you lots of time and effort, and it lets you focus on the more specialized parts of your program.

Managed and Unmanaged Programs

Visual C++ .NET lets you write programs for both Windows and the Microsoft .NET platform. In this book, we concentrate on .NET but also cover good ol' Windows. .NET is Microsoft's framework for developing Internet programs. It includes the Common Language Runtime (CLR) and the .NET Framework class library.

The CLR is the base of .NET — everything else runs on top of it. The CLR manages all the code it runs and provides all the low-level services that all programs need, such as memory management. The .NET Framework class library is an *application framework* with reusable object-oriented classes you can use in your programs. (You find out what the heck a reusable object-oriented class is later in the book.)

To take advantage of .NET and the CLR, your programs must be designed for them. Part of that requirement involves using the .NET Framework classes, but the rest involves using a compiler designed for .NET. Naturally, Visual C++ .NET qualifies. When you write code for .NET, it's known as *managed code*.

Code you write for Windows without using any .NET libraries or features is known as *unmanaged code*.

If you don't use an application framework, creating attractive graphical programs can be a chore. Users have an easier time learning and using graphical interfaces, but programmers find them difficult to create. For example, writing a simple Windows program that contains menus and prints "Hello World" on the screen can require 2000 to 4000 lines of code. (Programmers affectionately call this type of program Hello World. A Hello World program is often used to illustrate how easy or difficult a particular programming system is.) That's such a ridiculous number that .NET programs *have* to use the .NET

Framework class library. Hard-core geeks can tap into lower levels, but everyone else uses the .NET Framework.

Part of the reason a simple program such as Hello World is so difficult to write in Windows is that you need to remember about a thousand programming commands to manipulate Windows. That's a lot to cram into your head.

Most programs are much more complicated than Hello World, and you need to do a lot of programming tasks to get them to work. For instance, you must perform the following tasks just to start the program:

✔ Define a routine that receives Windows messages

✔ Determine whether shortcut keys caused these messages

✔ Determine which parts of your program should receive these messages

✔ Find out whether another instance of your program is running

✔ Register the names of portions of your program

All these steps don't even get you to the point of displaying something on the screen!

Application frameworks handle these and similar types of tasks automatically. For example, when you create a program, you can use the .NET Framework System.Windows.Forms.Application class, which handles all the code for starting a program. You can use the System.Windows.Forms.Form class to create a window. These classes handle the details of .NET programming for you automatically, so you can concentrate on the unique features of your program.

Visual C++ also includes other kinds of application frameworks: The Microsoft Foundation Classes (MFC) library includes C++ classes that represent Windows features. The Active Template Library (ATL) is a set of C++ templates that make it easy to create objects for the Component Object Model (COM), in much the same way that MFC makes creating programs for Windows easy. COM and ATL are both pretty cool, but even doctorates from Hacker U find them a bit of a challenge, so we won't get into them in this book.

Chapter 2

Get with the Program

In This Chapter

▶ Discovering the fundamentals of programming

▶ Finding out about statements, variables, comments, and libraries

▶ Reading a program

▶ Examining the fundamentals of object-oriented programming

*I*n this chapter, you get a brief overview of the fundamentals of programming: designing, writing, compiling, and debugging. You'll breeze through some theoretical mumbo jumbo about object-oriented programming. And you will also take a look at a real, live .NET program.

Intro to Programming 101

Designing a program (sometimes called *analyzing*) is when you figure out what a program is supposed to do. You examine the problem you're trying to solve and figure out a strategy for solving it.

Writing (often called *coding*) is when you sit down and, uh, write the program. Usually you do this by typing high-level instructions using a computer language. For example, you may tell the computer to print some text to the screen. Throughout this and the next section, you find out about many C++ commands so that you can tell the computer what to do.

Next, you *compile* the application. In this step, Visual C++ .NET converts the high-level C++ program into a low-level program that the computer understands. Programs are often broken down into several files during the development process (because it's easier to manage them that way). During the compilation phase, these separate files are linked into a single application. After a program has been compiled, the computer understands how to run it.

Now you *run* the program. If your program is more than a few lines long, it will probably have some errors in it. Because errors are par for the course, you need to test your program to make sure it behaves properly.

TECHNICAL STUFF

You take the high-level language road, and I'll take the low-level language road

In case you'd like to see the difference between a high-level language and a low-level language, here's a simple C++ line (high level) followed by the equivalent in assembly language (low level).

C++ example:

```
a = 3*a - b*2 + 1;
```

Assembly language equivalent:

```
mov eax, DWORD PTR _a$[ebp]
lea eax, DWORD PTR[eax+eax*2]
mov ecx, DWORD PTR _b$[ebp]
add ecx, ecx
sub eax, ecx
inc eax
mov DWORD PTR _a$[ebp], eax
```

Actually, even the assembly language code is at a higher level than the computer can understand. The computer understands only machine language, which is the numeric equivalent of the assembly language instructions.

Here's what machine language looks like:

```
8b 45 fc
8d 04 40
8b 4d f8
03 c9
2b c1
40
89 45 fc
```

Now, how would you like to program like that?

The process of finding and correcting mistakes is called *debugging*. You usually use the debugger to help you track down the cause of the problems. Then you go back to the editing stage to correct those problems.

Computer programs consist of commands telling the computer what to do and how to manipulate data. In fact, all that most programs do is acquire, process, and display (or store) data.

Even a video game does this. It acquires commands in the form of your keystrokes, mouse movements, or joystick movements, processes these commands to determine what to do, and then displays the resulting data (for example, a screen showing the next room in a maze, with the guts of a radioactive alien dripping down a wall).

Down on Function main Street

The place where a C++ program starts is called the main function. When a program begins, the first statement in the main function executes. A *statement* is a line of code — it's essentially an instruction to the computer.

(A *function* is a group of statements that are organized together, somewhat like a paragraph. You'll find out more about functions in a later chapter.) Then, all the following statements are executed, one statement at a time.

Some statements tell the program to execute different sections only when certain conditions are true. This type of statement is called a *conditional statement*. For example, a line may say the equivalent of "print the document only when the user chooses the Print command."

Variables represent data in programs. For example, if you want to store the name of a user, you can create a variable called name to do so. Then, anytime you need to know the name of the user, you can examine the value of the variable called name. The value inside a variable can change as the program runs. So, you can store "Miriam" in the name variable at one point and "Sarah" in the same variable at another point. The value in a variable doesn't change out of the blue without your knowing it, though. If you want to change the value in a variable, you have to write a statement in the program to specifically do so.

Program *comments* explain what's happening in a program. You use comments to describe the purpose of a section of code, to discuss assumptions, or to point out particular tricks. When you add comments to your code, the code is easier for other people to read. Comments also help when you're trying to correct something you wrote late at night — you may have written terrible code at that point, and the comment may be the only way you can tell what on earth you were trying to do. (Comments are also a good place to put in snide remarks about your manager. I've found swear words, complaints about bills not being paid, and all types of other good stuff when viewing the HTML source files on some major Web sites.) Comment lines are ignored by the compiler, which skips over them when it converts C++ to machine code.

Figure 2-1 shows a small program, with the main function, statements, and variables pointed out.

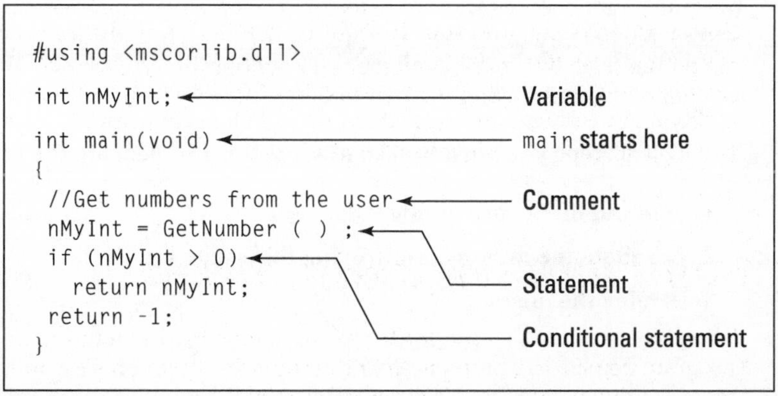

Figure 2-1: The basic features of a program.

```
#using <mscorlib.dll>

int nMyInt;                              Variable

int main(void)                           main starts here
{
  //Get numbers from the user            Comment
  nMyInt = GetNumber ( ) ;
  if (nMyInt > 0)                        Statement
    return nMyInt;
  return -1;                             Conditional statement
}
```

A Do-Run Runtime

Routines common to most programs are stored in the .NET *Common Language Runtime*. For example, almost every program prints values to the screen. Printing to the screen can, believe it or not, involve a lot of steps for the computer. Rather than reinvent these steps each time you write a program, you can just use the routine already provided by .NET.

When you are writing *unmanaged* programs (that is, old-style C++ applications) common routines are stored in things called *libraries*. What's the difference? Conceptually, nothing. Both are libraries. One just has a fancier name. The Common Language Runtime can be used by Visual Basic, C#, and Visual C++, whereas libraries are typically for a specific language. But the capabilities in the .NET Common Language Runtime are quite different (and far richer) than those in the standard C++ libraries.

There are two types of libraries: static and dynamic. With *static libraries,* routines used by your program are copied into the program itself, thus increasing the program's size. With *dynamic libraries* (called DLLs), the routines aren't copied into your program but are accessed when the program runs.

Solve Your Problems with a Program

When you begin the process of creating a program to solve a particular problem, you first need to break the problem down into logical pieces and then write functions to handle each piece. At first, you may find it difficult to chunk the program down into pieces. But the more you program, the more you develop your problem-solving skills. (And Computer Science courses teach all kinds of cool tricks and problem-solving strategies that you can use.)

As a quick example, here's how you can convert a real-world problem into a program. Suppose you want to calculate the area of a square. (Why? Who knows. Maybe you're trying to impress a bunch of friends at a party.) You remember from way back in elementary school that the area of a square is calculated by multiplying the length of one side by itself.

The logical steps you need to take to solve this problem are the following:

1. **Find out the length of one side.**

2. **Calculate the area by multiplying this value by itself.**

3. **Display the answer.**

Now that you've broken the problem into logical steps, you need to convert it into a computer language. For example, in C++ .NET, this program would be written as follows:

```
// SquareArea
// Computes the area of a square given the length of one side

#include "stdafx.h"

#using <mscorlib.dll>

using namespace System;

// This is the entry point for this application
#ifdef _UNICODE
int wmain(void)
#else
int main(void)
#endif
{
    String *pszSize;
    int nSize;
    int nArea;

    //Ask for the length of the side
    Console::WriteLine(L"What is the length of the side of the
            square?");

    //Read the answer
    pszSize = Console::ReadLine();

    //Convert the answer to a number
    nSize = nSize.Parse(pszSize);

    //Calculate the area of the square
    nArea = nSize*nSize;

    //Write the result
    //Note that we must convert the area into a string to do
            so
    Console::WriteLine(L"The square's area is {0} units.",
            nArea.ToString());

    //Hang out until the user is finished
    Console::WriteLine(L"Press the Enter key to stop the
            program");
    Console::ReadLine();
        return 0;
}
```

This program is in the SquareArea directory on the CD accompanying this book.

So now that you've seen what a program looks like, what the heck does all that stuff mean? Well, before we explore that, here's how you read a program, in case you've never read one before:

1. **Start at the top.**

2. **Read the program one line at a time.**

3. **Try to figure out what each line does.**

4. **If you can't figure something out, move on to the next line.**

This is what the compiler does, except that the compiler usually doesn't do Step 4.

The following scenario shows what can happen if you read the SquareArea program line by line and make your analysis after each line. Here's are the first two lines:

```
// SquareArea
// Computes the area of a square given the length of one side
```

You may say, "Hmm, that looks pretty reasonable. This is a program that calculates the area of a square." (The funny // at the beginning of the line means that it's a comment line.)

```
#using <mscorlib.dll>
using namespace System;
```

"Beats me. Looks like someone named Ms. Corlib is being used. With any luck, she's a friend of Lara Croft. I probably find out about it in a later chapter." (And you're right!)

```
#ifdef _UNICODE
int wmain(void)
#else
int main(void)
#endif
```

"That looks way strange. I guess I'll skip it for now."

```
String *pszSize;
int nSize;
int nArea;
```

"Not sure what these do, but *size* and *area* sure sound like they are part of the problem."

```
//Ask for the length of the side
   Console::WriteLine(L"What is the length of the side of the
          square?");
//Read the answer
pszSize = Console::ReadLine();
//Convert the answer to a number
nSize = nSize.Parse(pszSize);
```

"This looks bizarre, but I guess it's finding out the length of the side of the square."

```
//Calculate the area of the square
nArea = nSize*nSize;
```

"Aha, something I understand! This is a formula multiplying the length of the side by the length of the side to find the area."

And so forth.

Throughout the rest of this part, you will discover what these various programming commands do. In fact, instead of just reading programs, you will find out how to construct them. In other words, you will become fluent in programmerese.

And Now for Something Completely Different

You've just taken a brief tour of what a C++ program is like. The square area program, however, didn't take advantage of the object-oriented capabilities of C++. In fact, C++ is popular partly because of these object-oriented capabilities. Why? Here are some of the main reasons:

- With object-oriented programming, you can reuse code and thus save development time.
- Object-oriented programs are well structured, which makes it easier to figure out what a particular routine does.
- Object-oriented programs are easier to test. You can break an application into small components and isolate testing to specific components.
- Object-oriented programs are easier to expand as your needs change.

The basic idea of object-oriented programming is simple. Data and the routines to process the data are combined in a single entity called a *class*. If you want to access the data in the class, you use the routines from the class.

With the older-style procedural programming, on the other hand, the data and routines are separate and are thought of separately.

The object is the object

The basic idea behind object-oriented programming is this: Break a problem into a group of objects. *Objects* contain data and the routines that process the data. So a jukebox program, for example, can be composed of several objects for getting and processing information describing songs. The program can have one object to represent songs and another to represent the whole jukebox. Each of these objects can have data further describing it (for example, the Song object can have data indicating the length of time the song will play) and functions for processing the object (for example, the Song object can have a function to print the name and playing time of a song). Combining data and functions that process a particular type of object is called *encapsulation*.

You can combine several objects to create new objects. This is called *composition*. For example, you can create a Karaoke object by creating an object containing a Jukebox object and a Microphone object. (Or you can create a Breakfast object containing a Pizza object and a Soda object.)

You can also create a new object based on an existing one. For example, you can take an object that plays videos and turn it into an object for selling videos by adding capabilities for handling commerce transactions. Modifying or adding new capabilities to an existing object to create a new object is called *inheritance*.

Inheritance is one of the most powerful capabilities of object-oriented programming. By inheriting from an existing, working object, you can do the following:

- ✔ **Save code:** You don't have to retype what's in the original object.

- ✔ **Improve reliability:** You know that the original object works, so any bugs you encounter have to come from your new code. And if you do find bugs in the original object, the corrections automatically affect any object inherited from it.

- ✔ **Improve readability:** You can discover how a basic set of objects works. Then, any objects derived from those basic objects are easy to master — you have to examine only the new data and functions because you already understand most of the functionality.

Another property of object-oriented programming is that you can change how a particular function operates, depending on the object being used. This is called *polymorphism.* For example, printing a cell in a spreadsheet prints a value, whereas printing a chart prints an illustration. In both cases, you're printing, but because the objects are different (a cell and a chart), the results are also different.

Encapsulation

Encapsulation refers to combining data and the functions that process the data into a single entity, called an *object* or *class.* The data are called *data members* (sometimes called *member variables* or, depending upon their use, *properties*) of a class. The functions are called *member functions* (sometimes called *methods*) of a class.

The challenge in designing an object-oriented program is to define classes so that they accurately model the real-world problem you're trying to solve and can be reused frequently. This may be a bit difficult at first, but after you've programmed for a while, it becomes second nature.

Inheritance

Inheritance is one of the coolest things about object-oriented programming. With *inheritance,* you create new objects by expanding existing ones. When you create a new class from an existing class, the new class is called a *derived class.* The previously existing class is called the *base class.* (Sometimes derived classes are called *children* and base classes are called *parents.* And sometimes the act of creating a derived class is called *subclassing.* Or, in the case of creating children, it is called . . . ah, never mind.)

Figure 2-2 shows seven classes. The Sound class is the most elemental. The Sound class lists the title and playing time for a particular sound. Song is based on Sound, so it too lists a playing time and title. It adds information on the author of the song and the date it was performed. RockSong is a derived from Song. It contains all the items from Song (which contains all the items from Sound), in addition to other items. As you can see, you can use inheritance to build up complex things, such as an AlternativeRockSong, out of much more elemental items. At each step, the derived class inherits the features and capabilities of its base class.

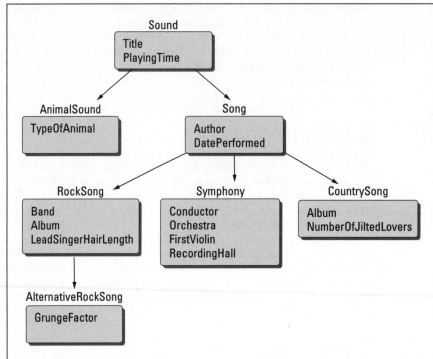

Figure 2-2:
You can create new classes by inheriting the features and capabilities of existing ones.

Polymorphism

Not only can you build up classes through inheritance, but you can also use polymorphism to specify a behavior for each class. In case you haven't memorized every Greek word you've encountered in this chapter, *polymorphism* lets you change the way a function behaves depending upon how it is used. For example, the Sound class may have a member function called GetMe. For the AnimalSound object, this function may tell you to go to the local zoo. For the RockSong object, the function may instruct you to drive to the nearest music store or go to a music Web site.

The combination of inheritance and polymorphism lets you easily create a series of similar but unique objects. Because of inheritance, such objects share many similar characteristics. But because of polymorphism, each object can have a unique behavior. So, when you use polymorphism, common functions, such as GetMe, behave one way for one object and another way for another.

If polymorphism isn't used for a particular function, the base class functionality is used. For example, if a particular object derived from RockSong doesn't *override* GetMe (that is, provide a version of a function specific to the derived class), RockSong's GetMe routine is used for that object. Because of this, functionality in base classes tends to be generic so that it can be used across derived classes. If it's not generic, the derived classes almost always use polymorphism to override the behavior of the base class.

The programmer who designs the Symphony or CountrySong class determines what the GetMe call will do. The person who uses Symphony or CountrySong needs to understand not all the details about what GetMe does, but merely that it performs the correct function for finding music. This additional benefit of polymorphism — namely, that the user of a class doesn't have to understand its details — is sometimes called *information hiding*.

Chapter 3

You Gotta Be Startin' Coding

*I*n this chapter, you create your first C++ program. In fact, you create several. You begin by creating a managed C++ program. This is .NET's fancy term for saying that Big Brother is watching out for the program and will help it succeed by giving it a lot of support (with the Common Language Runtime) and by making sure that it behaves properly (by keeping it from losing memory and doing other bad things.) You also create unmanaged programs, which is .NET's unfriendly term for a good old-fashioned (or standard) C++ program. To do so, you create the fundamental part of all C++ programs: a source file.

Man on Des Sources

Source files — sometimes called CPP files (for C Plus Plus files), implementation files, or CXX files — contain the main parts of the program. They're where you type functions, define data, and decide how the program flows. (*Program flow* refers to the order in which statements or sections in a program are executed.)

Source files are comprised of statements. *Statements* are program lines that tell the computer to do something.

For example, the following line is a statement that tells the computer to calculate the area of a square by multiplying the length of the sides by the length of the sides:

```
nArea = nSize * nSize;
```

Each statement must end with a semicolon. The semicolon tells the computer where one statement ends and the next statement begins, just like a period does in a sentence.

You can group a set of statements by surrounding them with { and } (a left curly brace and a right curly brace). For example, suppose you have a statement such as

```
if the pizza is cold, reheat it;
```

(The if command, which we describe in Chapter 11, lets you tell the computer to execute a particular statement if a particular condition holds true.) If you want to tell the computer to execute another statement at the same time, you can say something like:

```
if the pizza is cold {reheat it; take a 5-minute nap;}
```

The two statements are grouped together inside the { and }.

You also use { and } to define where functions begin and end. You can find out more about this in Chapter 12.

When you pass parameters to a function, you surround the parameters with (and). For example, you can say:

```
if the telephone line is busy {take a nap(5 minutes); try
                calling again;}
```

This tells the nap function how long you want to wait before making the phone call again. You can find out more about this (passing parameters, not making phone calls) in Chapter 12.

Here's a summary of the rules about statements:

- ✔ End lines with ;
- ✔ Group lines with { }
- ✔ Pass parameters with ( )

One Shell of a Program

Okay. Enough of the boring theory. It's time to get busy. You start by creating a .NET project:

1. Choose File⇨New⇨Project.

The New Project dialog box appears.

2. Under Project Types, select Visual C++ Projects.

3. Under Templates, select Managed C++ Application.

4. In the Name box, type HelloWorld.

This creates a folder named HelloWorld in the Visual Studio Projects folder in your My Documents folder. Take a look at Figure 3-1. If you want the HelloWorld folder to be created in some other folder, you can type the folder's name in the Location box or click the Browse button to display a folder browse window.

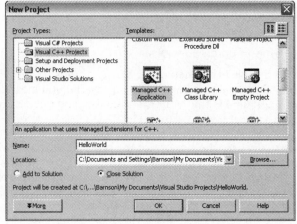

Figure 3-1:
Use the New Project dialog box to create a project called HelloWorld.

5. Click OK.

Visual C++ creates a bunch of files, including a *solution,* which is basically a group of projects. You'll have only one project in this solution. You can discover more about solutions in Chapter 4. Solution Explorer, which shows the files that make up your HelloWorld project, is shown in Figure 3-2.

Figure 3-2:
Solution Explorer shows the files in your solution.

This creates a brand new project containing a very simple program that prints "Hello World" on the screen. To see the source code for the program, double-click the HelloWorld.cpp icon in Solution Explorer. You can find this icon under Source Files under HelloWorld.

Fortunately, this simple "Hello World" printing program is exactly what you want to create for your first program. Before you examine your masterpiece, run it:

1. **Choose** <u>D</u>**ebug**⇨**Start Without Debugging.**

   Visual C++ displays a message telling you that the HelloWorld - Debug Win32 project configuration is out of date.

2. **Click Yes to have Visual C++ build the HelloWorld project.**

   The Output window opens so you can see the progress of the build.

   After your hard drive is finished doing a little drum solo, you'll see a black window flash on the screen and go away. Did you mess up already? Nope. What happened is that your program ran, and once it ended, went away.

So how do you actually see whether or not the program worked? Well, there are lots of ways. In Chapter 16, you can find out how to use the debugger to stop at the end of the program. Later in this chapter, you see how to add some code to cause the program to wait before it ends, which is a useful technique during development. But for now, try this:

1. **Open a command prompt window.**

   On Windows 2000 and Windows XP, choose Start⇨Programs⇨Accessories ⇨Command Prompt. On Windows NT, choose Start⇨Programs⇨Command Prompt.

2. **Use the CD command to change your current folder to where the HelloWorld project is located.**

   If you used the default folder it will contain spaces, so be sure to put the folder name in quotes. On Windows 2000 and Windows XP, the folder name will be something like "C:\Documents and Settings\MyUserName\My Documents\Visual Studio Projects\HelloWorld." (The actual location depends on how your computer is set up. Typically, though, if you replace C: with the drive where Windows is installed — probably C: — and replace MyUserName with your login name — such as boba — you'll find it.)

3. **To run your program, type** Debug\HelloWorld.

   Visual Studio builds a debugging version of your projects by default, so it puts the output — that is, your program in executable form — in a folder named Debug. See what it looks like in Figure 3-3.

Figure 3-3:
Running
HelloWorld
at the
command
prompt.

```
Command Prompt                                              _ □ ×
C:\Documents and Settings\Barnson\My Documents\Visual Studio Projects\HelloWorld
>debug\helloworld
Hello World

C:\Documents and Settings\Barnson\My Documents\Visual Studio Projects\HelloWorld
>
```

The main event

Now that you've run the program, let's find out more about how it actually
works. When you run a program, the computer needs to know where to find
the first line of the program. Rather than numbering the program lines (which
is a real pain, but was what they did in the old days of programming), you put
the first line in a function called `main`. The first line in `main` is the first line
that executes when you run the program. For example, here's a simple program that does nothing:

```
int main(void)
{
    //This does absolutely nothing.
}
```

This program starts with a function called `main`. That's where all C++ programs start. Because `main` can take parameters, you put ( ) after it. (In .NET,
you usually won't pass in any parameters, so you type `void` as a friendly
placeholder.) Next you see {, which tells the computer that the lines that
follow are part of `main`. The closing } tells the computer that this is the end
of `main`.

TECHNICAL STUFF

Poem for a castrati

All the managed C++ programs that you create
in this book will start with a slightly more complex looking `main`, as shown in the following
code:

```
#ifdef _UNICODE
int wmain(void)
#else
int main(void)
#endif
```

Unicode is a standard that indicates that text
can include international characters from a
broad variety of languages, including Asian languages. The `_UNICODE` in the first line pre-
pares the program to be run internationally. You
can set special options when you compile a
program to indicate that the program is a
Unicode program.

You may be wondering what int means (it appears before main in the program you just saw). It has to do with functions, which you can discover more about in Chapter 12. *Functions* are self-contained routines that perform some type of action (such as print), process data, or ask for input. Functions can return values. In C++, main is a function and can return an integer.

Console me

Although you can write programs that do nothing, usually you want to get some type of input from the user and then write some type of output. There are a million ways (well, five or so) to do this in .NET. One of the easiest is to use the Console functions. These let you read and write to the console window — the black window that popped up when you ran your first program.

To write to the screen, use Console::WriteLine. Give it a text value, and it will print it on the screen. For example, the following line writes "Hello World" to the screen (note that the text is placed in quotations marks):

```
Console::WriteLine("Hello World");
```

Suppose you want to write "You looking at me?" instead. That's easy:

```
Console::WriteLine("You looking at me?");
```

To get information from the user, you can use Console::ReadLine. This gets a line of text from the user. (In Chapter 7, you see how to convert what is typed to something useful.) For example, the following line waits for the user to type some text:

```
Console::ReadLine();
```

Note that Console::ReadLine doesn't display anything on the screen. So usually when you are looking for input from the user, you will first write a question with Console::WriteLine and then read in the answer with Console::ReadLine, as shown in the following lines:

```
Console::WriteLine(L"Press the Enter key to stop the
        program");
Console::ReadLine();
```

Using my religion

The Console functions are part of the .NET Common Language Runtime. So, before you can use them, you need to let Visual C++ .NET know how to find the functions. To do so, you use the #using keyword. The .NET Common Language Runtime is divided into many different dynamic libraries (DLLs).

The #using command tells which libraries the .NET program is going to use. (Remember, the Common Language Runtime is just a collection of libraries of useful functions, with a slick marketing name.)

Okay, typing *Common Language Runtime* over and over is making my fingers tired. I'm just going to use *CLR* from now on. It is my own abbreviation, so if you use it around a bunch of your programmer friends and they have no clue what you mean, just look at them like they are idiots.

The most basic .NET functions, including the Console functions, are found in a library called mscorlib. This stands for Microsoft core library, but if you are geeking out all night and don't want to admit it to your friends, you can always tell them you spent the evening with Ms. Corlib. The following line indicates that the program will use the mscorlib.dll library:

```
#using <mscorlib.dll>
```

Inside the CLR, functions are divided into various related groups, called *namespaces*. These namespaces contain a variety of classes (you can discover much more about classes in Chapter 17). And the classes contain the functions. For example, ReadLine and WriteLine are in the Console class. The Console class is in the System namespace. Thus, the official name for Console::WriteLine is System::Console::WriteLine.

The using namespace keyword lets you avoid typing all the namespace qualifiers for a function. It tells Visual C++ .NET what namespaces to assume when it tries to figure out what a function means. For example, you'll see the following in the HelloWorld program:

```
using namespace System;
```

As a result, we can write Console::WriteLine instead of System::Console::WriteLine.

Note that the #using and using namespace keywords are not part of standard C++. Nor are any of the .NET Common Language Runtime functions. So all the stuff you've found out so far will work when writing only .NET applications. Later in this chapter, you find out to write the same type of program using standard C++.

Color commentary

You may know exactly how your program operates. But if someone else looks at it, or if you return to it in a few years, you may forget what a particular line or function does. That's why it's important to put comments in your programs. *Comments* explain in English (or in whatever language you speak) what you've written in computerese.

Sure, use old-fashioned comments

C++ uses // to indicate comments. You can write comments also using the older C style, in which you enclose comments between a /* and a */. Here are several examples:

```
/* Old style comment */
a = 10; /*Set to 10*/
/*var a*/ a = 10; /*set to 10*/
```

If you use the older C-style comments, be sure that you end them! If you forget the */ at the end, the compiler ignores everything that you've typed after the first /*.

Note that when you use //, unlike when you use /* and */, you don't need to end the line with a special character. The two slashes indicate that all the following text on that line is a comment. But unlike using /* and */, you need to start each comment line with //.

You've already seen comments if you've looked at the sample programs in this book. Comments are indicated by // (two slash marks); when you see them, you know that all the following text on that line is a comment. (See the "Sure, use old-fashioned comments" sidebar for information about older C-style comments.)

Comments can be entered on separate lines, as in

```
//This is a comment.
```

Comments can occur also at the end of a line, as in

```
a = 10; //Give the variable a the value 10.
```

As the Hello World turns

Now that you've found out the basics of Visual C++ .NET programming, take a look at the source code of the program you created earlier in the chapter. You should now be able to read and understand what it does:

```
// This is the main project file for a VC++ application
// project generated using a wizard.

#include "stdafx.h"

#using <mscorlib.dll>

using namespace System;

// This is the entry point for this application
#ifdef _UNICODE
```

```
int wmain(void)
#else
int main(void)
#endif
{
    Console::WriteLine("Hello World");
    return 0;
}
```

As you can see, the program starts with some comments. That's easy enough. Next, it uses #using and using namespace to set up use of the CLR. After a few more comments, you hit the main function, which is where the program starts. It writes a line to the screen and ends. The mysterious return 0 at the end just returns a value from the main function. You can ignore that for now.

What Hello World needs now

Now, make some slight improvements to the Hello World program. First, mark that all the strings are .NET strings. And then add some lines to the end so that you can run the program from the Visual C++ .NET IDE and not have the program disappear before you get a chance to see if it runs. So, change the body of HelloWorld so that it looks like this:

```
Console::WriteLine(S"Hello World");
//Hang out until the user is finished
Console::WriteLine(S"Press the Enter key to stop the
             program");
Console::ReadLine();
```

TECHNICAL STUFF

Silly string

Text, such as "Hello World", is called a *string* in computerese. You can put funny letters in front of the text to give the compiler extra information about the string. For example, if you want the string to be treated as a Unicode string, precede it with an L:

```
Console::WriteLine(L"Hello
       World");
```

Unicode strings let you include all types of international characters, such as characters with accents or Kanji. In .NET, if you don't tell a string

to be Unicode, it is usually converted to Unicode at runtime, so you are better off marking that the string is Unicode.

Better yet, precede your strings with an S:

```
Console::WriteLine(S"Hello
       World");
```

This tells .NET to use its built-in string class, which is more efficient. And efficient is always good.

You can find this program in the HelloWorld3 directory on the accompanying CD-ROM.

Coding without a .NET

So far, all the programs you have created have been native .NET programs. As such, they won't run on anything besides a .NET system. C++, on the other hand, is a standardized language that runs on many different platforms. In this section, you see how to write Hello World as a standard C++ program. In the .NET world, programs that use standard C++ rather than .NET are called *unmanaged programs*.

Before you start coding, however, put on the secret agent terminology ring. In .NET, functionality is provided through the CLR. In standard C++, functionality is provided through a series of libraries. In .NET, you use #using to access the CLR. In standard C++, you include a *header file*. The header file tells the compiler the names and characteristics of routines you're using from other files or from libraries. For example, suppose that you want to use a routine called foo, and foo is in a library. To use foo, you include a header file that tells the compiler that foo is a routine and describes what types of data you may pass to foo.

If you create routines in one file that you plan to use in another file, you need to create a header file describing these routines. By reading the header file in the other source files, you can access the routines you created in those source files or in external libraries.

See me. Feel me. Touch me. Print me.

If you want to display something for the user to read, you must print it to the screen. We did this in .NET with Console::WriteLine. In unmanaged programs, we use the cout (pronounced "see-out" or to rhyme with *gout*) statement instead. When you send a value to cout, cout happily prints it. You use the << command to send a value to cout.

As with .NET, be sure to enclose text you want to print in quotation marks.

Here are some examples. Anytime you see cout <<, the value that follows will be printed:

```
//print "Hello World"
cout << "Hello World";
//print "The meaning of life is: 42"
cout << "The meaning of life is: 42";
```

The (not) missing linker

When you define an external function in a header file, you give only the function name and its parameters, not the name of the library or the source file containing the function. The compiler generates a list of all the functions it needs for a particular file, both external functions and those defined in that file. After compilation, the linker is called. Among other things, the *linker* looks at all the functions that are needed and searches for a match across all files and libraries. If it finds a match, it uses that function automatically. If it doesn't find a match, it spits out an error message.

You can also print several values at the same time. In the following two examples, two values are being printed. In the first of the two examples, "My name is" and "Michael" are two separate values. And as the second example shows, the values can be either text ("The meaning of life is") or numbers (42).

```
//print "My name is Michael"
cout << "My name is " << "Michael";
//print "The meaning of life is: 42"
cout << "The meaning of life is: " << 42;
```

As you can see, you can combine text and numbers easily. Also note that two statements end with a semicolon.

Ta da! That's all you need to do to start printing things with standard C++.

What's my new line?

You can print a number of special characters. The most commonly used special character is \n, which starts a new line. (As you may expect, this character is sometimes called the *newline character.*) For example, if you want the preceding examples to print text on separate lines, you type this:

```
//print "My name is Michael"
cout << "My name is " << "Michael\n";
//print "The meaning of life is: 42"
cout << "The meaning of life is: " << 42 << "\n";
```

The \n is treated like normal characters are treated. In other words, you can use \n by itself, as in the 42 << \n, or you can put it in the middle (or end) of any text, as in Michael\n. (You can also do something such as Mich\nael. This will print *Mich* on one line, start a new line when the \n is encountered, and then print *ael.*) Unlike normal characters, \n doesn't print anything visible to the screen — it just forces a new line to start.

Well, aren't these characters special?

You can use a number of special characters while printing. Here are a few:

\n Start a new line

\t Tab

\b Go back one space

\f Start a new page

\\ Print the \ character

\' Print the ' character

\" Print the " character

For example, suppose that you want to print the following:

```
He said "Ahoy"
```

You simply do this:

```
cout << "He said \"Ahoy\"\n";
```

At first, all these instances of << and \n might look rather outlandish, but you get used to them pretty quickly.

When you use cout, you don't have to use the \n special character to start a new line. C++ has a special function called endl (which stands for end of line) that you can use instead:

```
cout << "My name is Bob" << endl;
cout << "The meaning of life is approximately: "<< 42 <<
endl;
```

Unlike \n, you can't use endl in the middle or at the end of a string. Instead, you need to break the string into pieces, as shown in the code that follows:

```
cout << "My name " << endl << "is Bob" << endl;
```

Using endl instead of \n makes it more obvious that you want the output to appear on separate lines.

The original cin

Reading characters from the keyboard is as easy as writing them to the screen. You use cin and >>. (This is pronounced "see-in" or "sin." Your choice.) For example, to have the user type the number of songs, you can do this:

```
cin >> NumberOfSongs;
```

When you get input from the user, you typically save it into a variable. Chapter 8 discusses variables.

Borrowing a function from a library

At this point, you're almost ready to write your first unmanaged program. But the routines cout and cin are part of a library and, as this chapter discusses earlier, you need to include a header file that defines those routines if you want to use them in a program. You do so with the #include command. (This is pronounced "include" or "pound include.")

Any command that starts with # is called a *preprocessor directive.* This is a fancy term for a command that tells the compiler to do something. Preprocessor directives don't get turned into code. Rather, they control how the compiler operates.

For example, the #include preprocessor directive tells the compiler to load an include file. The definitions for cin and cout are made in an include file called iostream.h. (The .h is the standard extension for a header file.) To load these definitions, you add this line to the beginning of your program:

```
#include <iostream.h>
```

This line of code loads the definitions for cin, cout, and many other routines that are part of the iostream library.

Note that preprocessor directives aren't followed by a semicolon. Preprocessor directives can be only one line. Therefore, the compiler always knows that when the line ends, the preprocessor directive ends.

C++ is comprised of a small number of commands and a lot of library functions. Many library functions are common across all C++ compilers — no matter what C++ you use, you'll always find these helper functions. Other library functions are add-ons. For example, you can buy a library that contains functions for doing statistics or for manipulating images.

Future hackers read this: " " versus < >

The #include command is followed by the name of the header file to load. If the header file is one of the standard header files — that is, if it comes with the compiler — put the name inside < and > (a left and a right angle bracket):

```
#include <iostream.h>
```

The compiler knows where to find its own header files and will search there. If you're loading a header file that you created, put the name inside quotation marks. This tells the compiler to look in the current directory before searching the directory containing the standard header files:

```
#include "foo.h"
```

You can also give a full path name:

```
#include
    "\michael\jukebox\foo.h"
```

Hello, is there anybody out there?

Now it's time to write the unmanaged version of Hello World:

1. **Choose <u>F</u>ile⟹<u>N</u>ew⟹<u>P</u>roject.**

2. **Under Project Types, select Visual C++ Projects. Under Templates, select Win32 Project.**

3. **In the Name box, type** HelloWorld2.

   By default, Visual C++ selects the Close Solution option, which closes your current solution (for the original HelloWorld) and creates a new one for HelloWorld2. Keep that setting. You can have multiple projects in a single solution — that's what solutions are for, after all — but multiple projects complicate things; let's keep it simple for now.

4. **Click OK.**

   The Win32 Application Wizard appears (see Figure 3-4).

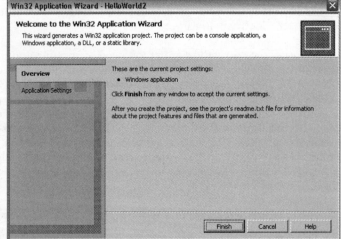

Figure 3-4:
The Win32
Application
Wizard lets
you make
HelloWorld2
a console
application.

5. **Click Application Settings.**

   The Wizard shows the settings you can change for HelloWorld2.

6. **Choose Console application instead of the default Windows application.**

   (FYI: A console application is also a genuine Windows application, but when most people hear "Windows application," they think of one with windows and icons and whiz-bang graphics. Apparently, so do the programmers who worked on Visual C++.)

7. **Click Finish.**

   Visual C++ grinds away for a bit, creating another solution and some source code.

8. **Double-click HelloWorld2.cpp in Solution Explorer.**

   Visual C++ opens the file in an editor window. You'll see that the Win32 Application Wizard wrote some code for you. That was very kind of it, don't you think? But we want our own code, thank you very much.

9. **Press Ctrl+A to select all the code, and then press Delete to get rid of it.**

10. **And now, type the following code:**

```
// HelloWorld2
// Prints hello world on the screen
// Unmanaged

#include "stdafx.h"
#include <iostream.h>

int _tmain(int argc, _TCHAR* argv[])
{
    //Write to the screen
    cout << "Hello World\n";
    return 0:
}
```

You can type this program, or you can load it from the HelloWorld2 directory on the CD accompanying this book.

You'll remember from running HelloWorld that running it from the Visual C++ IDE doesn't let you see the output. So let's not even bother with that this time. You need to run HelloWorld2 from the command prompt. But first, you must build it. (Visual C++ did that for us the last time when we tried to run it from the IDE.) To build and run HelloWorld2:

1. **Right-click HelloWorld2 (the one in bold, not HelloWorld2.cpp) and choose Build.**

   Visual C++ opens the Output window so you can see the progress of building and any errors. When Visual C++ has finished building HelloWorld2, the Output window displays Build: 1 succeeded, 0 failed, 0 skipped.

2. **Now that HelloWorld2 has been built, open a command prompt window.**

3. **Use the CD command to change your current folder to where the HelloWorld2 project is located.**

4. **Run your program by typing** Debug\HelloWorld2.

   See what the program looks like in Figure 3-5.

Those sooner-or-later-gotta-happen syntax errors

If you type a program incorrectly or use C++ commands improperly, the compiler will tell you that you have a syntax error. This just means that the compiler doesn't recognize the words you've used or that you've left something out of a command. Many types of syntax errors can occur. Chapters 23 and 24 discuss the most common syntax errors and how to correct them.

Figure 3-5:
Running
HelloWorld2
at the
command
prompt.

```
Command Prompt                                                    _ □ x

C:\Documents and Settings\Barnson\My Documents\Visual Studio Projects\HelloWorld
2>debug\HelloWorld2.exe
Hello World

C:\Documents and Settings\Barnson\My Documents\Visual Studio Projects\HelloWorld
2>
```

You may notice that standardized C++ passes two parameters to the main function. These are called the command-line parameters. If you invoke the program from a command prompt, you can pass in parameters. For example, you might type dir *.* at the command prompt. The *.* is a command-line parameter. If you were to type HelloWorld2 *.*, the *.* command-line parameter would be accessible through the argc and argv parameters. But, until you get ultra-geeky, you won't need to worry about this stuff.

Chapter 4

The Seven Percent Solution

*I*f you're reading this book in order, you've already created a few .NET programs. In the process, you used many aspects of the Visual C++ development tools. Throughout the rest of Part I, you find out more about the various
pieces that make up the Visual C++ environment. In this chapter, you focus
specifically on solutions and projects.

Solutions and *projects* make it easier to create programs by providing a way to
group all the source files and other junk you need. A project file shows the
different source files that make up a program. Project files also make it easier
to add source files to a program and change the various options that control
how a file is compiled. A solution is simply one or more projects.

Happiness Is a Warm Solution

Some programs consist of a single file. But most programs, such as the ones
that you create in Chapters 2, 3, and 4, are much larger. They involve many
different source-code files and many different header files and libraries. To
create the final executable, you need to compile each of these different
source-code files and then link them.

You can do this in two ways. One way is to use a command-line tool called
NMAKE and build something called a makefile. The other (kinder and gentler)
way is to use solutions and projects.

A *makefile* contains a list of commands that are executed to create an application. For example, the list might say compile foo, compile bar, link these
together with library muck, and so on. Creating a makefile can be rather complicated. You need to know lots of details about how files are compiled and
linked. You also need to know a special makefile language!

The great thing about makefiles, however, is that NMAKE determines what files have been changed since the last time you "made" your program. So when you build your application, only the files that have changed are recompiled. This saves a lot of time.

Project files are like makefiles that Visual C++ creates for you and lets you edit visually, without requiring you to know all the nitty-gritty details about how the compiler goes about compiling and linking a program.

Project files make your life easier

Project files, like makefiles, are used for organizing programming projects. But project files are a lot simpler than makefiles for several reasons. One, when you use project files, the compiler automatically looks through a source file and finds all the dependencies for you. (*Dependencies* are sets of files that, if changed, cause the project to be recompiled.

Two, manipulating project files visually is easy. Also, because Visual C++ automatically knows how to compile C++ files, how to link files, and so on, you don't have to tell it exactly how to do these things. In fact, all you have to do is simply add source files to a project file. The Visual C++ handles the rest. Pretty cool.

You may have already used a project file. If you created a program in the past few chapters, AppWizard created a project file that listed every source file in your program.

You can use Solution Explorer to do all kinds of programming tasks. For example, you can look at or edit any of the source files listed in your project file. You can control details that determine how your application is built. You can compile your application. See the "Common Things to Do from Solution Explorer" section for more information.

Solutions and projects

In the Visual C++ online documentation, you often see the words *solution* and *project* used together. Technically, the two words mean different things. A *solution* is a set of one or more projects. A solution with one project is the most common setup; you know you're a hacker when you have a solution with more than one project.

Because solutions and projects are so closely related, we refer to them interchangeably unless the topic applies to only one or the other but not both.

Your One-Stop Solution for Building Programs

You need to create a project file and a solution whenever you build a program. The project file tells the compiler what source files to compile when building the application. It also tells the compiler what libraries to link in. Visual C++ application wizards create solutions and projects for you.

Specifying details about the new project

Creating a new project is easy. To begin, choose File⇨New⇨Project to display the New Project dialog box (see Figure 4-1). This is where you specify details about a new project. For simple projects, you need to provide a project path and name. You also need to indicate what type of project you're creating and the prepackaged template you want.

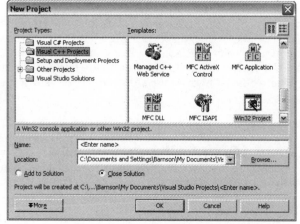

Figure 4-1: Use the New Project dialog box to create new projects.

✔ **Project Types:** Specify which type of project you want to create. In this book, we stick with Visual C++ Projects. Depending on which Visual C++ package you bought, you may have different entries in the Project Types list than those shown in Figure 4-1.

✔ **Templates:** Choose from the various kinds of projects that Visual C++ can create for you, based on what you selected in the Project Types list. Visual C++ projects have more than a dozen templates. Some of the templates are actually wizards, which give you a lot of control over what type of program Visual C++ creates for you. Two templates that you'll see often in this book are Win32 Project and Managed C++ Application. (There are all sorts of other choices, such as templates for various types of controls, libraries, and other geeky things.)

✔ **Name:** Type the name for the new project file. You usually use the same name for the project as the application you're building.

✔ **Location:** Choose the drive and folder where you want the project to go. You can click the Browse button to browse an existing folder. Visual C++ automatically creates the folder if it doesn't already exist. In general, it's a good idea to keep all source files associated with a project together in their own folder.

For example, suppose you want to create an application called Jukebox9, and you want to store it in the Myapps\Jukebox9 folder. First, use the Browse button or the Location field to switch to the Myapps folder. Then type **Jukebox9** for the Project name. Visual C++ creates the Jukebox9 folder as a subfolder under the Myapps folder.

✔ **Add to Solution/Close Solution:** As mentioned, solutions can hold more than one project. Therefore, when you create a project, you can add the project to the solution you're working in or tell Visual C++ to create a new, empty solution to hold the project.

After you supply the necessary information, click the OK button. For most types of projects, Visual C++ then displays a wizard that lets you specify what kind of project you want to create. Some wizards, such as the Win32 Application Wizard (which you see in Chapter 3), are fairly complicated, with several steps. Others consist of only one step and let you add some bare-bones files to your project.

Adding files to the project

To add a file that you haven't written yet, follow these steps:

1. **Choose File⇨New⇨File.**

   The New File dialog box appears, as shown in Figure 4-2.

2. **In the Categories list, select Visual C++.**

3. **In the Templates list, select C++ File (.cpp).**

4. **Click Open.**

   You've just added an empty C++ file.

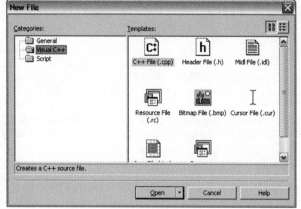

Figure 4-2:
Create a new source file on the New File dialog box.

To add a file that you've already written, follow these steps:

1. **Choose Project⇨Add Existing Item.**

   The Add Existing Item dialog box appears. This dialog box works like almost every file open dialog box in Windows.

2. **Click the filename you want to add to the project.**

   If you want to add more than one file, hold down the Ctrl key and click each filename. After you've added files to your project, Solution Explorer looks like Figure 4-3.

Figure 4-3:
Solution Explorer shows the files in your solution.

Common Things to Do from Solution Explorer

You can use Solution Explorer to do myriad tasks. Here are some common tasks you'll probably do over and over again with projects:

✔ **Look at or edit one of the files in the project:** Double-click a filename to load the file into an editor. If the file doesn't exist, Visual C++ asks whether you want to create a new file. Answer yes and you get a shiny new editor window.

✔ **Add a new file to the project:** Right-click *project*, where *project* is the name of your project, and choose Add⇨Add Existing Item (see Figure 4-4). Doing so is the equivalent of choosing Project⇨Add Existing Item.

Figure 4-4:
Add an existing source file to a project using Solution Explorer.

Solution Explorer shows you the dependencies for a project. As we mentioned, dependencies are sets of files that, if changed, cause the project to be recompiled. For example, if the file is a source file, the dependencies are usually the header files that are included when the file is compiled.

Suppose that you change something in a header file that the source file includes. Doing so changes the way the source file behaves because something is now defined differently in the header file. Thus, we say that the source file is dependent on the header file, and the source file needs to be recompiled so that the changed header file is accounted for.

Solution Explorer lists the project's dependencies under Header Files and Resource Files, as shown in Figure 4-5. Resource files are individual resources — such as bitmaps and icons — that are part of a program's resources. They're dependents just like header files.

Figure 4-5:
Solution
Explorer
shows a
project's
depen-
dencies.

Solutions and projects are an important part of Visual C++. Visual C++ needs them to build your programs, and you use them to quickly look at your source code. Solution Explorer is where you'll spend a lot of your time — after writing code, of course.

Chapter 5

All It Takes Is a Good Editor

• •

• •

*W*hen you get right down to it, the process of writing programs consists largely of typing code in an editor. And, just as a good word processor makes writing a book much easier — well, not *that* much easier — a good programmer's editor makes writing a program much easier. A *programmer's editor,* as its name implies, is an editor that lets you do special programming-related tasks in addition to the usual editing tasks, such as cutting, copying, and pasting text. (A really good programmer's editor has built-in links to late-night pizza joints and maybe a Tomb Raider button or two.)

Visual C++ contains a sophisticated, customizable programmer's editor that you can use to do programmer-type tasks, such as indenting groups of lines or quickly loading header files, in addition to the usual editing tasks. (The Visual C++ programmer's editor is called *the editor* for short in this book.) This chapter provides a quick guide to the most important features of the Visual C++ editor.

All the Code That's Fit to Edit

With Visual C++, you can edit as many files as you like (well, not quite an infinite amount, but an awful lot). If you edit several files at once, each appears in an editor window. Visual C++ supports both MDI-style windows and tabbed windows. (For those of you who were doing something real during the early 90s, like listening to Milli Vanilli, MDI means multiple document interface, which is a fancy way of saying that you can open a bunch of windows on the screen at one time and move them around.) Tabbed windows are the default. Figure 5-1 shows an editor window with some text in it.

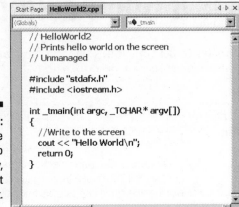

```
Start Page  HelloWorld2.cpp                    ◁ ▷ ×
(Globals)                          ▾  ⋄ _tmain              ▾
    // HelloWorld2
    // Prints hello world on the screen
    // Unmanaged

    #include "stdafx.h"
    #include <iostream.h>

    int _tmain(int argc, _TCHAR* argv[])
    {
        //Write to the screen
        cout << "Hello World\n";
        return 0;
    }
```

Figure 5-1:
Use the
editor to
display,
enter, or edit
text.

The most common ways to display an editor window follow:

- ✓ **Edit a file that's in a project:** Double-click a filename in Solution Explorer. This loads the file into an editor window.

- ✓ **Edit a member of a class:** Double-click a member name in the Class view. This loads the file into an editor window and positions the cursor on the specified member. You can also right-click a member name and choose Go to Definition to edit the .cpp source file or Go to Declaration to edit the .h header file.

- ✓ **Create a new file:** Choose File⇨New⇨File to display the New File dialog box. Choose the file category you want to create and then select a file type from the Template list.

- ✓ **Load an existing file:** Choose File⇨Open⇨File. Select the name of the file that you want to edit.

After you edit a file, you can easily save it. You can also save all the files that you edit in one fell swoop. Here are several ways to save:

- ✓ **Save a file:** Choose File⇨Save *filename*.

- ✓ **Save a file, giving it a new name:** Choose File⇨Save *filename* As. Type the new name that you want to give the file and click Save.

- ✓ **Save any files that have changed:** Choose File⇨Save All. It's usually a good idea to do this before you run a program that you've created, in case the program crashes the system.

Master of Editing Ceremonies

As you program, you may find yourself performing a number of editing tasks over and over (and over!) again. Some of these tasks are basic, such as cutting and copying text. Other tasks are specific to programming, such as indenting a group of lines or opening a header file.

Table 5-1 lists and describes ways to perform both basic and programming-specific editing tasks. The more basic tasks are described first.

Table 5-1	Editing Tasks for Nerds and Non-Nerds Alike
Task	*Description*
Select text	Click where you want the selection to begin. Hold down the left mouse button, move to the end of the selection, and release the button.
	Or click where you want the selection to begin, hold down the Shift key, and click where you want the selection to end.
	Or click (or use the arrow keys) until you get to where you want the selection to begin. Hold down the Shift key and use the arrow keys until you get where you want the selection to end.
Cut text	Select the text. Then choose Edit⇨Cut or press Ctrl+X. You can then paste the text somewhere else. (You can also right-click the selected text and choose Cut.)
Copy text	Select the text. Then choose Edit⇨Copy or press Ctrl+C. You can then paste the text somewhere else. (You can also right-click the selected text and choose Copy.)
Paste text	Choose Edit⇨Paste or press Ctrl+V. This pastes text from the Clipboard into the editor. (You can also right-click where you want the text to go and choose Paste.)
Move to the top of the file	Press Ctrl+Home.
Move to the end of the file	Press Ctrl+End.
Move up a page	Press PgUp.

(continued)

Table 5-1 *(continued)*

Task	Description
Move down a page	Press PgDn_
Move right one word	Press Ctrl+→_
Move left one word	Press Ctrl+←_
Indent a group of lines	Select the group of lines and then press Tab. You might do this if you've just added an if statement and you want to indent a section of code so that it's easier to read.
Outdent a group of lines	Select the group of lines and then press Shift+Tab. You might do this if you've copied a group of lines from one place to another, and now you don't need them indented so much.
Look for matching ( ) { } < > or [	Press Ctrl+] to move between the opening (, {, <, or [(the cursor must already be on one) and the closing), }, >, or]. You might do this if you have lots of nested statements and want to find where the block started. Or you might want to make sure that you remembered to end a function call with).
Set a bookmark	Move the cursor to where you want to place the bookmark. Press Ctrl+K, Ctrl+K to set it. This lets you mark a place in the code that you can easily pop back to. For example, if you want to copy code from one part of a file into a routine, you might set a bookmark at the beginning of the routine, scroll to find the code, copy it, jump to the bookmark you set, and paste in the code.
Jump to a bookmark	Press Ctrl+K, Ctrl+N to find the next bookmark in the file. Press Ctrl+K, Ctrl+P to find the previous bookmark.
Switch editor windows	Press Ctrl+Tab or Ctrl+F6 to cycle to the next editor window. Press Shift+Ctrl+Tab or Shift+Ctrl+F6 to cycle to the preceding editor window.

Task	Description
Open a related header file	Right-click anywhere in the #include file-name and choose Open Document *filename*.
	When you write C++ programs, you often need to modify the header file as well as the C++ file. Or you might want to check a header file quickly to see what has been defined.
Get help for a command	Click somewhere inside the call you need help on. Press the F1 key.
	For example, you might want to know the syntax for a library call, a Windows API call, or a C++ command.

Brought to You in Living Color

The editor in Visual C++ uses something called syntax coloring to make it easier for you to read the programs you've written. *Syntax coloring* highlights the different program elements — such as comments, keywords, numbers, and variables — so that you can identify them easily. Highlighting also helps you to find common syntax mistakes quickly.

For example, if your code always appears in black and your comments in blue, it's easy to see whether you forgot to close a comment block because you see a seemingly endless ocean of blue text before your eyes. Likewise, if you set up highlighting so that your keywords are green, you know that you misspelled a keyword if it isn't green. For instance, if you type *clasp* when you meant *class,* it won't show up green. And if a variable shows up green, you know it's a bad variable name because variables can't have the same names as keywords. (We discuss naming conventions for variables in Chapter 8.) If you want to customize the default colors for syntax coloring, just choose Tools⇨Options, and select Fonts and Colors under the Environment heading.

Figure 5-2 shows an edit window with syntax coloring turned on. (Well, because it's a black-and-white picture, it's looks more like syntax graying.)

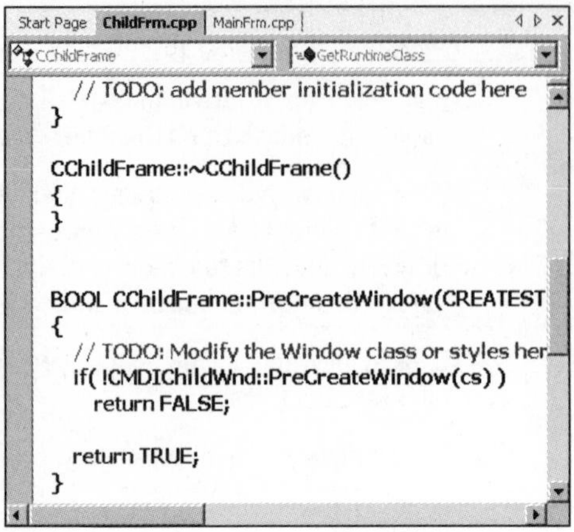

```
Start Page   ChildFrm.cpp   MainFrm.cpp                    ◀ ▷ ✕
CChildFrame                    ▼   GetRuntimeClass              ▼
        // TODO: add member initialization code here
    }

    CChildFrame::~CChildFrame()
    {
    }


    BOOL CChildFrame::PreCreateWindow(CREATEST
    {
        // TODO: Modify the Window class or styles her
        if( !CMDIChildWnd::PreCreateWindow(cs) )
            return FALSE;

        return TRUE;
    }
```

Figure 5-2:
Syntax
coloring
makes it
easy to see
the syntax
elements of
your source
files.

Online Help: Just Click Your Mouse One Time, Dorothy

If you're using a C++, .NET Framework, runtime library, Windows, or MFC feature but can't remember how that feature works, help is just a click away. For example, suppose that you're using the cout stream object from the standard C++ library, but you're not sure whether you're using it correctly:

```
cout << "Bob";
```

Just click somewhere on the word cout and then press F1, and online help appears.

As another example, suppose that you had this line:

```
while (strlen(bar) > 10)
```

You can click while and press F1 to get help about the while command or click strlen and press F1 to get help about the strlen library function.

Navigating by the Stars

When you're editing code, you'll end up moving between functions to see how a program operates almost as much as you navigate within a particular function to try to make it work correctly.

The navigation bar at the top of the editor window shows you the classes and member functions in the file you're editing. To move the cursor to a specific member function:

1. **Click the combo box on the left.**

   A list of classes is displayed.

2. **Select the class you're interested in.**

3. **Click the combo box on the right.**

   The member functions in the selected class are displayed, as shown in Figure 5-3.

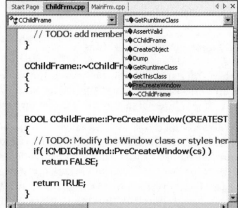

Figure 5-3:
The navigation bar makes for quick editing.

4. **Select the member function you want to edit.**

   Visual C++ moves the cursor to that function.

Note that the navigation bar shows only classes and member functions in the current file. If you want to look at another class's members, use the Class view.

Coding Hide and Seek

Sometimes a lot of code in a lot of windows with a lot of projects can get a bit overwhelming. The Visual C++ IDE feels your pain and has a way to lighten the load. By *outlining,* you can hide code you're not interested in seeing, but display it quickly when you want to see it all. Visual C++ outlines your code by creating or letting you create *regions* of code that appear with plus or minus signs to let you show and hide them (see Figure 5-4).

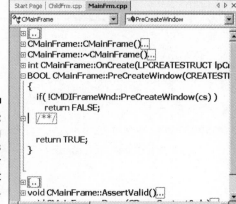

Figure 5-4:
Outlining
code makes
for
convenient
viewing.

Following are the two major approaches to outlining:

- **Outlining specific code:** You can easily outline any arbitrary code in a file. Just right-click it and choose Outlining⇨Hide Selection. (You can also choose Edit⇨Outlining⇨Hide Selection from the main menu.)

- **Outlining blocks of code:** Visual C++ knows how the C++ language is structured. It can outline code in blocks that reflect how you write C++ code. (You can find out more about blocks such as loops, flow-control statements, and functions in Part II.) To outline blocks, choose Edit⇨Outlining⇨Collapse to Definitions from the main menu. Visual C++ creates regions of code for each function definition, class definition, and any intervening code in the current window. Within each block, other blocks of code are outlined too.

Seek and Ye Shall Find

If you're like most programmers, you often find yourself trying to locate a particular block of code in your file. Instead of scrolling through the file until you find it, you can have the editor search through the code for you.

Use Edit⇨Find and Replace⇨Find (or press Ctrl+F) to find a particular piece of text. Use Edit⇨Find and Replace⇨Replace (Ctrl+H) to find the text and replace it at the same time. For example, you can use Edit⇨Find and Replace⇨Replace to replace every variable named foo with one named goo.

The Find and Replace dialog boxes let you enter a number of options to control how the search is performed. Figure 5-5 shows the Find dialog box.

Why do they use such fancy words?

Wildcards are sometimes called *regular expression matching commands.* This rather unwieldy term comes from the world of compilers.

When you build a compiler, you often need to build something called a *lexical analyzer,* which is a program that scans the text in your source files and breaks it into pieces that the compiler can understand. The lexical analyzer breaks the file into pieces by searching for patterns. These patterns are called (you guessed it) regular expressions.

Thus, regular expression matching just means looking for regular expressions, or patterns.

But you can just say wildcards.

The regular expressions in Table 5-3 are sometimes called *GREP-style regular expressions* because they're the same expressions used by the general text-searching program called GREP. GREP is a tool that became popular on UNIX systems. Many UNIX tools have rather guttural sounding names, such as MAWK, SED, DIFF — and GREP. When you're around computer people, feel free to use the word *grep* rather than search, as long as you're referring to searching text. You don't grep for your socks, for example. Or most people don't.

Figure 5-5: Find your way to happiness.

The options in the Find and Replace dialog boxes are described in the following list:

- **Match case:** C++ is a case-sensitive language. For example, C++ considers `Boogs` and `boogs` to be two different variables. If you set case sensitivity on, the search (or the replace) finds only those words where the capitalization matches the search string exactly. Use this option if you know exactly what you're looking for (that is, if you know the case). If you can't remember whether a name you're searching for is capitalized or not, turn off case sensitivity.

- **Match whole word only:** If this option is on, the search matches the word only when it's a separate word by itself (a word that's separated from other words by a space, a comma, or a bracket). When this option is off, the search finds the text, even if it's embedded in another word. For example, if you're searching for *const* when this option is off, the search finds *const* in the words *constant* and *deconstruct.*

- **Search hidden text:** If this option is on, text that is hidden (such as when you're using outlining) is also searched.

- **Search up:** Normally, the editor searches from the current location of the cursor to the end of the file. This option tells the editor to search from the current location to the beginning of the file instead.

- **Use regular expressions and wildcards:** *Wildcards* are special characters you use to represent other characters. For example, suppose you're looking for a particular variable that you know starts with an *S* and ends with an *h,* but you're not sure what's in the middle. You can use the * wildcard to find all variables that begin with *S*, end with *h,* and have any number or letters in the middle..

  Wildcards are a simpler form of regular expressions, which are more powerful. Table 5-2 lists some of the most useful wildcards; Table 5-3 lists some useful regular expressions.

- **Search: Current window/Current document:** This option tells the editor to search only the file that's in the current window.

- **Search: All open documents:** This option tells Visual C++ to search all the windows you currently have open. This is handy when you want to change the name of a class you use throughout a project.

- **Search: Only <current block>:** Searches can be limited to blocks of text or code. If a block search is supported, Visual C++ will enable this option and tell you the kind of block search.

- **Search: Selection only:** This option lets you replace text only in a selection block, which is useful when you need to change a variable name in a single function.

- **Mark All:** This button tells Visual C++ to find all the matches it can and, instead of displaying them, set a bookmark on them so you can come back to them later.

Table 5-2	Wildcards
Command	*Meaning*
?	Matches any single character. For example, this matches *Slip, Skip, Sbip,* and so on: `S?ip`
*	Matches any one or more characters. For example, this matches *Sl, Slug, Slip, Sliding,* and so on: `Sl*`

Command	Meaning
[ ]	Matches one of the characters that appear inside the brackets. For example, this matches *Smug and Slug:* `S[ml]ug`
[!]	Matches any character, except the character(s) inside the brackets. For example, this matches *Saug, Sbug,* and so on, but not *Smug* or *Slug:* `S[^ml]ug`

Table 5-3	Regular Expression Matching Commands
Command	**Meaning**
.	Matches any single character. For example, this matches *Slip, Skip, Sbip,* and so on: `S.ip`
*	Matches any number of characters. For example, this matches *Sl, Slug, Slip, Sliding,* and so on: `Sl*`
+	Matches one or more of the preceding characters. For example, this matches *Soon, Son,* and *So:* `So+`
^	Matches the beginning of a line. For example, this matches comments at the beginning of a line: `^//`
$	Matches the end of a line. For example, this matches `foo` only if it's at the end of a line: `foo$`
[ ]	Matches one of the characters that appear inside the brackets. For example, this matches *Smug* and *Slug:* `S[ml]ug`

(continued)

Table 5-3 *(continued)*

Command	Meaning
[^]	Matches any character, except the character(s) inside the brackets. For example, this matches *Saug, Sbug,* and so on, but not *Smug* or *Slug*: `S[^ml]ug`
[-]	Matches any letter in the range of characters separated by the hyphen (including the specified letters themselves). So, c-l means all the characters between c and l, inclusive. For example, this matches *Scug, Sdug, Seug, . . . Slug,* but nothing else: `S[c-l]ug`

Chapter 6

A Compile's Just a Frown, Upside Down

. . . .

In This Chapter

▶ Compiling a program

▶ Dealing with syntax errors and warnings

▶ Finding out the difference between compiles, builds, and rebuilds

. . . .

Writing programs can be wickedly good fun. You can include all types of zany formulas and approaches in your programs, and then type them and share them with friends at parties. And if you're a student, you can submit them to the creative writing department as avant-garde poems. For example, if Shakespeare had been a programmer, he might have written something like if (_2B) { } else { }. (And if he had been a real hacker, he would have written _2B ? {} : {}.)

But if you want the programs you write to actually *do* something, you need to compile them. *Compiling* a program turns source code, which is code that humans can understand, into machine instructions, which the computer can understand.

The process of turning source code into machine code is complex. It involves figuring out how to turn a set of high-level instructions into specific low-level machine instructions. When the process is complete, an *executable* is created. This is the program you can run.

Entire books are written on how to convert high-level programming languages into machine language. Fortunately for you, compiler vendors have read these books, so you don't have to understand how this process works. You just take the programs you've written and compile them with Visual C++.

It's Hard to Get by with Just a Compile

When you create a program, you edit, compile, and debug it. Along the way, you recompile it many, many times to correct and expand it. Fortunately, compiling a program with Visual C++ is easy. In fact, you've already compiled a program (several times) if you followed the steps in Chapter 3.

To compile a program, first open the solution for that program. (See Chapter 4 for more information on solutions.) Then choose Build➪Build or click the Build button on the Build toolbar (see Figure 6-1).

Figure 6-1:
The Build toolbar has buttons for common Build options.

Visual C++ goes through all the source files in the solution and converts them to machine code. The result is an executable program. You don't see anything on the screen, but the program is now on your hard disk. You can run the program, copy it to a disk and give it to a friend, or do whatever else you like doing with programs. (Nothing *too* wild, we hope.)

If you want to run the program, choose Debug➪Start or click the Start button on the Debug toolbar (see Figure 6-2). If you know that your program has no bugs (which means that you're well on your way to having a hacker ego), choose Debug➪Start Without Debugging, which runs the program without using the Visual C++ debugger.

Figure 6-2:
The Debug toolbar has buttons for starting, stopping, and stepping through your programs.

Blast! Syntax Errors

If you make a mistake while writing your program — for example, if you pass the wrong number of parameters to a function, misspell a command, or use the wrong name for a variable or a class — the compiler won't be able to understand your program.

If this happens (we should say *when* this happens, because it's going to happen), the compiler shows you the syntax errors in the Output window, as shown in Figure 6-3. *Syntax errors* are messages telling you that you've messed up somehow. You can double-click a syntax error in the Output window to go to the line containing that problem. You must correct each syntax error before the program can compile correctly.

Figure 6-3:
Syntax errors are displayed in the Output window.

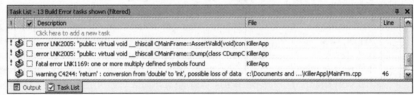

Sometimes it's clear what's wrong. Other times, you may have a hard time figuring out how to correct a syntax error, especially when you're new at it. After you mess up enough times, though, you start to see patterns, which can help you better figure out how to correct the problems.

Some simple rules:

✔ Save your program files before you compile them.

✔ If an error pops up and the line you're on looks perfectly fine, sometimes it's the preceding line that's messed up. Be sure to check it, too.

✔ Check for missing or extra ; and } characters.

✔ Compile your programs in small chunks. That way, you can focus on errors in one spot, rather than throughout the entire program.

✔ Messages that say Cannot convert from . . . to . . . usually mean that you're trying to assign the wrong type to a variable. For example, you may have a variable that's an integer but you're trying to turn it into a string.

✔ Make sure that you've typed things correctly. A common mistake is to name a variable one thing but then spell it wrong or use some other name later.

✔ Check out Chapters 23 and 24. They contain lists of common errors and ways to correct them.

✔ Sometimes, one simple problem can cause the compiler to find tons of errors. For example, putting in the wrong path for a header file can lead to 30 or more error messages. (You'll probably encounter this problem only in unmanaged programs.) Correcting that one line can make all those errors go away. So, if you compile a program and see screen after screen of problems, don't panic. Often a simple change corrects them all.

✔ If you can't figure out what's wrong, ask someone for help. If you're embarrassed about this, just say something like, "Geez, I've been up all night staring at this code and everything is just swimming. I sure could use help from a fresh pair of eyes." Fellow programmers will understand.

Warning, Will Robinson

Sometimes when you compile, you get warnings rather than (or in addition to) errors. *Warnings* occur when the compiler understands what you're doing but thinks you may be making a mistake. For example, if you create a variable but never give it a value, the compiler warns you by saying, in effect, "Why did you do that?" Or perhaps you're using a variable before assigning it a value. If you do this, you get a message similar to the one in Figure 6-4.

Figure 6-4:
Warnings
are
displayed
when the
compiler
finds code
that may
lead to
problems.

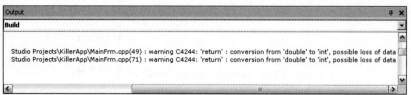

It's usually a good idea to heed warnings. Although warnings sometimes occur because the compiler is being overprotective, they usually occur because you did something careless. For example, if you accidentally forget to add a line to initialize a variable that you use, you get a warning. If you don't heed the warning, the variable will have a meaningless value wherever it's used, which can lead to all sorts of troublesome complications.

A good rule is to correct things until you have no warnings and no errors.

Why doesn't the compiler correct errors?

Even though the compiler knows where an error occurs and what type of error it is, the compiler doesn't know *why* the error occurred. For example, the compiler may detect that a semicolon is missing. Why doesn't it just add one? Well, the semicolon could be missing because you forgot to type one, or perhaps the entire line that's missing the semicolon wasn't meant to be there, or maybe you forgot a few other things in addition to the semicolon.

Rather than hazard a guess and get you into real trouble, the compiler just points out the problem and leaves it up to you to correct it. The compiler usually gets you close to the error, but beware: The actual problem could be several lines away. For example, the compiler may identify a certain line as missing a semicolon when the semicolon is actually missing from a previous line.

There's More Than One Way to Compile

You can compile files in three ways: by building them, compiling them, or rebuilding them.

Building (Build➪Build) compiles fresh OBJ files for any source files that changed. If there are fresh OBJs, the program is linked to create a new executable file (EXE). The result is a bunch of syntax errors or a full working program.

When you're working on a project and changing first one piece and then another, you usually build. That's because building recompiles only things that have changed, so you don't have to waste lots of time watching the compiler do unnecessary work. Most likely, you'll do a Build➪Build after you change source files and need a new EXE.

Compiling (Build➪Compile) compiles a single file, the one you're currently editing. It doesn't create a full program. You use this option when you want to check a particular file for syntax errors. If you compile a file successfully, the result is an object file (OBJ).

Rebuilding (Build➪Rebuild All) compiles all files in a project and links them to create an EXE. As with building, the result is a bunch of syntax errors or a full working program. Even if you just built a program, if you build it again, every single file is recompiled from scratch. (The result is a fresh OBJ for every single source file, plus an EXE formed by linking all the OBJs.) You usually rebuild when you want to make sure that *everything* in your project has been built again.

Part II

Everything You Always Wanted to Know about C++ but Were Afraid to Ask

The 5th Wave   By Rich Tennant

"It was at this point in time that there appeared to be some sort of mass insanity."

In this part . . .

*P*art II begins your serious nerd education. You find out about the fundamentals of Visual C++ .NET, from the parts that make up a program to variables, statements, and pointers. You also uncover one of the most important tools in a programmer's toolbox: the debugger.

You can discover a lot by example. Try out the sample programs as you run across them to make sure that you understand what's being discussed.

One of the most important parts of your nerd education is nerd humor. By the end of Part II, you'll be laughing uncontrollably at jokes like this:

What would you get if Lee Iacocca were bitten by a vampire?

    a. Winged convertibles with an aversion to garlic

    b. Cujo

    c. AUTOEXEC.BAT

Chapter 7

There's No Data Types Like Show Data Types

Computer programs process data — and you can have a lot of different types of data. Floating-point numbers in a spreadsheet program, order records in an inventory system, and shapes in a drawing program are only a few examples of different data types. Even though Hollywood directors think computers are omniscient, they really aren't, and thus don't have a clue as to what types of data they are meant to process unless they are explicitly programmed. In this chapter, you declare a variety of the basic data types and also dig in deeper with one of the most important data types: the String.

A Language for Jocks

Strongly typed languages, such as C++, require that the programmer describe what a piece of data is before using it. For example, if you want to save a number, you first need to tell the computer to expect a number.

Using a strongly typed language has many advantages. For example, if you make a mistake and treat an item that's a number as if it were an employee record, the compiler generates an error. That's good because, without type safety, you could accidentally destroy important information. Suppose that an employee record uses eight bytes of memory, and a number uses only two bytes of memory. If you clear an employee record, you clear eight bytes of memory. So if you cleared a number as if it were an employee record, you'd end up clearing the number plus six additional bytes in memory. And the six extra bytes you cleared may very well have contained important information. Clearing them could lead to some unexpected and undesirable results.

Some other languages, such as JavaScript, are *loosely typed*. In loosely typed languages, the computer figures out what an item is when you use it. For example, if you set a variable to contain the text foo, the language processor makes the variable a string. Loosely typed languages can be easier for new programmers, but they don't catch mistakes as well as strongly typed languages.

1 Do Declare a Variable's Type

In C++, you must declare each variable's type before you can use it — that is, you need to tell the compiler what type of data the variable will hold. (You can find out more about variables in Chapter 8. In the meantime, just know that a variable is a thing you store information in. Think of a variable as a cell in a spreadsheet, except that it has a name.) You have a few ways to declare a variable's type, but by far the most common is to indicate the type when you create the variable.

The process of creating a variable is called *defining the variable*. To define a variable, you simply indicate the type followed by the variable name. Several examples of variable definitions are provided here. This example creates a variable foo that is of type int (integer):

```
int foo;
```

This creates a variable bar that is of type char (character):

```
char bar;
```

And the following indicates that the function min takes two integers as parameters and returns an integer. (You find out more about what functions do and how to define them in Chapter 12.)

```
int min(int first, int second);
```

Note that *declare* and *define* are different. When you *declare* the type, you indicate what something is, but you don't set aside any memory for it. (It is not physically created.) When you *define* something, it is physically created. This difference doesn't matter much for variables. You almost always indicate their type when you define them, rather than declare their type in one place and define them in another place. In other words, with variables, declaration and definition are wrapped up in one. When you read about structures (see Chapter 9) and classes (see Chapter 17), you see declaration and definition occurring in two distinct steps.

The elemental data types

C++ provides a number of predefined data types that you can use. You can also create more complex data types by combining data types, as Chapter 9 discusses. Here are the three most commonly used data types:

- ✔ double: A floating-point number. (That doesn't mean that the number is a witch. Instead, it means numbers such as 4.3444, 42.0, and 3.14. It means the decimal point can float left or right, and is not in a fixed position.) Doubles represent numbers from $\pm1.7 \times 10\text{-}308$ to ±1.7 (10308. In math terms, they are real numbers.

- ✔ int: An integer. Integers are whole numbers. They can be positive, negative, or 0. For example, the numbers 0, 1, 3, 39, and -42 are all integers but 1.5 isn't.

- ✔ String: Some text, such as "Hello World".

Suppose you wanted to store the radius of a circle. You might use this code:

```
double dblRadius;
```

This says that the variable named dblRadius stores a floating-point number, such as 4.5. This is perfect for storing the radius of a circle.

When you write your application, you need to figure out what data types you need for the various data that you're going to be using. For example, if you were storing the number of attendees at a concert, you would use an integer, because it is unlikely that half a person would attend. (Of course, someone could be half out of it.) If you were storing the radius of a circle, you would use a double because the radius could be 2.3 units or 55.6 units or whatever. And if you need to store text, you'd use a string.

Less common data types

This section describes some other data types that aren't used as often as the ones in the preceding section:

- ✔ float: A floating-point number but with less precision than a double. A float represents numbers between $\pm3.4 \times 10\text{-}38$ to ±3.4 (1038.

- ✔ long: Can precede an int to tell it to use 32 bits to represent the number. Integers in Visual C++ .NET are 32-bit by default anyway, so there is no need for this.

- ✔ **short:** Can precede an int to tell it to use 16 bits to represent the number.

- ✔ **signed**: Can precede an int to indicate that the number is either positive or negative. (This is the default for Visual C++.)

- ✔ unsigned: Can precede an int to indicate that the number is always positive. This allows one more bit to be used to represent the size of the number. So, instead of integers ranging from -2,147,483,648 to 2,147,483,647, they range from 0 to 4,294,967,295.

- ✔ void: No type. Used to indicate that a function doesn't return a value. (See Chapter 12 for more information on functions.)

- ✔ char: A character. A, B, and & are all characters. (By the way, *char* can be pronounced like the "char" in "charcoal" or like "car" or even like "care.") You'll see this type in unmanaged programs but rarely in managed programs, because in managed programs you usually use the more powerful, built-in string type instead.

The type safety feature

Machine language doesn't care about data types. To machine language, data is just locations in memory. That's why a machine language program will blithely write integers all over your employee records, or write character values all over your program, or do whatever else a program may tell it to do. (Many computer viruses are designed to destroy data in just this way.)

But C++ *does* care about types. If you declare a variable as one type and then try to use it as another type, the compiler generates an error. This is referred to as *type safety,* and it is a very helpful feature of C++ because it means that the compiler finds some common errors. (This is certainly better than having the compiler ignore the errors, only to have your program crash as a result of them.)

So, the following program works well:

```
//Use an integer for the size.
int nSize;
//Set the size to 7
nSize = 7;
```

But if you try the following, you get an error because nSize is an integer and therefore can't be set to a string:

```
//Set size to something bogus.
nSize = "Hello World";
```

For some operations, the compiler automatically converts from one data type to another. For example, the compiler converts a floating-point number to an integer in the following situation:

```
int nSize;
nSize = 6.3;
```

One of these types is not like the others

Visual C++ goes to great lengths to make sure that no type mismatches occur. As the compiler compiles a C++ source file, it creates something called a symbol table. The *symbol table* contains detailed information about all the variables and functions used in the source file. Whenever you use variables (or functions), the compiler finds their type from the symbol table and makes sure that the correct types are used.

The compiler also contains detailed rules on how to convert data from one type to another. For example, if you have a function that expects a double (see Chapter 12 for more information on passing parameters to functions) and you pass in an integer, the compiler knows how to convert an integer to a floating-point value. If the compiler finds a type mismatch in a situation where it doesn't have a rule for converting the data, it reports an error.

When you compile a program that uses more than one source file, the situation is a bit more complex. One source file may use a function or variable that is declared in a different source file. The compiler needs to be able to match functions and variables across source files — and to make sure that correct types are used. Technically speaking, this step is performed during the linking phase.

Type checking across files (called *external resolution*) is performed with a technique called *name mangling.* When you declare a variable, a function, or another item, the compiler converts the name you've given the item to an internal name. The internal name includes information describing the type of the item. For example, suppose that the compiler uses the character *i* to indicate that an item is an integer and *cp* to indicate that an item is a character pointer. Then suppose that you have this function in one source file:

```
int NumberOfSongs();
```

Also suppose that, in a different file, you have this code:

```
char *MyText;
MyText = NumberOfSongs();
```

The compiler would convert the name `NumberOfSongs` to `iNumberOfSongs` and the name `MyText` to `cpMyText`. You never see these internal names (unless you're looking at assembly language listings), but the linker does.

As a result, the linker sees this:

```
cpMyText = iNumberOfSongs();
```

By looking at the mangled name, the compiler sees that a type mismatch has occurred (because type integer doesn't match type character pointer), so it prints an error.

After running this code, `nSize` is set to 6. (The compiler automatically truncates the number. That means it chucks all the digits to the right of the decimal point. The fancy word for this is *floor.*) The compiler warns you, however, that it had to make a conversion. When you get a warning from the compiler, you should pay attention. In fact, it's a good idea to make sure that programs compile with no warnings or errors. For this case, you should explicitly tell the compiler to convert from one type to another. This is called *typecasting*. To do this, just put a type name in parentheses before the item to convert:

```
int nSize;
double fltEntered;
nSize = (int) fltEntered;
```

In this example, the compiler converts (typecasts) the `double` variable to an integer. To do that, it lops off the fractional part of `fltEntered`. For example, if `fltEntered` were 3.141592653, `nSize` would be assigned the value 3.

Hope ToStrings Eternal

In standard C++, types are just structures that consume a certain amount of memory. In .NET, types also have built-in functionality. Technically, types are objects. (You find out more about objects in Chapter 17.) As such, they have a variety of built-in functions, the most useful of which convert types from one form to another. Table 7-1 shows the key conversion functions for common data types.

Table 7-1	The Conversion Functions	
Type	*Function*	*Meaning*
String	ToDouble()	Converts a string to a double
String	ToInt32()	Converts to an integer
double	ToString()	Converts to a string
double	Parse()	Converts a string to a double
int	ToString()	Converts to a string
int	Parse()	Converts a string to an int

For example, suppose you want to write a number. First you need to convert it to a string, as shown in the following code:

```
int nNumber = 3;
Console::WriteLine(nNumber.ToString());
```

Suppose, on the other hand, that you have a string and want to turn it into a double. You would do this:

```
String *szNumber = S"3.14"
double fltNumber;
fltNumber = Double::Parse(szNumber);
```

You may have noticed the * before the String variable name. It's there because you need to use pointers when dealing with strings. You can find out more about pointers in Chapter 13. In the interim, whenever you define a string, put * before the variable name. And whenever you call one of the built-in functions on a string, use -> instead of . (period).

And just in case you want to know what some of the other bizarre stuff is, the S before "3.14" tells the compiler to make a .NET string. You can create all types of strings (believe it or not), and S tells the compiler to use the type that is best for .NET. Also, the ::, as in Double::Parse, is a funky type of syntax that lets you call methods (such as Parse) on object types (such as double) without creating the object first. It's one of those convenient C++ capabilities.

Some Things Never Change: Constants

You'll find that you use certain numbers or words repeatedly in an application. For example, if you're doing mathematics, you know that _ is always 3.141592.... If you're writing a philosophy program, you know that the meaning of life, the universe, and everything is 42.

For cases like this, you can create a constant. A *constant* is just a name for an item that never changes. To make an item a constant, precede its declaration with const. For example, the following code makes PI a constant that always has the value 3.141592:

```
//Set the constant for pi.
const double PI = 3.141592;
```

Constants make your programs a lot easier to read because you provide a name for a particular value. Also, if you change the value of a constant, the change ripples out and affects the whole program. For example, if a sudden time warp occurs and you find yourself on the planet Transsexual (in the galaxy of Transylvania), where __is 7, you change only the constant. All related calculations update automatically, saving you from having to read through your whole program to find each place where you use _.

You can use a constant in a program anywhere that you can use an item of the same data type as the constant. For example, if you have a floating-point constant, you can pass in that constant anywhere that you can use a floating-point number in an equation. Thus, you can multiply the diameter of a circle by the constant PI to determine the circumference.

Adding constants to a program

Next, you create a program that uses constants and conversions. This program asks the user for the radius of a circle and then prints the area. Create a new .NET program and then type and run this application:

```cpp
// CircleArea
// Computes the area of a circle given the radius

#include "stdafx.h"

#using <mscorlib.dll>

using namespace System;

// This is the entry point for this application
#ifdef _UNICODE
int wmain(void)
#else
int main(void)
#endif
{
    double fltRadius;
    double fltArea;
    const double PI = 3.141592;

    //Ask for the size of the radius
    Console::WriteLine(S"What is the radius?");

    //Read in the answer and convert to a floating-point
            number
    fltRadius = Double::Parse(Console::ReadLine());
    //Calculate the area of the circle
    fltArea = PI*fltRadius*fltRadius;

    //Write the result
    //Note that we must convert the area into a string to do
            so
    Console::WriteLine(S"The circle's area is {0} units.",
            fltArea.ToString());

    //Hang out until the user is finished
    Console::WriteLine(S"Press the Enter key to stop the
            program");
        Console::ReadLine();

    return 0;
}
```

This program is in the CircleArea directory on the CD accompanying this book. Check out CircleArea2 for an unmanaged version of the same program.

Constants and bug prevention

Another nice thing about constants is that if you inadvertently try to change them, the compiler complains. For example, suppose that you accidentally included the following line in the middle of the program:

```
PI = 15;
```

When the compiler sees this line, it generates an error telling you that you're trying to change the value of a constant. This kind of early warning can prevent lots of hard-to-find bugs later on.

String Out on an All-Time High

Strings are a fundamental part of almost all applications. To use them effectively, you need to know some basics. Table 7-2 shows the instant, just-add-water set of things to do with strings.

Table 7-2	Stuff to Do with Strings
Need	*How to Do It*
Combine two strings	`pszResult = String::Concat(psz1, psz2);`
Write some text with values mixed in	`Console::WriteLine(S"Value 1: {0}` `Value 2 {1}", psz1, psz2);`
See whether two strings are the same	`fResult = psz1->Equals(psz2);`
Find where one string occurs within another	`nOffset = psz1->IndexOf(psz2);`
Get the *n* characters from the middle of a string, starting with the *m*th character	`pszResult = psz1->Substring(m, n);`
Find the length of a string	`nLength = psz1->Length;`
Get rid of leading and trailing whitespace	`pszResult = psz1->Trim();`

You manipulate strings throughout the programs in this book. Here's a simple program that illustrates various string techniques:

```
// Strings101
// Shows some basic string manipulations

#include "stdafx.h"

#using <mscorlib.dll>

using namespace System;

// This is the entry point for this application
#ifdef _UNICODE
int wmain(void)
#else
int main(void)
#endif
{
    String *pszString;
    int nNumber;
    double fltNumber;

    //Combine two strings
    pszString = String::Concat(S"Peanut butter", S" and
            jelly");
    Console::WriteLine(pszString);

    //Combine two strings while converting
    nNumber = 3;
    pszString = String::Concat(S"Converted ",
            nNumber.ToString());
    Console::WriteLine(pszString);

    //Convert to a floating-point number
    Console::WriteLine(S"Please enter a number");
    fltNumber = Double::Parse(Console::ReadLine());
    //Add a number to it
    fltNumber = fltNumber + 30.5;
    //Now write it out
    Console::WriteLine(String::Concat("The number is ",
            fltNumber.ToString()));

    //Write out some strings, concatenating in place
    Console::WriteLine(String::Concat(S"First ", S"Second ",
            S"Third"));

    //Write using format syntax
    Console::WriteLine(S"A string: {0}\nAn integer {1}", S"my
            string", nNumber.ToString());
```

```
    //Get rid of leading and trailing whitespace
    pszString = S"   Hello   World      ";
    Console::WriteLine(S"With: {0}\n and without
            leading/trailing whitespace: {1}", pszString,
            pszString->Trim());

    //Find the character in the middle of the string
    Console::WriteLine(S"The middle character of {0} is
            \"{1}\"", pszString, pszString-
            >Substring(pszString->Length/2, 1));

    //Hang out until the user is finished
    Console::WriteLine(S"Press the Enter key to stop the
            program");
    Console::ReadLine();
    return 0;
}
```

You can find this program in the Strings101 directory on the accompanying CD-ROM.

Chapter 8

These Variables, They Are A-Changin'

• •

In This Chapter

▶ Naming variables

▶ Defining and initializing variables

▶ Using a naming convention

• •

*P*rograms read, write, and manipulate data. When you want to save a particular value or save the results of a calculation, you use a variable. A *variable* is a name that represents a piece of information. You can store all types of things in variables, such as information about an employee, the length of a song, or the number of bicycles ordered.

Variables often have descriptive names. For example, the name nRadius tells you that this variable represents the radius of a circle. On the other hand, C3PO is not a great variable name. It can be a serial number, a license plate, a robot, or who knows what.

Whenever you want to access the information stored in a variable, you use the variable's name. Because C++ is strongly typed, you need to declare a variable's data type before using the variable.

In this chapter, you name, define, and initialize variables.

Naming Variables

When you choose a name for a child, you have lots of limitations. For example, maybe you hope that your child will grow up to be a Windows programmer. So instead of naming him Bob, you are tempted to name him pszBob. Or instead of naming her Gabrielle, you want to name her hWnd. Unfortunately, even though most (but not all) governments will let you do this, your child will face hopeless teasing from classmates and lots of scolding from teachers wanting to correct his or her capitalization.

When you choose the name for a variable, you needn't concern yourself with whether fellow variables will tease your newly named variable. In fact, you can name a variable pretty much anything that you want, with only a few (quite reasonable) limitations:

- ✔ Variable names can't start with numbers.
- ✔ Variable names can't have spaces in them.
- ✔ Variable names can't include special characters, such as . ; , " ' and +. It's easiest to just assume that _ (the underscore) is the only nonalphanumeric character that you can use in a variable name.
- ✔ Variables shouldn't be given the name of C++ library functions.
- ✔ Variables can't have the same name as keywords.

Table 8-1 is a list of the Visual C++ keywords, which are the commands that are part of the C++ language. You find out what most of these keywords do by the time you finish this book! The keywords that start with two underscores (_ _) are special Visual C++ extensions that make personal-computer programming easier. Don't use keywords for variable names.

Table 8-1	The C++ Keywords	
__abstract	__hook	__multiple_inheritance
__alignof	__identifier	__nogc
__asm	__if_exists	__noop
__assume	__if_not_exists	__pin
__based	__inline	__property
__box	__int8	__raise
__cdecl	__int16	__sealed
__declspec	__int32	__single_inheritance
__delegate	__int64	__stdcall
__event	__interface	__super
__except	__leave	__try_cast
__fastcall	__m64	__try/__except
__finally	__m128	__try/__finally
__forceinline	__m128d	__unhook
__gc	__m128i	__uuidof

__value	float	signed
__virtual_ inheritance	for	sizeof
__w64	friend	static
__wchar_t	goto	static_cast
bool	if	struct
break	inline	switch
case	int	template
catch	long	this
char	mutable	thread
class	naked	throw
const	namespace	true
const_cast	new	try
continue	noinline	typedef
default	noreturn	typeid
delete	nothrow	typename
deprecated	novtable	union
dllexport	operator	unsigned
dllimport	private	using
do	property	uuid
double	protected	virtual
dynamic_cast	public	void
else	register	volatile
enum	reinterpret_cast	wchar_t
explicit	return	while
extern	selectany	
false	short	

Here are some examples of legal variable names: way_cool, RightOn, Bits32. And here are some bad names: case (this is a keyword), 52PickUp (this starts with a number), A Louse (this has a space in it), +-v (this has illegal characters in it).

Variable names are case sensitive. So bart, Bart, bArt, and BART are all different variables.

Defining Variables

Before you use a variable, you need to define it. To do so, just state the data type for the variable, followed by the variable's name. Here are some examples:

```
int RevenueService;
double OrNothing;
long Johns;
```

If you want to, you can even combine definitions on a single line, as long as all the variables you are defining are of the same type. For example, if you had three floats, named Banana, Chocolate, and RootBeer, you could do this:

```
float Banana;
float Chocolate;
float RootBeer;
```

Or, you could do the following:

```
float Banana, Chocolate, RootBeer;
```

Initializing Variables

When you define a variable, you can also provide an *initial value*. This is the value the variable will have when it's first used. You provide an initial value by following the name with an = (equal sign) and a value. For example:

```
int NumberOfSongs = 3;
double dblRadius = 3.5;
long Johns = 32700;
```

Now, that wasn't so hard, was it?

That's the Name, Uh Huh, Uh Huh

Although you can name variables pretty much anything that you like, following a naming convention will make it easier to read your programs. One of the most common naming conventions is *Hungarian notation*, invented by a Hungarian dude who works at Microsoft. The idea behind Hungarian is to put a few characters at the beginning of every variable name to tell you what type of a variable it is. In this book, we use a variation of Hungarian called *Michael and Bob's Hungarian Lite*. Actually, it's just a simplified version of Hungarian notation without any particular name, but why not name it something pretentious.

For example, we put the letter *n* before integer variables, as in:

```
int nRadius;
int nCount = 0;
```

Table 8-2 shows the prefixes used before variables in this book. Following such a convention can help prevent bugs, but you can use it or lose it as you see fit.

Table 8-2	Variable Naming	
Type	*Prefix*	*Example*
Integer	n	nCount
Double	dbl	dblRadius
String	psz	pszName
Boolean	f	fFinished
object	o	oLine
object pointer	po	poCircle
array	a	aShapes
member	m_	m_nShapes

You may not have seen some of these types yet. For example, you find out about arrays in Chapter 14 and objects in Chapter 17.

Chapter 9

Struct by Lightning

• •

In This Chapter

▶ Declaring and using structures

▶ Combining structures

▶ Adding structures to an application

• •

*P*revious chapters in this book describe simple data types and how to store information in a variable. But suppose that you want to store something more complex than a simple data type — for example, a user's name, address, and phone number? You *could* do this by storing the information in three separate variables: one for the name, one for the address, and one for the phone number.

This strategy is awkward, though, because in the real world it's natural to group things. For example, suppose that you want to read or print an employee record. Although that record probably contains lots of parts (such as name, address, phone number, and salary), you probably think of it as a complete entity in and of itself. After all, it's a lot easier to say "print the employee record" than it is to say "print the employee name, address, phone number, salary. . . ."

This chapter shows you how to group a set of related variables into a single entity called a *structure*. Combining related items into a single structure can make a program much easier to understand. You'll probably use structures in every program you write — and you see them used throughout the book. And in Chapter 17, you see how structures turn into classes — the fundamental building blocks of object-oriented programs.

Declaring Structures

Declaring a structure is similar to declaring a simple data type (as Chapter 7 discusses). To declare a structure, you use the class keyword, followed by the name of the structure. Then, in curly brackets (some people also call these braces), you type public:, followed by a list of the variables that make up the structure.

For example, you can have the following:

```
class CircleInfo
{
public:
    double dblRadius;
    double dblArea;
};
```

In this case, the structure's name is `CircleInfo`. It contains a double named `dblRadius` (which will be used to store the radius of the circle) and a double named `dblArea` (which will be used to store the area of a circle).

To define a variable to be a structure, just follow the structure name with the variable name:

```
//Make a CircleInfo variable
CircleInfo oCircle;
```

What does it really mean to define a variable to be a structure? Well, now you have a variable called `oCircle` that is of type `CircleInfo`. That means the `oCircle` variable contains other variables — `dblRadius` and `dblArea` — because type `CircleInfo` contains two double variables. You can talk about the double variable called `dblRadius` inside the `CircleInfo` variable called `oCircle`. In this case, you are talking about a specific member (`dblRadius`) of a variable (`oCircle`) whose type is `CircleInfo`.

By combining variables to make structures, you can organize information more easily. Throughout this chapter, you find out how to use variables that are structures.

Defying clarification by defining declaration

In C++, *declaration* and *definition* are technical terms. They have slightly different meanings and are often used interchangeably (although doing so is incorrect).

Declaring a structure means telling the compiler what's in the structure, as in:

```
class CircleInfo
{
public:
    double dblRadius;
    double dblArea;
};
```

No memory is set aside for the structure.

Defining a variable means telling the compiler to create a variable. This causes memory to be allocated for a variable:

```
CircleInfo oCircle;
```

Using Those Marvelous Structures

After you create a structure, you can access its members (the variables in it) by typing the structure variable, followed by a . (that's a period), followed by the member name.

For example, to print the radius of a circle, you can type this:

```
//Make a CircleInfo variable
CircleInfo oCircle;
//Now print the value of the data member called
//dblRadius
Console::WriteLine(oCircle.dblRadius.ToString());
```

As you can see, `oCircle.dblRadius` acts just like a normal variable. Using members of structures is no different than using a plain old stand-all-by-its-lonesome variable.

Building Big Structures from Little Structures

You can combine structures to create more complex structures. Sometimes this is called *nesting* structures.

Any structure that you include in another structure must be declared before it is used. For example, before the `CrazyEight` structure can use a `CircleInfo`, `CircleInfo` must be declared. This isn't a big deal. You just need to make sure you do things in the right order. If you don't, Visual C++ .NET will flip you some error messages.

For example, the following structure contains two `CircleInfo` structures:

```
class CrazyEight
{
public:
    CircleInfo oTopCircle;
    CircleInfo oBottomCircle;
};
```

An In-struct-ional Program

Take another look at the CircleArea application, this time changing it so that it uses structures:

```
// CircleArea3
// Computes the area of a circle given the radius
// Uses a structure for storing the information

#include "stdafx.h"

#using <mscorlib.dll>

using namespace System;


//Set up a structure for storing information about circles
class CircleInfo
{
public:
    double dblRadius;
    double dblArea;
};

// This is the entry point for this application
#ifdef _UNICODE
int wmain(void)
#else
int main(void)
#endif
{
    const double PI = 3.141592;
    CircleInfo oCircle;

    //Ask for the size of the radius
    Console::WriteLine(S"What is the radius?");

    //Convert the answer to a floating-point number
    oCircle.dblRadius = Double::Parse(Console::ReadLine());

    //Calculate the area of the circle
    oCircle.dblArea = PI*oCircle.dblRadius*oCircle.dblRadius;

    //Write out the result
    //Note that we must convert the area into a string to do
           so
    Console::WriteLine(S"The circle's area is {0} units.",
           oCircle.dblArea.ToString());

    //Hang out until the user is finished
    Console::WriteLine(S"Press the Enter key to stop the
           program");
    Console::ReadLine();

    return 0;
}
```

You can type this program in, or you can load it from the CircleArea3 directory on the CD accompanying this book.

You may notice some interesting things about this program. First, the CircleInfo structure is declared before the function named main. (main is the name of the function where the program begins.) That's because you need to declare things before you use them. In this case, CircleInfo is used inside main, so it's declared before main. You see this over and over again in C++ programs. A class is declared. Its various member functions are defined. And then the class is used.

At first, you may think that things seem a little backward because the lowest, most elementary items are declared first, followed by the items that use them. You get used to this as you do more programming in C++. For now, if you want to see the big picture, you can start toward the bottom of the source file and then work your way back up.

Wait, my teacher is instructing me about struct!

In this book, you use the class keyword when you create structures. You use the class keyword also when you create classes. (See Chapter 17 for more information on classes.)

C++ actually has two different commands that you can use to declare structures (and classes): class and struct. struct is similar to class, except that you don't need to use public: before you list the items that make up the structure. Some people use struct anytime they declare structures and use class anytime they declare classes (which are structures that also contain functions). Note, though, that you can just as easily use struct to declare classes.

When you read about classes (starting in Chapter 17), you find out what the public keyword means. You find out also about private and protected, and use these keywords frequently. struct items are public by default, whereas class items are private by default. Rather than remember which is which, it's easier to just use class anytime you declare a structure or a class.

Why are there two keywords for doing almost the same thing? struct is a holdover from C. It's kept so that you can compile C programs with a C++ compiler, and it was given some new functionality that makes it similar to class. Because you're a C++ programmer, you should use class.

Chapter 10

Express Yourself

*P*rograms process data and, as part of this processing, they perform a variety of calculations. A set of calculations (or formulas, as they're sometimes called) is known as an *expression* in Visual C++ .NET. If you've used a spreadsheet, you're probably already familiar with expressions: When you type a formula into a cell, you type an expression.

Expressions are used to calculate new information based on existing information. For example, you can use expressions to calculate the area of a circle, a monthly mortgage payment, or far more complex things such as the outcome of an election.

Cappuccino, Expresso?

Expressions are vital for creating complex applications. If you have been reading the chapters in order, you've already seen expressions for calculating the area of a square and the area of a circle. For example, the following line from CircleArea3 (Chapter 9) calculates the area of a circle given the radius:

```
oCircle.dblArea = PI * oCircle.dblRadius * oCircle.dblRadius;
```

You use expressions also to determine whether certain conditions are met. For example, if you want to see whether you've exceeded your credit limit, you can use an expression to compare your limit with the amount you've charged.

When you create a program to match a real-world situation, you usually need to determine the expressions that define what's happening. Here are some sample expressions:

```
2 + 2
3.1415 * Radius * Radius
ChargedAmount < CreditLimit
```

As you can see, without expressions, you can't even add two numbers together!

Smooth Operators

Table 10-1 describes five common operators that you use repeatedly to create expressions. An *operator* is simply a math symbol that indicates what type of mathematical operation to use when you write a formula. In the expression 4+5, for example, + is an operator.

Table 10-1		Math Operators
Operator	*Usage*	*Meaning*
*	foo * bar	Multiplies two numbers. For example, 6 * 3 is 18.
/	foo / bar	Divides two numbers. For example, 18 / 3 is 6.
+	foo + bar	Adds two numbers. For example, 6 + 3 is 9.
-	foo - bar	Subtracts two numbers. For example, 9 – 3 is 6.
%	foo % bar	Modulo. Returns the remainder of dividing two numbers. For example, 10 % 3 is 1, because 10 / 3 is 3, remainder 1.

Modulo is often used to constrain a set of integers to a range. For example, suppose that you have a spaceship that moves across the bottom of a screen (such as with the Space Invaders video game). If you want the spaceship to reappear on the left side of the screen after it has gone off the right edge, you can use modulo. If the screen is 10 units wide and pos is the position of the spaceship, pos % 10 will always be between 0 and 9, no matter what you add to pos. Thus, when the spaceship gets to position 9 and you add 1 to the position to move it right, pos % 10 returns 0, and the spaceship shows up on the left.

Slightly More Complex Operators

Table 10-2 describes operators that are more complex than the operators described in Table 10-1. You probably won't need to use these complex operators right away. But as your programming skills increase, you'll find that they're quite useful. Several of the complex operators are described further in their own separate sections outside the table. (You guessed it — they're too complex to describe fully in a table!)

Table 10-2		Increment, Decrement, and Shift Operators
Operator	*Usage*	*Meaning*
++	foo++, ++foo	Increment. Adds 1 to the value of an item. For example, if variable nAge is 1, nAge++ is 2. (By the way, the ++ operator is what gives C++ its name.)
--	foo--, --foo	Decrement. Works the same as the increment operator, but it decreases instead of increases a value. If a is 2, for example, a-- is 1.
>>	foo >> bar	Bit shift right. Using foo >> bar is the same as finding the integer result of foo/2bar. See "The >> operator" section for examples and more discussion.
<<	foo << bar	Bit shift left. Similar to >>, but the numbers get bigger. foo << bar is the equivalent of foo ¥ 2bar. See "The << operator" section for examples and more discussion.

The ++ operator

The increment operator can be tricky because the amount added depends on the type of item incremented. For example, if you have a pointer to an item foo and foo is four bytes long, incrementing the pointer actually adds 4 to its value, because that way it points to the next foo. Confused? You can find out more about pointers in Chapter 13.

There are two flavors of ++. You can put ++ before a variable *(preincrement),* as in ++bar, or you can put ++ after a variable *(postincrement),* as in bar++.

++bar increments the value of bar, and then evaluates bar. So if you do this:

```
int bar = 1;
Console::WriteLine(++bar.ToString());
```

bar is set to 2, and 2 is printed on the screen.

By contrast, bar++ evaluates bar and then increments it, so that this:

```
int bar = 1;
cout << bar++;
```

sets bar to 2, but prints 1. That's because bar is evaluated before it's incremented. (By the way, for fun, the first example uses managed code and the second uses old-fashioned, unmanaged, C++ code.)

++ is often used in loops and iterators. (Does that sound complex? Don't worry, they're discussed in the Chapter 11.)

The same basic rules apply to the -- operator, except values are decremented by 1. (Okay, it isn't always decreased by 1. For certain operations, such as manipulating pointers, the value can be decreased by more than 1. But for most of the stuff you'll do, it goes down by one. Phew.)

The >> operator

The shift operators are often useful for manipulating binary numbers. Here are some examples of the >> operator in action:

16 >> 1 is 8

16 >> 2 is 4

16 >> 3 is 2

15 >> 1 is 7

15 >> 2 is 3

These answers result from determining the binary representation of foo and then shifting all bits right bar times. Note that when you shift bits right, the number gets smaller.

For example, the binary representation of 16 is

1 0 0 0 0

If you shift these bits right once, you get

    0 1 0 0 0

which is 23, or 8. Thus, 16 >> 1 = 8.

Here's another example. The binary representation of 15 is

    0 1 1 1 1

So, 15 >> 2 is

    0 0 0 1 1

which is 3.

The << operator

Here are two examples of the << operator:

    16 << 1 is 32
    15 << 2 is 60

If the value of the variable exceeds the precision, bits will be cut off. For example, suppose that you have only 8 bits to represent a number. If you shift the number to the left 8 times, the result is 0. That's because all the bits that contained a value were shifted away.

Note that << looks just the same as the << used with cout. (Just to remind you, cout is the unmanaged C++ way to output values to the screen.) When used in an expression, it means bit shifting. But the << of a cout takes priority (because the expression is evaluated left to right and the cout << is found first).

Therefore, if you want to print the result of a bit shift, you should enclose the shift in parentheses, as in this example:

```
cout << (16 << 2) << endl;
```

True or False with Boolean Expressions

So far, all the operators covered in this chapter are used for calculating the result of an expression. For example, you've seen how to calculate the area of a circle by multiplying the radius by two times pi.

Now you find out about Boolean expressions. With *Boolean expressions,* you're concerned not about the result of a particular expression, but with determining whether the expression is true or false.

For example, you might say, "Does he love me?" or "Has my credit limit been exceeded?" or "Did the user ask to print a page?" Boolean expressions are almost always used with questions. Generally, these questions are turned into statements equivalent to "If the Boolean expression is true, then do a bunch of things."

If the result of a Boolean expression is 0, the answer is considered false. If the result is not 0, the answer is considered true.

Boolean expressions are so common with C++ that there is a data type just to deal with them: bool. A bool can be set to either true or false, two other C++ keywords.

The following sections and Table 10-3 describe the operators used in Boolean expressions. Naturally enough, these operators are known as *Boolean operators.* In Chapter 11, you can find out how to combine Boolean operators with questioning statements, such as the if statement.

Table 10-3		Comparison (Boolean) Operators
Operator	*Usage*	*Meaning*
>	foo > bar	Greater than. Returns true if the expression on the left is greater than the expression on the right. For example:
		3 > 5 is false
		3 > 1 is true
		3 > 3 is false because 3 is equal to but not greater than 3
>=	foo >= bar	Greater than or equal to. Similar to >, but it returns true if the left expression is greater than or equal to the right expression. For example:
		3 >= 5 is false
		3 >= 1 is true
		3 >= 3 is true, because 3 equals 3
<	foo < bar	Less than. Returns true if the expression on the left is less than the expression on the right. For example:

Operator	Usage	Meaning
		`3 < 5` is `true`
		`3 < 1` is `false`
		`3 < 3` is `false`
`<=`	`foo <= bar`	Less than or equal to. Returns `true` if the expression on the left is less than or equal to the expression on the right. For example:
		`3 <= 5` is `true`
		`3 <= 1` is `false`
		`3 <= 3` is `true`
`==`	`foo == bar`	Equals. Returns `true` if the expression on the left equals the expression on the right. For example:
		`1 == 2` is `false`
		`1 == 1` is `true`
`!=`	`foo != bar`	Not equal. Returns `true` if the value on the left is not equal to the value on the right. For example:
		`1 != 2` is `true`
		`1 != 1` is `false`
`!`	`!foo`	Not. Takes a single argument. If the argument is `true`, it returns `false`. If the argument is `false`, it returns `true`. For example:
		`!1` is `false`
		`!0` is `true`
`&&`	`foo && bar`	Logical AND. Returns `true` if the expression on the left and the expression on the right are both `true`. For example:
		`1 && 1` is `true`
		`0 && 1` is `false`
		Used for questions such as "If the spirit is willing && the body is weak, then . . ."

(continued)

Table 10-3 *(continued)*

Operator	Usage	Meaning
`||`	`foo || bar`	Logical OR. Returns `true` if either the expression on the left or the expression on the right is `true`. For example:
		`1 || 0` is `true`
		`1 || 1` is `true`
		`0 || 0` is `false`

Give Me an Assignment Operator

You use the assignment operator (=) when you want to give a variable a value, such as when you want to store some information in a variable or save the results of a calculation. For example, you've seen the assignment operator used in lines like this:

```
oCircle.dblArea = PI * oCircle.dblRadius * oCircle.dblRadius;
```

When you assign a value, the value of the expression on the right side of the = is copied to the variable on the left side of the =.

You can use multiple assignments in a single statement. For example, this line sets several variables to 0:

```
a = b = c = 0;
```

You can assign to a variable only a value of the same type as the variable or a value that can be converted to the type of the variable. The examples that follow illustrate this point. The following is okay, because a and 10 are both integers:

```
int a = 10;
```

The following, however, is not legal (in fact, to put it in non-C++ terms, you can probably call it a "Bozo no-no"):

```
int a = "bozo";
```

That's because a is an integer and "bozo" is not. (Bozo is a clown, remember?)

TIP

Look out for this one

Note that the Boolean operator == is different than the assignment operator =. The assignment operator = sets the variable on the left equal to the value on the right. The Boolean operator == checks to see whether the value on the left is the same as the value on the right, but doesn't alter any variables. Using = where you want == is a common mistake that can make a big mess.

For example, the following fragment always sets a to 2. Notice that in the if statement, a is set to 1. Because 1 is a Boolean true, the a = a + 1 line executes:

```
if (a = 1)
   a = a + 1;
```

This is quite different from the following, which adds 1 to a only if a is 1:

```
if (a == 1)
   a = a + 1;
```

You can use a simple trick to help avoid using = when you really mean == in comparisons. If you are comparing a variable to some number or other constant value, list the value first, followed by the variable. That is, rather than do this:

```
if (a == 1)
   a = a + 1;
```

write this:

```
if (1 == a)
   a = a + 1;
```

The two programs will work the same. But if you inadvertently type:

```
if (1 = a)
   a = a + 1;
```

you get a syntax error. Thus, by using this trick, you get syntax errors rather than crashed programs when you use the assignment operator rather than the comparison operator. This error is so common that the compiler warns you about it, so pay attention if any warnings show up!

All the Lonely Operators

You'll probably find that you frequently need to perform some simple operations on a variable. For example, you may want to add a value to a score, or you may want to multiply a variable by a constant.

Of course, you can always do these things using statements such as these:

```
foo = foo * 3;
bar = bar + 2;
```

However, C++ is known for providing a variety of shortcuts that can help you spend less time typing. Table 10-4 shows a number of shortcuts you can use to operate on a variable. All these shortcuts replace statements of the form:

```
foo = foo operator bar
```

with statements of the form:

```
foo operator bar
```

For example, rather than do this:

```
b = b + 1;
```

you can do this:

```
b += 1;
```

Table 10-4	Assignment Operator Shortcuts	
Assignment Operator Shortcut	*Usage*	*Meaning*
+=	foo += bar	Add the value on the right to the variable on the left. For example, this adds 3 to foo:
		foo += 3;
-=	foo -= bar	Subtract the value on the right from the variable on the left. For example, this subtracts 3 from foo:
		foo -= 3;
*=	foo *= bar	Multiply the variable on the left by the value on the right. For example, this multiplies foo by 3:
		foo *= 3;
/=	foo /= bar	Divide the variable on the left by the value on the right. For example, this divides foo by 3:
		foo /= 3;
%=	foo %= bar	Save the modulo of the variable on the left with the value on the right. For example, this sets foo to the modulo of foo and 10:
		foo %= 10;

Assignment Operator Shortcut	Usage	Meaning
`<<=`	`foo <<= bar`	Perform a left shift of the variable on the left by the number of bits specified on the right. For example, this shifts `foo` two bits to the left, thus multiplying `foo` by 4:
		`foo <<= 2;`
`>>=`	`foo >>= bar`	Perform a right shift of the variable on the left by the number of bits specified on the right. For example, this shifts `foo` two bits to the right, thus dividing `foo` by 4:
		`foo >>= 2;`
`&=`	`foo &= bar`	Perform a bitwise AND with the variable on the left. For example, if `foo` is 10, this is 2:
		`foo &= 2;`
`|=`	`foo |= bar`	Perform a bitwise OR with the variable on the left. For example, if `foo` is 10, this is 11:
		`foo |= 1;`
`^=`	`foo ^= bar`	Perform a bitwise inversion of the variable on the left. For example, if `foo` is 10, this is 8:
		`foo ^= 2;`

Operator and a haircut, two bits

Integers are stored in the computer as a series of bits. For example, an integer is stored using 32 bits. The number of bits determines the maximum value the integer can take.

Boolean values are typically saved as integers, even though the value of a Boolean can be only `true` or `false`. If you're using a large number of Booleans, you can save lots of space by using a single bit to represent each Boolean value.

For example, suppose that you survey 10,000 people, asking each person the same 32 simple yes-or-no questions. Saving the results of your survey in a program requires $10,000 \times 32$ (320,000) integers. That's more memory than computers in the early days ever had!

If you save the result of each answer as a single bit instead, where you set bit 0 to true if question 1 is answered yes, bit 1 to true if question 2 is answered yes, and so on, you can save a lot of space. In this particular case, you can save 32 answers in each integer — and you need only 10,000 integers to save the results of the survey. That's quite a difference.

When you pack information into an integer in this way, it's sometimes called creating *bit fields* or *bit packing*. (Not to be confused with backpacking, which is something completely different.)

You can use the bit operators in Table 10-5 to operate on specific bits in a variable.

Table 10-5		Bit Operators
Bit Operator	*Usage*	*Meaning*
~	~foo	Computes a bitwise NOT. If a bit is 0, it's set to 1. If a bit is 1, it's set to 0. For example, given a four-bit binary number:
		~1011 is 0100
<<	foo << bar	Shifts a number left by a number of bits. For example, given a four-digit binary number:
		1011 << 2 is 1100
		(See also Table 10-2.)
>>	foo >> bar	Shifts a number right by a number of bits. For example:
		1011 >> 2 is 0010
		(See also Table 10-2.)
&	foo & bar	Performs a bitwise AND. When the bit on the left and the bit in the corresponding position on the right are both 1, it returns 1. Otherwise, it returns 0. For example:
		1011 & 1010 is 1010

Bit Operator	Usage	Meaning
`|`	`foo	bar`	Performs a bitwise OR. When the bit on the left or the bit on the corresponding position on the right is 1, it returns 1. Otherwise, it returns 0. For example:
		`1011	1010` is **1011**
`^`	`foo ^ bar`	Performs a bitwise exclusive OR (also known as an XOR). When one, but not two, of the bits on the right and left are 1, it returns 1. Otherwise, it returns 0. For example:
		1011^1010 is **0001**

If you think I'm nerdy: The if operator

The `if` operator (also called the *conditional* operator) is similar to the IF function in a spreadsheet. The `if` operator takes three expressions. It evaluates the first expression. If the first expression is true, it returns the value of the second expression. But if the first expression is false, it returns the value of the third expression.

In a spreadsheet, this is written as follows:

```
IF(expr1, expr2, expr3)
```

This really means: If `expr1` is true, return the value of `expr2`. Otherwise, return `expr3`.

In C++, this is written as follows:

```
expr1 ? expr2 : expr3
```

So, you can write something like this in a blackjack game:

```
UserMessage = (ValueOfCards > 21) ? "You're busted!" : "Hit
        again?";
```

We call these operators to order

If you recall the time when you studied addition and division in school, you may remember that the order in which you write things does matter. (You may even remember words such as *noncommutative property* and stuff like that.)

A little voodoo magic: hex (and binary and decimal)

If you're new to computers, all this talk about binary numbers may be a bit confusing. The number system that you use every day is called a *base ten,* or *decimal,* system. In base ten, every time you move left in a number, it represents ten times as much, so that 10 is ten times as big as 1, and 200 is ten times as big as 20. Each digit represents a power of ten, so, for example, the number 125 is really 100 + 20 + 5. This is the same as $1 \times 10^2 + 2 \times 10^1 + 5 \times 10^0$. (Remember from high-school math classes that any number to the zeroth power is 1.)

Computers can't represent ten different options for each digit, though. Instead, they can tell only whether a number is on or off — each digit can be only a 0 or a 1. Such numbers are called *base two,* or *binary,* numbers. A digit in a binary system is often called a *bit* (short for *binary digit*). For example, the binary number 1101 is the same as $1 \times 2^3 + 1 \times 2^2 + 0 \times 2^1 + 1 \times 2^0$. In base ten, that's 8 + 4 + 1, or 13.

Computers store numbers in groups eight bits long, called *bytes.* A byte can represent 256 (or 2^8) unique values. When two bytes are put together, they're called a *word.* A word has 2^{16} bits and can represent up to 65,536 (2^{16}) values. Four bytes put together is called a *double word.*

2^{10} is a magic number for computer people. This is 1024, which is frequently called a K. Even though *K,* or *kilo,* means one thousand, for computer people a K means 1024. So, 64K of memory means 64×1024, or 65,536 bytes.

Likewise, *M,* or *mega,* normally means one million. But for computer people, it means 1024×1024, or 1,048,576.

Because it can be a pain to write out binary numbers (they have too many digits), *hex,* or *hexadecimal,* notation is sometimes used instead. Hexadecimal numbers are numbers that are base 16. When writing a hex number, every four bits from a number are combined to form a single hex digit, also known as a *hexit.* Because each hexit can range between 0 and 15, the letters *A* through *F* are used to represent the decimal values 10 through 15. In other words, *A* is 10, *B* is 11, and so on. When you write a hex number in C++, you precede it with 0x. So, 0x0A is the same as 10 in the decimal system. And 0xFF is the same as 255. If you hang out with enough computer people, someone will inevitably ask you your age in hex.

And why are computers binary? A lot of the reason has to do with how chips operate, and in particular, with the characteristics of transistors. It's a pretty involved explanation, so I guess you have to read my upcoming bestseller *Solid-State Particle Physics For Dummies* to find out more.

The computer follows the same rules that you learned (and probably forgot) from math class. Expressions are evaluated left to right, but some things are evaluated first. For example, if you have $3 + 2 \times 3$, the answer is 9. Why? Because multiplication takes priority over addition. So the 2×3 is evaluated before it's added to 3. If you simply read things left to right, you'd get 15 instead.

You can use parentheses to change the order of operation. For example, you can write $(3 + 2) \times 3$. In this case, $3 + 2$ is evaluated first, and then multiplied. If you aren't sure about which things are evaluated first, it doesn't hurt to add parentheses.

Table 10-6 lists the *order of operations*. The items at the top of the table are evaluated before (or have a *higher precedence* than) those at the bottom. For example, + appears before >. So, for example, 1 + 0 > 1 is the same as (1 + 0) > 1. The answer (of course) is false.

All items on the same row have the same priority, so they are always evaluated left to right when found in an expression. For example, 3 × 4 / 2 is the same as (3 × 4) / 2.

Table 10-6	Order of Operations
Precedence Level	*Operation*
Highest precedence	( )
	++ -- ~ !
	* / %
	+ -
	>> <<
	< <= > >=
	== !=
	&
	^
	|
	&&
	||
Lowest precedence	? :

If you're not sure about the order of operations, always add plenty of parentheses so that you can understand what's going on.

Some operator examples

Take a quick look at some examples that show operators in action.

Example 1: This statement determines the area of a circle:

```
dblArea = PI * dblRadius * dblRadius;
```

Example 2: This statement calculates how much tax you pay on a purchase given a particular tax rate:

```
dblTax = dblPurchase * dblTaxRate;
```

Example 3: Given the information from Example 2, this statement calculates the total price for the item. Essentially, the amount of the tax is added to the purchase price.

```
dblPrice = (1 + dblTaxRate) * dblPurchase;
```

Example 4: Given the price from Example 3, the following statement checks to see whether the credit limit is exceeded. If the credit limit is exceeded, the credit limit is increased by 500. (This is an advanced example.)

```
dblCreditLimit = (dblPrice > dblCreditLimit) ? dblCreditLimit
            + 500
  : dblCreditLimit;
```

Mathive Attack

All the expressions you have used so far use very simple operators. Suppose you want to do something more complex, such as something involving trigonometry? The CLR (Common Language Runtime) provides a whole set of math functions for your use and abuse. These are all in the Math class. Table 10-7 shows the most useful math functions.

Table 10-7	Math Functions	
Function	*Usage*	*Meaning*
Abs	Math::Abs(-4)	Returns the absolute value of a number.
Ceil	Math::Ceil(4.2)	Rounds up to the nearest integer. For example, the ceiling of 4.2 is 5.
Cos	Math::Cos(.03)	Returns the cosine of the number. The number is in radians.
E	Math::E	Returns the value of e, the mysterious base of natural logarithms, which is roughly 2.718.

Function	Usage	Meaning
Exp	Math::Exp(4)	Returns e^n. If you aren't sure what e is all about, don't worry about it.
Floor	Math::Floor(4.2)	Rounds down to the nearest integer. For example, the floor of 4.2 is 4.
Log	Math::Log(4)	Returns the log, or base e, of a number. This is called the natural logarithm, perhaps because logs floating in the water seem very natural.
Max	Math::Max(4.5, 88.2)	Returns the larger of two numbers.
Min	Math::Min(4.5, 88.2)	Returns the smaller of two numbers.
PI	Math::PI	Returns the value of (, which is roughly 3.141592.
Pow	Math::Pow(4, 2)	Returns x^n. In this example, returns 4^2, or 16. In case you are wondering, *Pow* is short for *power*, not the sound Batman makes when eradicating criminals.
Round	Math::Round(4.2)	Rounds to the nearest integer. For example, 4.2 rounds to 4, and 4.8 rounds to 5.
Sin	Math::Sin(.03)	Returns the sine of the number. The number is in radians.
Sqrt	Math::Sqrt(4)	Returns the square root of a number.
Tan	Math::Tan(.03)	Returns a number that has been in the sun for a while. Or the tangent of the number. The number is in radians.

You can check out some of these math functions in action in the following program, which, once again, calculates the area of a circle:

```
// CircleArea4
// Computes the area of a circle given the radius
// Uses math functions

#include "stdafx.h"

#using <mscorlib.dll>

using namespace System;

//Set up a structure for storing information about circles
class CircleInfo
{
public:
   double dblRadius;
   double dblArea;
};


// This is the entry point for this application
#ifdef _UNICODE
int wmain(void)
#else
int main(void)
#endif
{
   CircleInfo oCircle;

   //Ask for the size of the radius
   Console::WriteLine(S"What is the radius?");

   //Read in the radius and convert to a floating-point
          number
   oCircle.dblRadius = Double::Parse(Console::ReadLine());

   //Calculate the area of the circle
   oCircle.dblArea =
          Math::PI*oCircle.dblRadius*oCircle.dblRadius;

   //Write out the result
   //Note that we must convert the area into a string to do
          so
   Console::WriteLine(S"The circle's area is {0} units.",
          oCircle.dblArea.ToString());

   //And now do some gratuitous math
   Console::WriteLine(S"And in case you were wondering, the
          square root of the radius is {0}",
          Math::Sqrt(oCircle.dblRadius).ToString());

   //Hang out until the user is finished
```

```
Console::WriteLine(S"Press the Enter key to stop the
          program");
Console::ReadLine();

return 0;
}
```

You can find this program in the CircleArea4 directory on the accompanying CD. You can find an unmanaged version of CircleArea4 in the CircleArea5 directory on the accompanying CD.

Old-Fashioned Math

Naturally, all the cool math functions that are available in .NET are also available in standard C++. Such functions are part of the math library, which is loaded with the following line:

```
#include <math.h>
```

Table 10-8 shows the key math functions from the C++ math library. Remember, these are the guys to use if you're writing unmanaged programs.

Table 10-8	Standard C++ Math Functions	
Function	*Usage*	*Meaning*
abs	abs(-4)	Returns the absolute value of a number.
ceil	ceil(4.2)	Rounds up to the nearest integer.
cos	cos(.03)	Returns the cosine of the number. The number is in radians.
exp	exp(4)	Returns e^n.
floor	floor(4.2)	Rounds down to the nearest integer.
log	log(4)	Returns the log, or base e, of a number.
pow	pow(4, 2)	Returns x^n.
sin	sin(.03)	Returns the sine of the number. The number is in radians.
sqrt	sqrt(4)	Returns the square root of a number.
tan	tan(.03)	Returns the tangent of the number. The number is in radians.

Chapter 11

How Low Can You Flow?

In This Chapter

▶ Finding out about keywords used in control statements

▶ Using if to create conditions

▶ Creating loops with for and while

▶ Using switch, case, and break to create complex condition blocks

*B*y this point, you've found out about almost all the fundamental aspects of programming. But your programs still execute only sequentially. That is, your programs start with the first line in main and continue, statement after statement after statement, never deviating from their course for even one single moment.

But, as you've probably discovered, life doesn't really work that way. Sometimes a little variety is called for, in life and in your programs. In some cases, it's okay to have a program flow directly from one line to the next. But in many other cases, you probably want to divert or change the flow to suit your needs. That's why C++ has a number of statements that help you control the flow through your programs. (As you might guess from the use of the word *flow* three times so far, these statements are often called *flow control* statements.) These statements let you perform certain actions only if particular conditions are true, or they let you repeat an action until something happens.

There are lots of reasons to use statements like these. Here are some examples of typical scenarios in which you may need to repeatedly perform some type of operation:

✔ Continue adding the price of each item until there are no more groceries.

✔ Pump gas until the tank is full.

✔ Find the average grade of the 32 students in a class by repeatedly adding the grades of each student and then dividing the total by 32.

In other situations, you need to make a choice. Such choices are usually of this form: If some condition is true, perform a certain action. Here are several examples that illustrate this:

✔ If the professor insists that you do your homework, do it. (But not if your professor doesn't insist.)

✔ If a customer orders more than 3000 widgets, give them a discount.

✔ If the light is yellow, speed up. If it's red, stop.

As you can see, numerous situations exist in which you need to repeat a task or make a choice. Flow control statements let you write programs to handle these situations. In this chapter, you use flow control statements to enrich your programs.

The Big Three Keywords: if, for, and while

Three flow control statements are used in almost every application: if, for, and while. The if statement (which is sometimes referred to as a *conditional*) performs a set of actions when, and only when, a particular condition is true. The for and while statements (which are sometimes referred to as for loops and while loops) repeat a set of statements over and over again.

If you leave me now: The if keyword

The syntax for if is pretty simple:

```
if (expr1)
    stmt;
```

(Note that here — and in subsequent sections — expr means an expression such as i < 1, and stmt means a *statement*, such as cost = cost + 1.)

expr1 can be any expression. If it's true, stmt is executed. (An expression is true if its value is not 0. That is, expressions in conditionals are always Boolean expressions.) You can use { } to perform a group of statements. For example, the following code assigns values if the Boolean variable fIWereARichMan is true:

```
if (fIWereARichMan)
{
    nDeedle = 0;
```

```
    nDidle = 1;
    nDum = 0;
}
```

And this sets a discount value if a large order is placed:

```
if (nOrderSize > 3000)
{
    dblDiscount = .2;
}
```

You can make the if statement a bit more powerful by using the else option along with it:

```
if (expr1)
    stmt1;
else
    stmt2;
```

In this case, if expr1 isn't true, stmt2 is executed.

The following code checks a blackjack hand to see whether the player has busted. If the player hasn't busted, the dealer tries to deal a new card:

```
if (nHandValue > 21)
{
    //The player busted.
    nUserScore -= nBet;
    fBusted = true;
}
else
{
    //Does the player want another card?
    cout << "Hit?\n";
    cin >> fHitMe;
}
```

The following routine determines a discount based on the size of an order:

```
//Ordering 5000 units gives a 30% discount
if (nOrderSize > 5000)
{
    dblDiscount = 0.3;
}
else
{
    //Ordering 3000 units gives a 20% discount
    if (nOrderSize > 3000)
    {
        dblDiscount = 0.2;
    }
```

```
    //Otherwise, there is no discount
    else
    {
        dblDiscount = 0.0;
    }
}
```

Sometimes, as in the preceding example, you may have ifs within ifs. This is called *nesting*. When you nest ifs, be sure to indent in a way that makes it easy to read the program.

A beginner's guide to formatting programs (1001 ways to indent your code)

Programmers format code in lots of different ways. Although there's no official guideline, you can do certain things to make your programs easier to read.

Any time you place code within { }, indent the code. That way, it's easy to see that those lines go together. For example, the following is easy to read because of indentation:

```
if (nHandValue > 21)
{
    //The player busted
    nUserScore -= nBet;
    fBusted = true;
}
else
{
    //Does the player want
    //another card?
    cout << "Hit?\n";
    cin >> fHitMe;
}
```

Here's the same code but without indentation. In fact, some lines are combined (which is legal, but ugly):

```
if (nHandValue > 21) {
//The player busted
nUserScore -= nBet; fBusted = true;} else {
//Does the player want another card?
cout << "Hit?\n"; cin >> fHitMe;}
```

The first is a lot easier to read because it's pretty clear which statements are executed if the hand is greater than 21.

If you've read the chapters in order, you've seen the same rule apply to statements in main. All the lines in main were indented. And you see a slight variation of this rule when you create structures.

If you have nested statements, indent each time you nest:

```
if (foo)
{
    bar++;
    if (bar > 3)
    {
        baz = 2;
    }
    if (goober < 7)
    {
        flibber = 3;
    }
}
```

Another way to make your programs easier to read is to place the } at the same indentation level as the block that started it:

```
if (fFoo)
{
}
```

This makes it easier to see where a particular block ends. Also, although you need to use { } in an if statement only when there is more than one statement to execute when a condition is met, if you always use { } you can avoid some silly mistakes. For example, no brackets were used in the following:

```
if (fFoo)
    nVal++;
nCheck++;
```

Although the following is equivalent, it's a little easier to read and doesn't require a change if you need multiple lines inside the if:

```
if (fFoo)
{
    nVal++;
}
nCheck++;
```

Visual C++ .NET automatically formats your code for you. For example, if you indent a line, it will indent subsequent lines so that they match up. If you type a }, it will outdent it to match the beginning {.

for-get about it

The `for` keyword is used to repeat statements over and over. `for` has the following syntax:

```
for (expr1; expr2; expr3)
    stmt1;
```

This type of repetition is called a `for` loop.

When the `for` loop starts, `expr1` is evaluated. `expr1` is usually where you initialize variables that will be used in the loop. Then `expr2` is evaluated. (It's evaluated each time the loop is entered, which is how you control how many times the loop executes.) If `expr2` is true, `stmt1` is executed. And if `stmt1` is executed, `expr3` is evaluated; `expr3` is usually used to modify what happens in `expr2`. If `expr2` is false, however, the loop ends and the program moves on to the next statement after the `for` loop.

A simple example using for

Did the preceding explanation seem confusing? Look at a simple example:

```
int i;
for (i = 0; i < 2; i++)
{
    Console::WriteLine(i.ToString());
}
```

Here's what's happening in this example:

1. When the loop begins, `expr1` is evaluated. In this case, `i` is given the value 0.

2. Then `expr2` is evaluated. This expression asks, is `i < 2`? Because `i` was just set to 0, `i` is less than 2. (That is, 0 is less than 2.) Therefore, `stmt1` is executed. In this case, the statement that executes is

   ```
   Console::WriteLine(i.ToString());
   ```

   This prints the value of i to the screen.

3. Next, `expr3` is evaluated. In this case, it's `i++`, so `i` is incremented from 0 to 1.

4. Because `expr2` is always evaluated before the `for` loop repeats, we go back to `expr2`. Is `i < 2`? Well, `i` is now 1, so it's less than 2. Therefore we execute `stmt1`, printing the value of `i` once more.

5. Then `expr3` is evaluated again, and therefore `i` is incremented to 2.

6. Once again, expr2 is evaluated. Is i < 2? No, because now i is equal to 2. Therefore, the loop ends.

By making expr2 more complex, you can do all types of things to determine when the loop ends. for loops are often used when traversing data structures. If you're studying computer science, you'll see them often.

Crimson and clover, over and over

If you want to repeat something a number of times, use the following loop:

```
for (i = 0; i < n; i++)
{
    //Statements to repeat go here.
}
```

The variable n controls how many times the loop repeats. For example, if you need to print "I repeat myself when under stress" 50 times, do this:

```
for (i = 0; i < 50; i++)
{
    Console::WriteLine(S"I repeat myself when under stress");
}
```

Sure beats writing it by hand.

If you want to be fancy, ask the user for the number of times to repeat:

```
int nCount;
Console::WriteLine(S"How many times do you want to repeat?");
nCount = Console::ReadLine()->ToInt32();
```

```
for (i = 0; i < nCount; i++)
{
    Console::WriteLine(S"I repeat myself when under stress");
}
```

Willy Wonka and the Chocolate Factorial

Here's a typical computer science homework problem: How do you find n factorial?

n factorial is n × (n – 1) ((n – 2) × . . . × 1. So, 2 factorial (written 2! in math books, but not in computer code) is 2 × 1. And 3! is 3 × 2 × 1.

The awful, takes-all-day approach is this:

```
//compute n!
n = Int32::Parse(Console::ReadLine());
if (n == 1)
{
    Console::WriteLine(S"1");
}
else if (n == 2)
{
    Console::WriteLine(S"2");
}
else if (n == 3)
{
    Console::WriteLine(S"6");
}
```

You can see how long typing this program would take. A much easier way is to use a for loop, as shown in the following program:

```
// Factorial
// Computes n!

#include "stdafx.h"

#using <mscorlib.dll>

using namespace System;

// This is the entry point for this application
#ifdef _UNICODE
int wmain(void)
#else
int main(void)
#endif
{
    int nNumber;    //The number the user types in
    int nResult = 1;

    int i;    //Loop variable

    //Get the value
    Console::WriteLine("What is the number?");
    nNumber = Int32::Parse(Console::ReadLine());

    //Now loop through. Each time through the loop,
    //multiply the result by i. This will give
    //1*2*3...n because i starts at 1 and increases
    //until it is n
    for (i=1; i<=nNumber; i++)
    {
        nResult *= i;
    }
```

```
//Print the result
Console::WriteLine(S"n! is {0}", nResult.ToString());

//Hang out until the user is finished
Console::WriteLine(L"Press the Enter key to stop the
        program");
Console::ReadLine();

return 0;
}
```

This program is in the Factorial directory on the CD accompanying this book. You can find an unmanaged version of it in the Factorial2 directory.

While thing, you make my heart sing

Like the `for` loop, the `while` loop is used to repeat something a number of times. It's simpler than the `for` loop, though, as you see here:

```
while (expr1)
    stmt;
```

When the `while` loop begins, expr1 is evaluated. If it's true, stmt is executed. Then expr1 is evaluated again. If it's still true, stmt is executed. This procedure is repeated until expr1 is no longer true.

For example, to repeat 10 times, do the following:

```
int i = 0;
while (i < 10)
{
    i++;
}
```

Make sure that what happens in stmt (the part that executes inside the while loop) affects the value of expr1. Otherwise, you'll never leave the loop.

Flow Down Moses

Two other flow keywords that you need to know about are the `switch` and `do` keywords.

Hangin' out with your computer

Here's a simple program you can write that will completely hang your computer. If you do this, you'll need to nuke your program with Task Manager.

```
//Hang the system
int main(void)
{
```

```
    while (1);
}
```

Why does this hang the computer? The program stays in the `while` loop until `expr1` is false. In this case, `expr1` is 1, so it's never false. The computer will never exit the loop. Bummer. This is called an *infinite loop*.

I'd rather code than switch

The switch statement is like an if statement with a lot of branches. (Each branch starts with the case keyword.) So, if you find yourself with a problem such as "if the country is Germany then . . ., else if it's France then . . . , else if it's Hungary then . . . ," you can use a switch statement rather than an if statement. Here's what it looks like:

```
switch (expr)
{
    case val1:
        stmt1;
    case val2:
        stmt2;
    ...
    default:
        dfltstmt;
}
```

First, expr is evaluated and compared against val1. (Here, val is some value, such as 1 or 45.3.) If expr is val1, stmt1 and all following statements are executed. If expr isn't val1, the process is repeated with val2, and so on. You should always include a default item (as shown in the preceding code) so that if nothing else matches, the dfltstmt (default statement) runs. Because all statements following a match are executed, you can use the break statement to leave the switch.

If you're a Visual Basic programmer, you may think that you can use strings for val1, just as you can in Visual Basic. Unfortunately, you can't. You can compare only numeric values, not string values.

Here's a quick example that prints the text name of a number:

```
//For demo purposes, n is handled only for 1 to 4
switch (n)
{
   case 1:
       Console::WriteLine(S"one");
       break;
   case 2:
       Console::WriteLine(S"two");
       break;
   case 3:
       Console::WriteLine(S"three");
       break;
   case 4:
       Console::WriteLine(S"four");
       break;
   default:
       Console::WriteLine(S"unknown number");
}
```

Note the use of break in each case statement. If you didn't use break statements, you'd get the following, undesired results:

n	Result
1	onetwothreefourunknown number
2	twothreefourunknown number

And so on.

Make sure that you don't forget the break after you execute a case in a switch. If you forget it, you'll keep executing lines in the switch even though you didn't intend to.

Do-wah diddy, diddy-dum, diddy-do: The do keyword

The do keyword is similar to while. The difference is that with a while loop, the expression is evaluated before the statements inside are executed. So, with while, it's possible that none of the statements will get executed. With do, the statements are executed and then a condition is checked to determine whether to continue. If the condition is true, the statements are run again. Otherwise, the loop stops:

```
do
    stmt;
while (expr);
```

Here's a quick example that loops until i is n:

```
int i = 0;
do
{
    Console::WriteLine(i.ToString());
    i++;
}
while (i < n);
```

If n happens to be 0, a number is still printed because expr isn't evaluated (in this case, i < n) until after the statements are executed.

i = i + 1 and i++ have the same effect.

"I can't really explain it, but everytime I animate someone swinging a golf club, a little divot of code comes up missing on the home page."

Chapter 12

Play That Function
Music Right, Boys

- -

In This Chapter

▶ Discovering what functions are

▶ Creating functions

▶ Passing arguments to functions

▶ Passing return values from functions

▶ Finding out about recursion and default initializers

- -

*P*rograms are often complex and lengthy. Some programs require thousands or even millions of lines of code. When you create a large program, a good strategy is to break it down into manageable sections that you (and other people reading it) can easily understand.

Visual C++ .NET lets you break programs down by grouping related statements together and naming them. This type of group is called a *function*. (Functions are also frequently called *routines* or *procedures*. In this book, we usually call them functions, but all three terms are common. BASIC programmers often call them *subroutines*.)

Functions can be called in various ways. *Global functions* can be called from any part of your program. *Library functions* can be called by lots of different programs. Most of your functions, however, will probably operate with a specific object. This type of function, called a *member function,* is discussed in Chapter 17.

You can also combine functions to build new functions. Building large functions from small functions can help make your programs easier to write, read, and test. In this chapter, you add functions to your programs to break them into more manageable, understandable chunks.

First, Some Opening Statements

If you've read some of the previous chapters, you've seen lots of sample programs. In Chapter 3, you find out that every time you write a statement, you need to follow it with a ; (semicolon). But you may have noticed that this isn't always the case in the sample programs. That's because, as with most things in life, exceptions and special cases exist for almost every rule.

Here's the general rule:

Most statements should be followed by a ; (semicolon).

The exceptions and special cases follow:

- ✔ If the statement starts with a # (pound sign), don't end it with a ; (semicolon).

- ✔ If the statement begins with a //, you don't need to end it with a ;, although it doesn't hurt anything if you do use a ;.

- ✔ If the statement ends with a }, you don't need a ; unless the reason the statement ends with a } is because you've just declared a `class` (or `struct` or `enum`), in which case you must end it with a ; .

Conjunction Junction, Making Functions

You define a function by giving it a name, followed by ( ) (left and right parentheses). (Later, you'll be putting some things called *arguments* inside the parentheses.) Then list the statements that make up the function. The rules for naming variables (described in Chapter 8) apply to naming functions, too. Here's how you define a function:

```
void function_name()
{
    stmt;
}
```

For example, the following makes a function that prints "Hello World":

```
void PrintHelloWorld()
{
    Console::WriteLine(S"Hello World");
}
```

Then, whenever you want to use that function, simply use its name followed by ( ). The process of using a function is referred to as *calling* (or *invoking*) a function. You can call functions as many times as you want.

Just as with structures, you need to define a function before you use it, as shown in the following program. Here's the HelloWorld application, but the code to hang out waiting for the user to press a key after the program ends is now moved to a function called HangOut. HangOut is defined at the top of the program and then invoked in main:

```
// HelloWorld4
// Uses a function for waiting for user input

#include "stdafx.h"

#using <mscorlib.dll>

using namespace System;

//Hang out until the user is finished
void HangOut()
{
    Console::WriteLine(S"Press the Enter key to stop the
            program");
    Console::ReadLine();
}

// This is the entry point for this application
#ifdef _UNICODE
int wmain(void)
#else
int main(void)
#endif
{
    //Write to the screen
    Console::WriteLine(S"Hello World");

    //Hang out until the user is finished
    HangOut();
    return 0;
}
```

This program is in the HelloWorld4 directory on the CD accompanying this book.

Arguments (Yes. No. Yes. No.)

You can *pass in* values to a function. These values, called *arguments* (or *parameters*), each need a data type and a name. By passing in arguments, you create a general function that can be used over and over again in an application. You can pass any number of arguments to a function, and you can use any of the data types.

This is how you define arguments:

```
void function_name(data_type1 arg1, data_type2 arg2, ...)

{
}
```

For example, the following function prints the factorial of a number. The number, called n, is passed in as an argument. Note that this value is then used throughout the function:

```
//Computes and prints the factorial of a number
void Factorial(int nNumber)
{
    int nResult = 1;
    int i;    //Loop variable

    //Now loop through. Each time through the loop
    //multiply the result by i.
    for (i=1; i<=nNumber; i++)
        {
            nResult *= i;
        }

    //Now print the result
    Console::WriteLine(nResult.ToString());
}
```

Anytime you want to print the factorial of a number, call this function. For example, the following program has a loop that iterates three times. Inside the loop, the program asks for a number and calls the Factorial function to print the factorial of the number:

```
int nNumber;
int i;
//Loop three times.
for (i = 0; i < 3; i++)
{
    //Get the number.
    nNumber = Int32::Parse(Console::ReadLine());
    //Call the factorial routine with nNumber.
    Factorial(nNumber);
}
```

You can easily write functions that have several arguments. For example, the following function prints the value of foo*n!, where both foo and n are passed to the routine:

```
//Computes and prints the factorial of a number
void Fooctorial(int nFoo, int nNumber)
{
    int nResult = 1;
    int i;    //Loop variable

    //Now loop through. Each time through the loop
    //multiply the result by i.
    for (i=1; i<=nNumber; i++)
        {
            nResult *= i;
        }

    //Now multiply by foo
    nResult *= nFoo;

    //Now print the result
    Console::WriteLine(nResult.ToString());
}
```

Functions that return values

All the functions discussed so far have performed actions (such as calculating and printing the factorial of a number). But functions can also return values. This capability is useful because it lets you use functions inside expressions. For example, you can use a mathematical library function such as Math::Cos( ) in the middle of a formula, as in 3*Math::Cos(angle).

You can write your own functions that return values. For example, you may want to create a routine that reads through a database and returns the names of customers who have placed three or more orders in the last six months. Or you may want to create a function that returns the moving average of a lot of numbers.

You need to do two things if you want a function to return a value:

 ✔ Precede the declaration with the data type that the function returns, instead of with void.
 ✔ Use the return keyword in the function before you leave it.

The return keyword immediately leaves a function and returns a value. If you use return in the middle of a function and the return is executed, the code following the return is not executed. (Not all returns are executed.

For example, some returns are in code that is executed only under certain conditions.)

Here's an example of a factorial function that returns the factorial of n. It's similar to the preceding factorial function, but instead of printing the value in the function, it returns the value:

```
//Computes and returns the factorial of a number
int Factorial(int nNumber)
{
    int nResult = 1;
    int i;    //Loop variable

    //Now loop through. Each time through the loop
    //multiply the result by i.
    for (i=1; i<=nNumber; i++)
    {
        nResult *= i;
    }

    //Now return the result
    return nResult;
}
```

Because the Factorial function returns a value, you can use it in expressions. This provides you with more flexibility regarding the ways and places you can use the Factorial function. For example, this code lets you print the factorial in the middle of a sentence:

```
nNumber = Int32::Parse(Console::ReadLine());
Console::WriteLine(S"The factorial of {0} is {1}",
        nNumber.ToString(),
        Factorial(nNumber).ToString());
```

Functions that return a value can be used anywhere that you can use a value of the return type. Thus, if a function returns an integer, you can use the function any place that you can use an integer. This can be inside an expression, such as:

```
nMyNum = 3*Factorial(nNumber);
```

You can also use functions to compute values that are passed as arguments to other functions. For example, the Factorial function takes an integer argument. Because the Factorial function returns an integer, you can pass in the factorial of a number as an argument to the Factorial function. The following code computes the factorial of a factorial:

```
nNumber = Int32::Parse(Console::ReadLine());
Console::WriteLine(Factorial(Factorial(nNumber)).ToString());
```

Ozone depletion and a global warning

After you leave a function, any variables that are declared inside that function are destroyed. So, any information they contain is lost. If you need to use this information after the function is called, you should return the information by using the `return` keyword.

For example, suppose that you need the name of the highest-paid employee in your company. If you only want to print the name and never look at it again, print the name inside the function and don't return anything. But if you need to use the name outside the function, such as to incorporate it in a form letter, return the name.

You can get access to the information in other ways besides returning it. One way is to use *global variables,* which are variables that are declared before `main`. Global variables are called global because they can be used from anywhere inside a program. Continuing with the example, the global variable approach to saving the name of the highest-paid employee is to copy the name into a global variable. Because

the variable is global, it sticks around after the routine has ended, and you can then look at its value.

Unfortunately, using global variables can lead to *spaghetti code* (code that's hard to read). When you set a global variable in a function, understanding what's happening is impossible without looking at every line of code. That's not in keeping with good coding practice, which says that when you look at the arguments passed to a function, you should be able to tell what is used by the function and what is changed within the function. Being able to do this is important because it lets you look at and understand the high-level use of the function without having to examine all the code.

All types of hard-to-find logic errors can occur if you aren't careful when using global variables. In general, you should return values instead of using global variables. If you need to return lots of values, use a structure or a pointer to a structure.

And this code determines whether the factorial of a number is greater than 72:

```
//Is the factorial greater than 72?
if (Factorial(nNumber) > 72)
{
    Console::WriteLine(S"It is greater.");
}
```

Revisiting the Factorial Example

In this section, you look at the factorial program again. But this time, the program is put together using functions. As you read the program, notice that even though it's getting complex, the `main` routine is fairly simple. In fact, you can now figure out what `main` does by reading only four statements (the other stuff inside `main` consists of comments).

The program now contains two functions: Factorial and GetNumber. Factorial computes the factorial of a number. This is the same function as in the "Functions that return values" section — it takes an integer as a parameter and returns the resulting factorial. GetNumber is used to get input; it asks the user for a number and then returns that number.

The main routine uses the GetNumber routine repeatedly to ask the user for a number. It then uses the Factorial function to display the factorial of the number. It keeps asking for new numbers until the user types a 0 (zero).

Note that the main routine is using a fancy trick to determine when to stop:

```
while (nNumber = GetNumber())
```

Remember that the while statement takes an expression as a parameter. The lines in the while statement are executed if this expression is true. In this case, the expression first calls the GetNumber routine to get a number. It then assigns the result to the variable named nNumber. This has three effects. First, the user is asked for a number. Second, if the user types 0, the while loop stops. And third, if the user doesn't type 0, the number entered is already stored in a variable that can be used in the while loop. You often see this type of shortcut in C++ programs. (By the way, if you are a troublemaker or a tester, you'll type a negative number in this program and note that it returns an incorrect answer. For extra credit, add a check to prevent the user from typing negative numbers.)

Here's the new factorial program:

```
// Factorial3
// Compute factorials until the user types in 0

#include "stdafx.h"

#using <mscorlib.dll>

using namespace System;

//Computes and returns the factorial of a number
int Factorial(int nNumber)
{
    int nResult = 1;
    int i;    //Loop variable

    //Now loop through. Each time through the loop,
    //multiply the result by i.
    for (i=1; i<=nNumber; i++)
    {
        nResult *= i;
    }
```

```
    //Now return the result
    return nResult;
}

//This routine prompts the user for a number.
//It returns the value of the number
int GetNumber()
{
    int nNumber;

    Console::WriteLine(S"What is the number?");
    nNumber = Int32::Parse(Console::ReadLine());
    return nNumber;
}

// This is the entry point for this application
#ifdef _UNICODE
int wmain(void)
#else
int main(void)
#endif
{
    int nNumber;

    //Get numbers from the user, until the user
    //types 0
    while (nNumber = GetNumber())
    {
        //Now we will output the result
        //Note that we are calling the function
        //Factorial
        Console::WriteLine(S"The factorial of {0} is {1}",
            nNumber.ToString(),
            Factorial(nNumber).ToString());
    }

    //Now we are finished
    Console::WriteLine(S"Bye");
    return 0;
}
```

This program is in the Factorial3 directory on the CD accompanying this book.

Reading programs that contain functions

When programs contain functions, the functions are usually defined before they're used. Therefore, if you read a program line-by-line, from start to finish, you end up looking at all the nitty-gritty details before you get a chance to see how the whole thing fits together.

Here are several tips to make your life easier:

✔ If the file has a `main` function in it, skip to `main` and see what it does. Work backwards from the highest-level functions to the ones with the most details.

✔ If the file contains only a lot of functions, look at the names of all the functions first.

Read the comments to get a clue about what they do. After you've looked at all the functions, figure out which ones are worth checking out and which ones are low-level utility functions that you can ignore.

✔ Usually the highest-level functions occur at the end of the file.

If you're wondering why you can give a variable in a function the same name as a variable that already exists outside the function, don't worry — this is explained in Chapter 15.

Recursion, Foiled Again

If a function calls itself, it's said to be *recursive*. Recursive routines are often used when completing a process is made easier if you can repeat the process on a smaller subset of items.

For example, suppose that you want to sort a lot of numbers. (This happens to be a classic and time-consuming computer science homework problem. I'll probably get into trouble for revealing this, but solving problems by using recursion happens way more often in computer science classes than it does in real life.) Sorting a large set of numbers can be a complicated task. The easiest way to do it is to search through the set for the smallest number, place it in a result list, and repeat the process until all the numbers are sorted. The problem with this approach is that you keep looking at the same list over and over and over again. And that takes a long time. That's why entire books are devoted to finding faster ways to sort numbers.

A common way to speed up this process is to use recursion and thus break the sorting problem into smaller problems. For example, suppose that instead of sorting one list, you wanted to merge two sets of already sorted numbers. That's a lot easier.

Why? Well, call the set that starts with the smallest number A. And call the other set B. Call the answer Result. To merge A and B, append the first item in A to Result. Now look at the second item. Is that smaller than the first item in B? If so, also put it in Result. Keep doing this until the item in B is smaller than the item in A. Now add the first item in B to Result. Keep looking at all the items in B until one in A is smaller. It may sound a little complicated on paper, but it's a heck of a lot easier and much faster than traversing all the numbers. In fact, you may want to try it out on paper to prove that it works.

Now the problem is to break the task of sorting numbers into merging two lists of sorted numbers. You can do that by breaking the set of numbers in half and sorting each half. How do you sort a half? Well, you break that half in half and sort it. As you continue this process, you'll eventually end up with a set that has one or two numbers in it. And that's a pretty easy set to sort.

Now you just go backward, merging the smaller sets into bigger sets. Eventually you end up with two halves that you merge to create one sorted list. So, by using recursion, you made the problem easier by using the same tasks on smaller pieces.

Look at this in a little more detail:

1. **Start with a set of unsorted numbers.**

   1 3 7 5 9 2 7

2. **Break these into two smaller sets.**

   1 3 7 5   9 2 7

3. **These are still too big; break them again.**

   1 3   7 5   9 2   7

4. **Now they're easy to sort; sort each set.**

   1 3   5 7   2 9   7

5. **Now go backwards and merge the newly sorted sets together.**

   1 3 5 7   2 7 9

6. **And merge once more.**

   1 2 3 5 7 7 9

Voila!

The code looks something like this:

```
numberlist
Sort( numberlist)
{
    if (NumberOfItemsIn(numberlist) == 1)
    {
        return numberlist;
    }
    if (NumberOfItemsIn(numberlist) == 2)
    {
```

```
        sort the two items //A simple compare
        return sortedlist;
    }
    //The list is larger, so split it in two and call
    //sort again
    Merge(Sort(first half of numberlist), Sort(second    half
        of numberlist));
}
```

Determining the factorial of a number, as you do previously in this chapter, is often accomplished using recursion. The following Factorial function is similar to that shown in the section "Revisiting the Factorial Example," but instead of using a for loop, the factorial routine calls itself with n - 1. In other words, n! = n2 (n - 1)*(n - 2). . . . This is the same as saying n! = n 2((n - 1)!).

Of course, (n - 1)! is the same as (n - 1) 2 ((n - 2)!). So, the factorial routine keeps multiplying the value passed in by the factorial of that value minus 1.

```
// Factorial4
// Compute factorials using recursion

#include "stdafx.h"

#using <mscorlib.dll>

using namespace System;

//Computes and returns the factorial of a number using
        recursion
//The factorial of 1 is 1, so that is easy.
//For the other ones, call Factorial again for
//something easier to solve.
int Factorial(int nNumber)
{
    if (nNumber > 1)
        return nNumber*Factorial(nNumber-1);
    return nNumber;
}


//This routine prompts the user for a number
//and returns the value of the number
int GetNumber()
{
    int nNumber;

    Console::WriteLine(S"What is the number?");
    nNumber = Int32::Parse(Console::ReadLine());
    return nNumber;
```

```
    }

    // This is the entry point for this application
    #ifdef _UNICODE
    int wmain(void)
    #else
    int main(void)
    #endif
    {
        int nNumber;
        //Get numbers from the user, until the user
        //types 0
        while (nNumber = GetNumber())
        {
            //Now we will output the result
            //Note that we are calling the function
            //Factorial
            Console::WriteLine(S"The factorial of {0} is {1}",
                nNumber.ToString(),
                Factorial(nNumber).ToString());
        }

        //Now we are finished
        Console::WriteLine(S"Bye");
        return 0;
    }
```

This program is in the Factorial4 directory on the CD accompanying this book. An unmanaged version is in the Factorial5 directory.

Connect the Dots: Using Ellipses

To indicate that a function can take any number of parameters, use . . . (ellipsis) in the argument list. For example, the following code tells the compiler that any number of parameters can be passed in — it's up to the function to figure out their type and what to do with them:

```
int factorial(...)
{
}
```

In general, though, using . . . when you define functions is a bad idea because you can inadvertently pass any type of junk into the function. This can cause things to choke pretty badly. Although you see . . . used in a few unmanaged library functions, avoid using it in functions that you write.

Hey, It's Not My Default

Default initializers specify default values for function arguments. For example, suppose that you have a function called foo that takes three integer arguments, a, b, and c. Also suppose that in most cases the programmer using your function will never need to use the c argument. You can assign a default value for c. c will always have this value unless a value for c is passed into the function. In other words, you can call foo(1,2), in which case a = 1, b = 2, and c is set to the default; or you can call foo(1,2,3), in which case a = 1, b = 2, and c = 3.

Default initializers are useful in functions that contain arguments needed only in special cases. Someone who uses the function can ignore these special arguments and the routine will work just fine. But for the special cases, the defaults can be overridden.

To specify default initializers, list the values along with the argument list when you define the function:

```
int foo(int a, int b, int c = 3)
{
}
```

Chapter 13

Pointer of No Return

· ·

In This Chapter

▶ Outlining the reasons for using pointers

▶ Finding out how to use pointers

▶ Drawing graphics with .NET

▶ Creating a linked list

▶ Freeing memory

▶ Avoiding crashes

▶ Using garbage collection

▶ Using unmanaged strings

· ·

Some people think that learning about pointers is really, really hard. This is usually the time when many computer science majors decide to study philosophy instead. But actually, pointers aren't so bad. As soon as you get over the initial shock, you find them incredibly useful and not as difficult as you thought.

This chapter helps you understand how and why to use pointers. But to keep readers wanting to join the Future Nerds of the World club, this chapter also has several technical sections and sidebars that you can read for further details. And just for extra fun, you start to create more interesting .NET applications, incorporating some simple graphics.

Why Pointers?

In other chapters, you find a lot of techniques for manipulating data. But as data becomes more and more complex, processing it efficiently using named variables becomes harder and harder. For example, you may want a list of arbitrarily sized pieces of information. Perhaps you know that you'll be scanning photographs, but you don't know their sizes in advance. With named variables, you'd need to know the size of the photographs in advance. With pointers, you can be more flexible.

As another example, you may want to keep track of the shapes a user wants to draw. With named variables, you'd need to know the number of shapes in advance. Using pointers, users can draw whatever number of shapes they want.

Another reason pointers are useful is that, even though a pointer is small, it can point to a very large thing. For example, suppose that you have a large computerized collection of patients' medical records, with each record consuming a lot of bytes — some up to several thousand bytes. If you wanted to reorder the records so that they were sorted by city, you'd be faced with a time-consuming job if you had to do it by recopying each record to its new position in the new sort order. But if you had a pointer to each record, you could quickly reorder the pointers. Then, even though the medical records themselves would never move, the changed pointer order would let you view the records in a new sort order.

You've already been using them

Pointers sound useful, but with all the bad press they get, you may be hoping that you can go on vacation for a few weeks and discover on your return that pointers are no longer needed. To paraphrase a famous song from the '70s, "Too late Ethel, you just got pointed." You can't avoid pointers. In fact, you've used them in every single program you've written so far. You just didn't know it.

Pointers and variables

To see why pointers are so useful, you need to go over how variables work. All computer data is stored in memory. When you assign a value to a variable, you fill in a block of memory with the value. When you use the variable, you read the value from memory. So, a variable is just a name for a region of memory in the computer.

A pointer is the same thing — it's just the address of something in memory. A pointer points to a portion of memory, just like a variable does. Every time you use a variable, you're really using a pointer.

The difference between a variable and a pointer is that a variable always points to the same spot in memory, but you can change a pointer so that it points to different spots in memory.

Figure 13-1 shows three variables called foo, bar, and dribble. You can see their memory addresses and their values. bar, for example, has the value 17 and is located at memory address 4. Two pointers, baz and goo, are in the figure also. baz has the value 4, which means it points to memory address 4. Thus, you can use the pointer baz to find out the value of the variable bar. If you change the value of baz to 8, you can use it to find the value of dribble (which is "Hey there").

Pointers are one of the most useful items in creating programs because they add great flexibility.

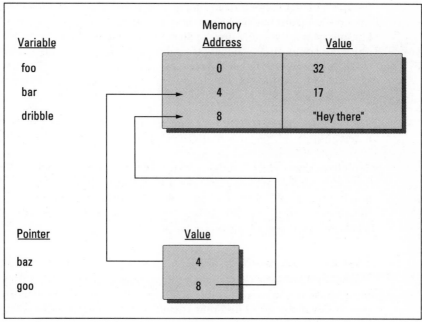

Figure 13-1: Variables are stored in memory. Pointers point to memory locations and can be used to access information stored in memory.

I'm pointing and I can't get up: Pointer troubles

Pointers sometimes drive beginning programmers nuts for two reasons. The first reason is that you often use pointers to obtain *two* different pieces of information. The second reason is that pointers can point to things that don't have names.

Double, double, value and address trouble

As just stated, you can use pointers to get two different pieces of information:

- ✔ **The value stored inside the pointer.** This is always the memory address of another piece of information. For example, if the pointer contains the value 4, that means it's pointing to memory address 4.

- ✔ **The value of the item pointed to by the pointer.** For example, if memory address 4 contains the value 17, a pointer containing the value 4 would be pointing to an item that had the value 17.

The value stored in the pointer is simply a memory location. If you print a pointer, you get some funky number that's just the memory address stored in the pointer. (And because there isn't much value in printing out a funky number, you most likely never will print this value.) But the pointer also points to something — because a value is stored inside the memory address that the pointer contains. This is usually the value you want to get at. Looking at the value contained by what the pointer points to is called *dereferencing* the pointer.

For example, the value of baz (refer to Figure 13-1) is 4. If you dereferenced baz, you'd get 17 because that's what is stored in memory location 4.

Sound abstract? Nah! You dereference all the time in real life. When you ask for a number 5 at your favorite restaurant, the waitperson says "Okay, number 5 is a cold, double-cheese pizza." In other words, 5 is the value contained in a pointer that points to a type of food. And double-cheese pizza is what you get when you dereference the pointer.

Tomb of the unnamed memory

The second potentially confusing thing about pointers is that they can point to things that don't have names. In Figure 13-1, you saw how to use a pointer to access the values of different variables. In that figure, the pointer baz points to the variable named bar. You can dereference baz to get the value stored in the variable bar. In this case, the pointer is pointing to an area in memory to which you've given a name (the variable's name, in this case bar).

You can also ask the computer to set aside a chunk of information and not give it a name. You often do this when you want to allocate memory dynamically. The unnamed chunk is in memory, though, so it has an address. You can store the address of this unnamed chunk in a pointer and then read from and write to this memory by using the pointer.

Another way to trash your computer

Computers keep special information in certain areas of memory. For example, the first 1000 bytes or so of memory contain lots of information telling the computer how to process keystrokes, timer ticks, and so forth. Then the operating system is loaded in a certain area. In other areas, you can find the memory for the video display card.

If you know where these areas are, you can point to them with a pointer and start writing in new values. Sometimes this does good things. For example, most video games know the exact memory area where video information is stored and use this knowledge to write to the screen very quickly or to perform special effects.

On the other hand, if you fill these special areas with junk, you can cause all types of strange behavior. This is known as *trashing* your computer because you filled up sensitive areas with trash. When your computer is trashed, anything can happen, but what happens is usually not good.

Windows tries to keep your programs well behaved. It can usually detect when you use a bad pointer and stop your program before it goes gooey ka-blooey. See the section "Whose GP fault is it, anyway?" later in this chapter for more details.

The motto? Be careful when you use pointers.

You are the weakest linked list

In this section, you look at a specific example in which you use a pointer to access a block of memory. Suppose that you want to create a program that stores lines to draw. Every time the user types a new set of coordinates, you dynamically allocate a new structure for storing them. And then you just save the address of this memory in a pointer.

Now comes the tricky part. Before the program begins, you don't know how many lines the user will draw. But you still need a way to store all the information about the lines. You could declare a whole bunch of pointers (say, LinePointer1, LinePointer2, LinePointer3, and so on) and then use the next pointer you had each time you needed to store information about another line. This strategy is yucky, though, because you need to make sure that you have more variables defined than lines the user might draw (what if the user wants to draw 20,000 lines?), and you need to use a gigantic switch statement to figure out what pointer you should use when.

A more elegant approach is to use something called a linked list. A *linked list* is a set of items in which the first item in the list points to the next item in the list. It's like a train. The first car of the train is hooked to the second car of the train, and so on (until you get to the caboose).

To store the swarm of lines to draw, you can create a linked list of lines. Each structure for storing line information will store the information about the line as well as a pointer to the next line. Figure 13-2 shows a linked list of three lines. Each line-information object stores information about the line as well as a pointer to the next one.

The linked list is a powerful and common way to store multiple items when the number of items or the size of each item isn't known in advance.

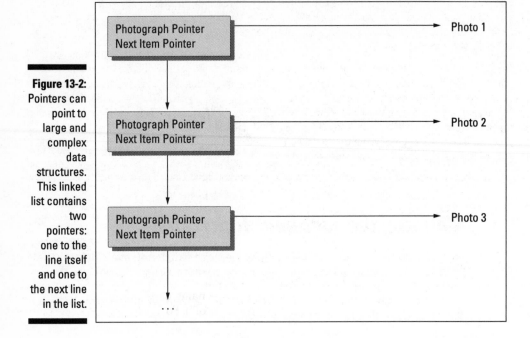

Figure 13-2:
Pointers can point to large and complex data structures. This linked list contains two pointers: one to the line itself and one to the next line in the list.

Using Pointers with C++

To make a pointer to a data type, you create a variable of that data type just like you usually do but precede its name with a * (pronounced "star").

For example, to create a pointer to an integer, you would do the following, which says that foo is a pointer to an integer:

```
int *pnFoo;
```

If you are following the naming convention used in this book, start pointer names with a *p,* followed by whatever letters you use for the type. For example, pn is a pointer to an integer. pdbl is a pointer to a double.

You need to declare the data type that the pointer points to. This makes your programs safer because the compiler makes sure that you don't accidentally point to something of the wrong type. After all, pointers are simply memory addresses. By giving a type to the pointer, if you accidentally try to copy, say, a photograph into an area of memory that's supposed to store information about a line, the compiler will flag the mistake for you. (This is good, because mistakes of this type can cause very nasty side effects.)

int *pnFoo doesn't mean that the pointer is called *pnFoo. The pointer is called pnFoo. The * tells the compiler that pnFoo is a pointer, but the * isn't part of the variable's name.

Give your pointer an address

When you define a pointer, it doesn't have a value. It just points into random space. But an undefined pointer is a dangerous thing. Before you use a pointer, you need to assign it a value. (That is, you need to fill it with the address of the piece of memory it's going to point to.)

Many times, you want to use a pointer to point to information stored in a variable. In other words, you fill the pointer with the address of a variable in your program. When you dereference the pointer, you can see what's stored in the variable.

To find the address of a variable, precede its name with an & (this is pronounced "amper," "ampersand," or "address of"). For example, you can do the following:

```
//Create a pointer to an integer
int *pnPosition;
//Here is an integer
int nXPosition = 3;
//Make the pointer point to nXPosition
pnPosition = &nXPosition;
```

These statements create a pointer called pnPosition that is filled with the address of an integer called nXPosition. If you dereference the pointer, you can find out the x position.

A pointer can point to only something of the correct data type. That is, if you have a pointer to an integer, you can fill the pointer with only the address of a variable that contains an integer.

Can 1 check your dereferences?

Dereferencing a pointer is easy: You just precede the pointer name with a *. For example, to find the value of what pnPosition points to, you can do the following:

```
//Print the number of songs
Console::WriteLine((*pnPosition).ToString());
```

This statement dereferences pnPosition. pnPosition contains the address of nXPosition, so the dereference returns the value stored inside the nXPosition variable.

A simple program that dereferences pointers

In this section, you write a simple program using pointers. (Don't worry, we'll get more complex soon.) This program contains an integer and a pointer to an integer. The pointer points to the integer number:

```
pnNumber = &nNumber;
```

The user types a value. First, the program prints the value directly with this fragment:

```
nNumber.ToString()
```

Next, it prints the value by dereferencing the pointer. Dereferencing pnNumber returns the value stored in the address that pnNumber points to. In this case, that means it returns the value stored in nNumber:

```
(*pnNumber).ToString()
```

When you call a function from a dereferenced pointer, such as calling the ToString function, always surround the dereferenced pointer with parentheses.

This example program is in the Point directory on the CD accompanying this book. Point2 contains an unmanaged version of this program. In addition to dereferencing the pointer, Point2 also prints the address contained in it.

```
// Point
// Shows how to declare and dereference pointers

#include "stdafx.h"

#using <mscorlib.dll>

using namespace System;

//Hang out until the user is finished
void HangOut()
{
```

```
      Console::WriteLine(L"Press the Enter key to stop the
            program");
      Console::ReadLine();
}

// This is the entry point for this application
#ifdef _UNICODE
int wmain(void)
#else
int main(void)
#endif
{
    int *pnNumber;
    int nNumber;

    //Have pnNumber point to nNumber
    pnNumber = &nNumber;

    //Get a number from the user
    Console::WriteLine(S"Please type in a number");
    nNumber = Int32::Parse(Console::ReadLine());

    //Now print this value back
    Console::WriteLine(S"The number is {0}",
            nNumber.ToString());

    //Now print it using a pointer
    Console::WriteLine(S"Using a pointer {0}",
            (*pnNumber).ToString());

    HangOut();
    return 0;
}
```

Changing the value of what you're pointing at

You can not only look at what a pointer points to but also change the value of something that is pointed to. In other words, you can not only read from the memory location but also write to it.

To do this, just use the *. For example, if pnPosition points to an integer (as in the preceding example), you can change the value stored in the integer by doing this:

```
*pnPosition = 5;
```

Changing the value in a structure

If you have a pointer to a structure, you can change an item in that structure. In the following code, `MyStruct` is a structure, and `poFoo` points to that structure. This means you can use `*poFoo` anyplace you can use the structure. To access a member of the structure, you can do this:

```
(*poFoo).value = 7.6;
```

Here's the code:

```
class MyStruct
{
public:
    int nData;
    double dblValue;
};
//Here is a pointer to the structure
MyStruct *poFoo;
//Here is the structure itself
MyStruct oRecord1;
//Point to the structure
poFoo = &oRecord1;
//Change something in the structure
(*poFoo).dblValue = 7.6;
```

Saved by the green arrow

Because using the `(*pointer).member` syntax can be a bit awkward, C++ has a shortcut:

```
//Change something in the structure
poFoo->dblValue = 7.6;
```

You see this `pointer->member` notation in almost all C++ programs that use pointers.

What's new?

Anytime you need to process an unknown number of items or store something of an unknown size, you end up allocating memory *dynamically* (this is also called allocating memory on-the-fly).

A linked list of lines is an example of this: You don't know how many lines you need to store, so each time the user types line coordinates, you allocate a new line-information object.

The new command allocates memory on-the-fly. You just tell new the data type that you want to create, and it returns a pointer to the area it allocated. If you wanted to create a new integer on-the-fly, you could do this:

```
//Point to an integer
int *pnPosition;
//Now allocate some memory for an integer
//and use pnPosition to point to it
pnPosition = new int;
```

If you wanted to create a new PointList structure on-the-fly, you could do this:

```
//Point to a PointList structure
PointList *poPoint;
//Allocate a new structure and point to it
poPoint = new PointList;
```

When you use new to create an item, the pointer is the only thing that remembers where the new item is stored. You must be very careful that you don't accidentally clear the pointer. Otherwise, you'll never be able to find the item again. For example, look at this code:

```
//A forgetful application
//Start with a pointer to an integer
int *pnPosition;
//Create a new integer
pnPosition = new int;
//Set the value to 3
*pnPosition = 3;
//Now create a new integer
pnPosition = new int;
```

The last line of this code allocated memory for a new integer. The address of the new integer was stored in pnPosition. But what happens to the integer that was set to 3? It's still floating around in memory but, because pnPosition no longer stores its address, you have no way to access it.

When you forget to save the address for something you created dynamically, that item is left hanging out in memory. This is called a *memory leak*. The item will keep using up memory — and you'll be unable to get rid of it — until your program ends. (.NET has a lot of features to help out with this problem, as discussed later.)

When you use new, be careful to keep pointers to the memory items until they are no longer needed. Then you can get rid of the memory safely by using the delete command, which is discussed later in this chapter in the "Free, free, set them free" section.

Warning: Graphic Material

Now that you have some basic understanding of pointers, you can start to create more interesting .NET programs. In this section, you dig into .NET's graphics capabilities. Just as you can use the Console functions to read and write text, you can use the Graphics functions to draw pictures on the screen.

To draw graphics, you first need to create a Graphics object. You do that with code like this:

```
Form *poForm = new Form();
Graphics *poGraphics = poForm->CreateGraphics();
```

Wow, pointers galore! When you draw graphics, you need to draw them on a window (a window not like the one in your house but like a screen in a Microsoft Windows operating system). One of the easiest ways to create a window is to create a Form. Then you can call CreateGraphics to create a drawing surface, called a Graphics object. As you can see, you use pointers to store the Form and the Graphics object and use the -> notation to call methods on these objects.

Before you view any graphics, you need to make the Form visible, with code such as:

```
poForm->Show();
```

Then, you can call any of the .NET graphics functions, as shown in Table 13-1. When you are finished drawing, you call the Dispose method:

```
poGraphics->Dispose();
```

Table 13-1	Useful Graphics Commands	
Method	*Usage*	*Meaning*
Clear	poG->Clear(Color::Red)	Fills the entire drawing surface with the specified color. See also Table 13-2.
Dispose	poG->Dispose()	Frees up memory associated with the graphics object. Call when you are finished drawing.

Method	Usage	Meaning
DrawEllipse	poG->DrawEllipse (poPen, 10, 20, 150, 200)	Draws an ellipse, using the specified pen. (Pens are discussed shortly) shortly). The other values set the x and y position of the top-left part of the ellipse, as well as its width and height. In particular, the x, y, width, and height parameters specify a rectangle into which the ellipse is drawn. If the width and the height have the same value, the result is a circle.
DrawLine	poG->DrawLine (poPen, 10, 20, 160, 220)	Draws a line from one point to another. In this example, it draws from the point at (10, 20) to the point at (160, 220).
DrawRectangle	poG->DrawRectangle (poPen, 10, 20, 150, 200)	Draws a rectangle, where the parameters set the x and y position of the top-left corner of the rectangle, followed by the width and height.
DrawString	poG->DrawString (S"Test", poFont, poBrush, 10, 20)	Draws text, with the specified font, brush, and starting position. Fonts and brushes are discussed shortly.
FillEllipse	poG->FillEllipse (poBrush, 10, 20, 150, 200)	Draws an ellipse, filling it in using the specified brush.
	poG->FillRectangle (poBrush, 10, 20, 150, 200)	Draws a rectangle, filling it in with the specified brush.

Color me purple

Whenever you draw, you need to specify a color to draw with. You do so with the Color structure. (Gee, I never would have guessed.) You can use the Color structure in two ways: using a predefined color value and using the FromArgb method.

Table 13-2 shows the predefined colors. The only caution with using them is to avoid eating when you type a color name such as PapayaWhip or LemonChiffon. You might spew.

Table 13-2	**Predefined Colors**	
AliceBlue	DarkOrange	Khaki
AntiqueWhite	DarkOrchid	Lavender
Aqua	DarkRed	LavenderBlush
Aquamarine	DarkSalmon	LawnGreen
Azure	DarkSeaGreen	LemonChiffon
Beige	DarkSlateBlue	LightBlue
Bisque	DarkSlateGray	LightCoral
Black	DarkTurquoise	LightCyan
BlanchedAlmond	DarkViolet	LightGoldenrodYellow
Blue	DeepPink	LightGray
BlueViolet	DeepSkyBlue	LightGreen
Brown	DimGray	LightPink
BurlyWood	DodgerBlue	LightSalmon
CadetBlue	Firebrick	LightSeaGreen
Chartreuse	FloralWhite	LightSlateGray
Chocolate	ForestGreen	LightSteelBlue
Coral	Fuchsia	LightYellow
Cornflower	Gainsboro	Lime
Cornsilk	GhostWhite	LimeGreen
Crimson	Gold	Linen
Cyan	Goldenrod	Magenta
DarkBlue	Gray	Maroon
DarkCyan	Green	MediumAquamarine
DarkGoldenrod	GreenYellow	MediumBlue
DarkGray	Honeydew	MediumOrchid
DarkGreen	HotPink	MediumPurple
DarkKhaki	IndianRed	MediumSeaGreen
DarkMagenta	Indigo	MediumSlateBlue
DarkOliveGreen	Ivory	MediumSpringGreen

MediumTurquoise	PaleVioletRed	SlateBlue
MediumVioletRed	PapayaWhip	SlateGray
MidnightBlue	PeachPuff	Snow
MintCream	Peru	SpringGreen
MistyRose	Pink	SteelBlue
Moccasin	Plum	Tan
NavajoWhite	PowderBlue	Teal
Navy	Purple	Thistle
OldLace	Red	Tomato
Olive	RosyBrown	Transparent
OliveDrab	RoyalBlue	Turquoise
Orange	SaddleBrown	Violet
OrangeRed	Salmon	Wheat
Orchid	SandyBrownSeaShell	White
PaleGoldenrod	Sienna	WhiteSmoke
PaleGreen	Silver	Yellow
PaleTurquoise	SkyBlue	YellowGreen

Despite its appearance, `FromArgb` is not the sound you make when you swallow a shoe. It stands for Alpha-Red-Green-Blue. You can use it to create a new color based on a red, blue, and green amount for making up the color. The values can range from 0 (meaning none) to 255 (meaning a whole bunch). For example, if you specify that red is 255, blue is 0, and green is 0, you get bright red as the color. If you specify red is 128, blue is 128, and green is 128 you get a light gray as the color. I'd love to tell you what every possible combination leads to, but it would fill the rest of the book. (For fun, calculate how many color values you can represent with this system.)

If you want to find out the red, green, and blue values for a color, load any graphics program such as Adobe Photoshop. In the color picker, find your favorite color. The color picker will show you the magic red, green, and blue numbers for that color.

If you want to use the color blue, you can do this:

```
Color::Blue
```

If instead you want to make up your own color, you can use code such as:

```
Color::FromArgb(255, 128, 0);
```

You use color in the sample program shown in the "You draw me crazy" section.

The example here sets the red, green, and blue values. You can also pass in four values to `FromArgb`, in which case the first value is the alpha level, followed by the red, green, and blue values. Alpha lets you set transparency level. If you're adventurous, play around with it.

When you use the `Color` object, you don't create a new object with the `new` keyword as you did for the `Graphics` object. Instead, you use `::` to refer to one of the color constants or to call the `FromArgb` method.

The pen is mightier than the sword

When you draw a line (using `DrawLine`) or an outline (using `DrawEllipse` or `DrawRectangle`), you use a `Pen` object. A `Pen` object represents the concept of a good old pen. It has a color (an ink color, if you will) and a width. To create a one-pixel-wide red pen, do this:

```
poPen = new Pen(Color::Red);
```

To create a five-pixel-wide teal pen, do this:

```
poPen = new Pen(Color::Teal, 5);
```

After you create a `Pen` object, you can dynamically change its color or width by setting the `Color` and `Width` properties, as shown in this code:

```
poPen->Width = 12;
poPen->Color = Color::SaddleBrown;
```

The .NET graphics functions are sometimes called GDI+.

Brush me off

When you draw a filled shape, such as with `FillEllipse` or `FillRectangle`, you specify a brush instead of a pen. As you would expect, a brush represents the concept of a painting brush. There are two kinds of brushes: `SolidBrush` and `TextureBrush`. `SolidBrush` paints with a solid color, whereas the more sophisticated `TextureBrush` lets you paint with an image.

To create a new brush, use code such as the following:

```
poBrush = new SolidBrush(Color::Red);
```

To change the color of the brush, sets its `Color` property:

```
poBrush->Color = Color::Thistle;
```

Fontastic

When you display text on the screen using `DrawString` (isn't that the thing that keeps your sweatpants up?) you need to specify a font. Here's how:

```
poFont = new Font("Arial", 12);
```

The first parameter indicates the typeface to use, and the second is the size of the font. You can use any font on the computer. Figure 13-3 shows some of the typical fonts.

Font	*Example*
Arial	Hello 123
Courier New	Hello 123
Times New Roman	Hello 123
Symbol	Ηελλο 123
Verdana	Hello 123
WingDings	✏︎♏︎●●◻︎ 👉📄📑

Figure 13-3: Common Fonts

You can use the Character Map accessory program to explore what characters look like in various fonts. This is especially useful for seeing what's in picture fonts such as Symbol and WingDings. If you are feeling bored, you can construct whole sentences from the ideograms in WingDings, look at the corresponding letters in a normal font, and then send them to friends to see whether they can decrypt your messages.

You draw me crazy

Now that you've explored the basics of .NET graphics, it's time to create a very simple graphics program. It uses brushes, pens, fonts, and various graphics commands to draw some shapes on the screen. Here's the code:

```
// Graphics
// Demonstrates .NET graphics

#include "stdafx.h"

#using <mscorlib.dll>
#using <System.Windows.Forms.dll>
#using <System.dll>
#using <System.Drawing.dll>

using namespace System;
using namespace System::Drawing;
using namespace System::Windows::Forms;


// This is the entry point for this application
#ifdef _UNICODE
int wmain(void)
#else
int main(void)
#endif
{
    //Structures for drawing graphics
    Form *poForm = new Form();
    Graphics *poGraphics = poForm->CreateGraphics();

    //Create a red pen with which to draw
    Pen *poPen = new Pen(Color::Red);

    //Show the display surface
    poForm->Show();

    //Draw a line
    poGraphics->DrawLine(poPen, 10, 10, 120, 150);

    //Now use a different color and width
    poPen->Color = Color::FromArgb(100, 255, 200);
    poPen->Width = 5;
    poGraphics->DrawLine(poPen, 120, 150, 10, 150);

    //Use the same pen to draw an ellipse
    poGraphics->DrawEllipse(poPen, 10, 150, 40, 60);

    //Create a new brush
    SolidBrush *poBrush = new SolidBrush(Color::Tomato);
    //Draw a filled rectangle with it
```

```
poGraphics->FillRectangle(poBrush, 50, 150, 40, 60);

//Create a font
Font *poFont = new Font("Helvetica", 22);
//Draw some text with it
poGraphics->DrawString(S"Hello", poFont, poBrush, 200,
        200);

//Free up the graphics surface
poGraphics->Dispose();

//Hang out until the user closes the form
Application::Run(poForm);
}
```

There are a few interesting things to note. First, a bunch of #using and using namespace commands are at the top of the program. That's because to use graphics and forms in .NET, you need to load a lot of stuff.

Next, notice Application::Run at the end of the program. Whenever you create a form, you can tell .NET to hang out until the user shuts down the form. That's a lot more convenient than the HangOut function you use in previous chapters. The form shows up, the user can watch it or interact, and when they click the close button on the form, the .NET program ends.

You can find this program in the Graphics directory on the accompanying CD.

Just Another Linked List in the Wall

Now that you've used pointers a bit — after all, you used them throughout the Graphics program — it's time to use them in a more classic, Computer Science way. In this section, you use pointers to create a linked list of points. The user types the coordinates for a series of points and you store them in a linked list. Then, when the user is finished, you connect the dots using the .NET graphics commands.

How the program works

The program creates a linked list of items. Each item structure contains coordinates for a point as well as a pointer to the next structure in the list. The last item in the list has a pointer with the value 0. This is sometimes called a *null pointer.*

The fundamental part of a linked list is the structure that contains information, along with a pointer to the next item in the list. Here, `PointList` contains two integers and a pointer to the next `PointList`:

```
class PointList
{
public:
    int nX;
    int nY;
    PointList  *poNext;
};
```

The program contains code to add new items to the list and display the list. Three pointers are needed. The first pointer points to the beginning of the list. That way, no matter what, the first element in the list can always be found. After all, if you want to draw all items in the list, you need to know where the list begins:

```
PointList *poPoints = 0;
```

The second pointer points to new items when an item is added to the list:

```
PointList *poNew;
```

The third pointer points to the last item in the list:

```
PointList *poLast;
```

This pointer is needed when you add items to the list. It points to the last item created, so that when you add a new item, the old last item points to the new item.

Take a look at how linked-list creation works in the program. First, the new item is created:

```
//Create a new point structure
poNew = new PointList;
```

If this is the very first `PointList` created, no `poPoints` points to it.. (If you are on a bus or a subway, be sure to read the previous sentence out loud and see whether people move away from you.) Remember, `poPoints` is the pointer that points to the beginning of the linked list:

```
if (!poPoints)
{
    //If it is the first one, initialize poPoints
    poPoints = poNew;
}
```

The if clause checks to see whether poPoints is null. That is what the funky ! in front of poPoints does. Now, if poPoints isn't null, you've already created an item in the list, so you hook up the new item to the end of the list:

```
//Connect it to the last one
poLast->poNext = poNew;
```

Note that all you did here was find the object pointed to by the poLast pointer and have its poNext pointer point to the object you just created.

Finally, you update the poLast pointer so that it now points to the object you just created, and you call a function to set the PointList coordinates:

```
poLast = poNew;
NewPoint(poNew);
```

After the user has typed a set of numbers, the program draws them by traversing the list. It starts with the first item in the list, draws a line from that point to the next point, and then moves to the next item in the list. The program does this until the pointer to the next item is null, because that means the end of the list has been reached:

```
poLast = poPoints;
while (poLast)
{
   //Draw it
   DrawPoint(poGraphics, poLast);
   //Advance
   poLast = poLast->poNext;
}
```

After all the lines are drawn, the program cleans up memory (you find out about this in the "Free, free, set them free" section):

```
poLast = poPoints;
while (poLast)
{
    PointList *poNext;
    poNext = poLast->poNext;

    //Free up the memory
    delete poLast;

    //Now advance
    poLast = poNext;
}
```

The code

The managed version of the program, which follows, is called Draw. Draw2 is an unmanaged version of the same program. The unmanaged version prints the coordinate values to the screen rather than drawing them with the nifty .NET drawing commands.

```cpp
// Draw
// Uses a linked list to store a list of points to draw
// Draws them using GDI+

#include "stdafx.h"

#using <mscorlib.dll>
#using <System.dll>
#using <System.Windows.Forms.dll>
#using <System.Drawing.dll>

using namespace System;
using namespace System::Drawing;
using namespace System::Windows::Forms;


//Stores point information
//Uses a linked list
class PointList
{
public:
    int nX;
    int nY;
    PointList  *poNext;
};

//Gets the values for a new point
void NewPoint(PointList *poNew)
{
    //Read the x and y positions and store them in the
            structure
    Console::WriteLine(S"What is the x position?");
    poNew->nX = Int32::Parse(Console::ReadLine());
    Console::WriteLine(S"What is the y position?");
    poNew->nY = Int32::Parse(Console::ReadLine());
    //Set the pointer to null
    poNew->poNext = 0;
}

//Draws the points
void DrawPoint(Graphics *poGraphics, PointList *poPoint)
{
    //Is there a place to draw to?
    if (poPoint->poNext)
    {
```

```
            //Create a pen to draw with
            Pen *poPen = new Pen(Color::Red);
            //Draw a line between the current point and the next
                point
            poGraphics->DrawLine(poPen, poPoint->nX, poPoint->nY,
                poPoint->poNext->nX, poPoint->poNext->nY);
        }

}

// This is the entry point for this application
#ifdef _UNICODE
int wmain(void)
#else
int main(void)
#endif
{
    //Points to the list of coordinates
    PointList *poPoints = 0;
    //Points to the last PointList created
    PointList *poLast;
    //Points to a new PointList
    PointList *poNew;
    //For storing the user response
    String *pszMore;

    //Structures for drawing graphics
    Form *poForm = new Form();
    Graphics *poGraphics = poForm->CreateGraphics();

    //A flag to tell us to stop
    bool fFinished = false;

    while (!fFinished)
    {
        //Create a new point structure
        poNew = new PointList;
        if (!poPoints)
        {
            //If it is the first one, initialize poPoints
            poPoints = poNew;
        }
        else
        {
            //Connect it to the last one
            poLast->poNext = poNew;
        }
        //Now update poLast
        poLast = poNew;

        //Read in the values
        NewPoint(poNew);
```

```
    //Should we read more in?
    Console::WriteLine("Press y to enter a new point");
    pszMore = Console::ReadLine();
    if (!pszMore->Equals(S"y"))
    {
        fFinished = true;
    }

}

//Show the display surface
poForm->Show();

//Now draw the points
poLast = poPoints;
while (poLast)
{
    //Draw it
    DrawPoint(poGraphics, poLast);
    //Advance
    poLast = poLast->poNext;
}

//Free up the graphics surface
poGraphics->Dispose();

//Now clean up memory
poLast = poPoints;
while (poLast)
{
    PointList *poNext;
    poNext = poLast->poNext;

    //Free up memory
    delete poLast;

    //Now advance
    poLast = poNext;
}

//Hang out until the user closes the form
Application::Run(poForm);

}
```

This program is in the Draw directory on the CD accompanying this book.
The unmanaged version is in the Draw2 directory.

Passing arguments by reference

Modifying global variables in a function is dangerous. A better approach is to return a value from a function and set the values outside the function. (This avoids mysterious side effects inside functions.)

If you'd rather have a function modify several items or modify items in an existing structure, you can pass a pointer to those items to the function. The function can dereference the pointer and change the values. This is better than changing global variables (or variables outside the local scope) because when you indicate that pointers are passed to a function, programmers using the function know that the thing the pointer points to may get changed.

Another approach is to use *reference arguments.* When you do this, a pointer to the argument (not the argument itself) is passed in.

Because a pointer is passed in, anytime you change something in the routine, the values themselves are changed.

Using reference arguments is easier than passing in pointers because you don't need to explicitly dereference the parameters inside the function. To pass an argument by reference, you can precede the name of the item in the argument list with &:

```
int Factorial(int &Number)
{
}
```

Then, any changes made to Number (or whatever the reference data is) in the function are permanent — they have an effect outside the function itself.

Pointer Pitfalls

As the saying goes, with power comes responsibility, and the same is true of pointers. C++ is a powerful language and pointers give you access to the computer's raw memory. That means you have to be careful. This section covers things you need to keep in mind when working with pointers and how .NET provides some relief.

Free, free, set them free

If you find that you no longer need some memory that you allocated, you should free it so that you don't use more space than you need. The process of doing this is called *freeing memory.*

To free memory, use the delete command, which works like new but in reverse:

```
//Pointer to a PointList
PointList *pnPoint = new PointList;
//Get rid of the PointList you just created
delete pnPoint;
//Clear the pointer
pnPoint = 0;
```

Note that when you delete a pointer, you don't use *. That's because you're deleting the memory that the pointer points to, not the value of what is pointed to.

When you delete an item, the pointer itself isn't changed. The item that it pointed to, however, is cleared from memory. So the pointer still contains a memory address, but the memory address is now empty. If you dereference the pointer, you get junk. After you delete what a pointer points to, you should set the pointer to 0. That way, you know not to use the pointer until you make it point to something meaningful.

Whose GP fault is it, anyway?

If you mess up with pointers, you can get some strange results; usually, that means you get a GP fault. (This is short for general protection violation and pretty much means that some program is hosed. If you're unlucky, you may have to shut down a bunch of apps or even reboot.) Windows watches for GP faults and stops your program in its tracks when one occurs. Figure 13-4 shows what the typical GP fault dialog box looks like.

Constant reference arguments: Don't change that structure!

Passing big structures in as arguments can be somewhat time-consuming because the computer has to make a new copy of all the items in the structure. To speed this process, pass the structure in *by reference*. That way, only a pointer is passed (and pointers are very small).

The catch is that now the structure can be changed within the routine. To get around this problem, use a *constant reference argument*.

This tells the compiler "I'm doing this only to make it faster. Don't let this thing be changed."

Here's an example:

```
int DrawIt(const PointList
    &MyPoint)
{

}
```

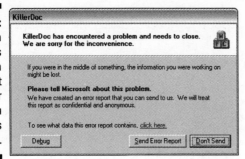

Figure 13-4:
When
Windows
detects a
GP fault, it
closes your
program
and displays
a warning.

Here are some common reasons why you can get yourself into deep water when you use pointers:

- **You copy something when a pointer is null.** For example, if `foo` is null, `*foo = x` tries to write information to la-la land. Windows doesn't like that. Neither does any system. The result is bad.

- **You copy something to the wrong place.** For example, suppose that `foo` points to the beginning of the list and `bar` points to the end of the list. If you use `bar` where you intended to use `foo`, you won't be doing what you think you're doing.

- **You delete memory and forget to clear the pointer**. For example, after freeing a chunk of memory, you merrily write a few million characters to the memory area that is now used by something else. Strange things will happen.

So, don't do these things, or you'll be foo-barred!

Garbage in, garbage out

In Draw, you went through a lot of work to clean up all the memory that you used. If you want, .NET can do this for you automatically using a feature called *garbage collection*. If you declare that an object is garbage collected, .NET watches how you use it. When nothing is using the object, .NET frees the memory associated with it. (Because garbage collection can be time-consuming as well as smelly, .NET waits until a convenient time to do the garbage collection.)

To make an object garbage-collected, put __gc before the object declaration, such as in the following code:

Avoid the void*

You might think that it would be handy to create a pointer that can point to anything. These types of pointers are called `void` pointers. Although `void` pointers are versatile (because you can use them anywhere to point to any kind of variable), they're also dangerous (because the compiler lets you use them anywhere).

Here's how you make one (if you were going to, which I'm sure you're not, right?):

```
//Let pOff point to anything
void *pOff;
```

`void` pointers are dangerous because no type is checking for them and their use can accidentally scramble memory.

For example, if you use void pointers in the linked list of points discussed earlier in the chapter, you can accidentally add employee records, integers, songs, and who knows what else to the linked list of points. The compiler would never know that you were doing something bad. Your customers sure would, though.

To sum up, unless you really, really need to, don't use `void` pointers.

```
__gc class  PointList
{
public:
    int nX;
    int nY;
    PointList  *poNext;
};
```

Check out Draw3 on the accompanying CD. It uses a garbage collected class for maintaining the point structure, and as a result, doesn't need to do the clean up at the end.

Stringing Us Along

As you have discovered earlier, *string* is a computer-speak term for a bunch of text or, rather, a set of contiguous characters. .NET has a built-in `String` class for manipulating strings. If you are writing unmanaged code, however, you need to deal with strings all by your self by using `char *`. Lots of library routines are devoted to processing strings. Pointers are also quite useful for processing strings.

Strings are stored in the computer as a contiguous array of characters, ending with a byte containing the value 0. (This zero, or null, byte at the end gives strings another name: *null-terminated strings*.) Strings are accessed by a pointer to the first item in the string. If you want to create a string, you can do this:

Some simple pointer pointers

Here are some simple reminders and tips that can help keep you sane when you use pointers:

✔ A pointer contains an address of something in memory. If you add, subtract, or do something else with the pointer, you are manipulating the address itself, not what is located at the address. Usually you don't want to do that. Instead, you usually want to manipulate what the pointer points to. You do this by dereferencing the pointer.

✔ The name of the pointer isn't *pFoo; it's pFoo. *pFoo dereferences the pointer.

✔ If pnFoo is a pointer to an integer, you can use *pnFoo anywhere you can use an integer variable inside your application. If poFoo is a pointer to something of data type *x,* you can use *poFoo anywhere you can use a variable of data type *x.* That means you can do *poFoo = jupiter; and jupiter = *poFoo; and so on.

✔ If you create some memory dynamically, be sure to save its address in a pointer. If you don't save the address, you'll never be able to use the memory.

✔ When you delete some memory that you've created dynamically, the pointer itself isn't deleted or changed — just the stuff pointed to. To avoid problems, set the pointer to null after you do a delete.

✔ If you're doing a lot of work with dynamically created objects, use .NET's garbage collection feature.

✔ If your head feels fuzzy, get some rest or put away those funny cigarettes.

```
//Create a string
char *szMyWord = "sensitive new-age guy";
```

This creates a string with the text "sensitive new-age guy" in it. The variable szMyWord points to this. You can print this string as follows:

```
//Print the string
cout << szMyWord;
```

You may want to look at the string library functions to see what else you can do with a string. Most of the library functions for processing strings start with str. For example, strlen returns the number of characters in a string.

C++ also includes an object called the ANSI string class that can help you create and manipulate strings.

When you allocate memory for a string, remember that it needs to end with a 0 byte, which takes up one byte. Make sure you include that ending byte in the size of the memory you allocate. Otherwise, you'll crash or trash memory.

Because you can use char * to point to a string of text, you can do lots of things with pointers to manipulate the text. C++ ends strings with a 0 (a byte containing a zero). That's how the library functions know when a string ends.

If you want to print the characters in a string one at a time, you can increment the pointer itself. If you have a pointer to a letter in a string, you can add 1 to the pointer to move to the next letter in the string. For example:

```
//A string
char *szMyString = "hello world";
//Another char *
char *szCharPtr;
//Change the first character
szCharPtr = szMyString;
*szCharPtr = 'j';
//Now move on to the next character
//Do so by incrementing the pointer
szCharPtr++;
//Now change the second  character
*szCharPtr = 'o';
//The string is now changed
//to "jollo world"
cout << szMyString;
```

Give Yourself a Pointer on the Back

Guess what? You now know an awful lot about pointers. In this chapter, you discovered that pointers are simply variables that point to areas in memory. You use pointers to access memory that is allocated dynamically (for example, when you don't know the amount of memory you need to allocate in advance). You use pointers also when you want to create linked lists (because you don't know the number of items in advance). Pointers have many other uses. You see them any time we use .NET features such as graphics commands or string conversion methods.

Even though you're now a pointer expert, if you do find yourself getting a little confused, don't be ashamed to look at the "Some simple pointer pointers" sidebar every now and then.

Chapter 14

Arrays and Shine

· ·

· ·

Arrays are a powerful data type used throughout many programs. An array is similar to a row (or column) in a spreadsheet: Basically, you have a lot of cells in which you can store information. This makes the array a very useful structure for storing information in a program.

In this chapter, you use arrays to store a list of items to draw. You also find out about a variety of special .NET classes that help you store data in your programs.

Up, Up, and Arrays

The great thing about arrays is that each element in the array has a number, called an *index,* that you can use to access the information in that element. You can also use loops to look at all the elements (or a range of elements) in a particular array. The array index lets you access any of the items in the array immediately. This makes *random access* much faster than using lists to store information.

For example, you could use an array to keep a list of playing times for songs. Then, if you wanted to find the playing time for song number 1, you would look at array element 1. Likewise, you could use arrays to store exchange rates for various currency markets, names of various employees, or any number of other things.

Before you create an array, you need to state how many elements will be in it. So, unlike lists, you need to know the size of the array before you create it. (Although, later in this chapter, you will find out about the .NET `ArrayList` class, which lets you have the best of both worlds.)

For example, suppose that `anFoo` is an array of integers. It might look like this:

Index Value

0	32
1	10
2	17
3	–5
4	10

As you can see, the first element in the array has an index of 0, the second element has an index of 1, and so on. And in this particular array, element 0 has the value 32, and element 4 has the value 10.

If you follow the naming convention used in this book, you'll start the array variable name with the letter *a*, followed by the letter for the type, such as *an* for integers, *adbl* for doubles, and so on.

To create an array, you simply list the data type, the name, and the number of elements that you want within [ ] (square brackets).

For example, to create an array of integers, you can do this:

```
//Create an array containing 20 integers, with indices
//0..19
int anFoo[20];
```

You need to remember that the first element in an array is element 0, and that if you create an array with *n* elements, the last item is *n* – 1. For example, in the array shown a few paragraphs back, *n* is 5 (because there are five elements). The first element in the array is 0, and the last element in the array is 4 (or 5 – 1).

When beginners first start using arrays, they commonly use a 1 (instead of a 0) for the first element and then wonder why the values in the array aren't what they expected.

Likewise, beginners commonly use *n* (instead of *n* - 1) for the last item in the array, and then they get strange data or GP faults. The GP fault occurs because C++ does not prevent you from accessing beyond the last element in the array. With reference to the sample code just shown, if you mistakenly wrote data to anFoo[20], that would be beyond the array itself and into the next memory location. Boom!

Element Array, My Dear Watson

To access an element in an array, use the variable name followed by the index in square brackets. For example, in the following code, anFoo is an array of 20 integers:

```
//anFoo is an array of 20 integers
int anFoo[20];
//Set the first element to 20 and the second element to 3
anFoo[0] = 20;
anFoo[1] = 3;
//Print the value of the second element
Console::WriteLine(anFoo[1]);
//Print 3 times the fifth element
Console::WriteLine(3*anFoo[4]);
```

 Note that if you're printing a number all by itself with Console::WriteLine, you don't need to call ToString explicitly. .NET knows how to do that automatically. If you use a more complex form of Console::WriteLine, such as using a formatting string, you must call ToString explicitly.

Initializing Arrays

You can initialize arrays in several ways. One way is to set each element by hand:

```
anFoo[0] = 1;
anFoo[1] = 3;
    .
    .
    .
```

Another way is to use a loop. Loops are especially powerful if the values in the array have a pattern or if the initial values can be read from a data file. For example, to create an array containing the numbers 1 through 20, you can do this:

```
//anIntegers is an array of 20 integers
```

```
int anIntegers[20];
//Loop through, setting the value of each element
//in the array
//Note that we are setting it to 1 + the array index
for (int i = 0; i < 20; i++)
  anIntegers[i] = i + 1;
```

Yet another way to initialize an array is to type the values for the elements when you declare the array. You can type as few items as you like (the remaining items are given a default value of 0). For example, you can initialize an array of integers with the following:

```
int anMyInts[10] = {1, 4, 5, 6, 7, 8};
```

In this case, the first six elements are assigned the values listed (element zero is assigned the value 1, element one is assigned 4, and so on), and the remaining four elements are assigned a default value of 0.

The relationship between arrays and pointers

An array of items of type *x* is really a pointer to an item of type *x*. That is, if you do this:

```
    int foo[8];
```

you can treat foo just as if you did this:

```
    int *foo;
```

The difference is that when you create an array, a block of memory is allocated, whereas when you create the pointer, a block of memory isn't allocated. The array variable is a pointer to the first element in the array.

Sometimes pointers are used to iterate through arrays. Consider the following code:

```
    //An array of integers
    int foo[8];
    //A pointer to an integer
    int *bar;
```

```
//Point to the first element
//in the array
bar = foo;
//This prints the first
//item in the array
cout << *bar;
//This prints the next
//item in the array
//Note that this is
//equivalent to foo[1]
cout << *(bar + 1);
```

When you use pointers to iterate through an array, each time you add a value to a pointer, you are actually adding the size of each array element to the pointer.

You can also make and initialize arrays of strings to use in your programs. In this case, don't give the size of the array when you create it. Use code such as this:

```
//Create a string array
String *aszFoo[] = {S"hello", S"goodbye"};
Console::WriteLine(S"The String array has {0} in it",
        aszFoo[1]);
```

If you want to create an array of strings in an unmanaged program, you need to do something slightly different. As you may recall, a string is an array of characters (or a `char *`). The following code creates and initializes an array of strings and then prints them:

```
//Create an array of three strings
//Assign initial values
char *aszFoo[3] = {"hello", "goodbye", "how are you"};
//Print the strings
cout << aszFoo[0] << aszFoo[1] << aszFoo[2] << endl;
```

A Dr. Lizardo Special: Multidimensional Arrays

(If you're not familiar with Dr. Lizardo, a character in the movie *The Adventures of Buckaroo Banzai,* your education is sadly lacking. This movie is a must-see for programmers. Dr. Lizardo travels to other dimensions and encounters all sorts of bizarre creatures named John.)

Anyway, to return to the main topic, the arrays discussed so far have been *single-dimensional* arrays. But *multidimensional* arrays also exist and are useful in many problem-solving situations. For example, suppose that you want to determine how many houses are in each grid of a city map. Because the map is two dimensional, a two-dimensional array is helpful in this situation, as shown in Figure 14-1.

Or, for another example, if you want to keep track of how many subatomic particles are in a particular area of space, you can break space into cubic regions and use a three-dimensional array. You can use multidimensional arrays also when physical space isn't involved. Matrices, which are often used for image processing, are two-dimensional arrays. Many data-processing problems can be broken into multidimensional arrays.

To define a multidimensional array, use as many [ ] as you have dimensions for the array. For example, the following code creates an array for a chessboard, which is eight squares high by eight squares wide:

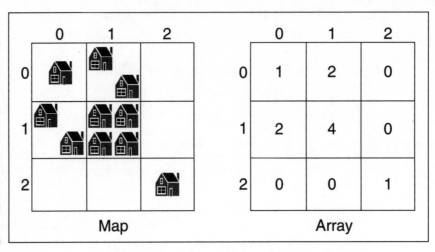

Figure 14-1:
Each grid in the 2-D city map corresponds to an element in the 2-D array used to store the number of houses.

```
int anChessBoard[8][8];
```

To access an item, you also supply as many [ ] as you have dimensions:

```
//Find the value at position 3, 4
anFull = anChessBoard[3][4];
```

The .NET ArrayList Class

Creating your own arrays is a ton of fun, and creating linked lists (as you do in Chapter 13) is even more fun, but sometimes it's okay to be boring. And if you're feeling boring and lazy, you might consider using some of the data structure classes that come with .NET. Actually, we suggest using them rather than rolling your own, uh, structures. That way, you can let Microsoft do all the hard work as well as find and correct the bugs. Meanwhile, you can sit back and make your own brand-new bugs.

One of the cool structures .NET provides is `ArrayList`. An `ArrayList` is like an array, in that you can ask for a specific item (such as item number 42), but it's also like a list in that it is open ended and you can just keep adding new items to the end. And, to make things even better, you can store any type of garbage-collected object you want in an `ArrayList`. The first item in could be a String, and the next item in could be a PointInfo.

Here's how you create an `ArrayList`:

```
ArrayList *poArray = new ArrayList();
```

These aren't your average everyday tips; they're multidimensional tips

The following is a list of tips to keep in mind when you use multidimensional arrays:

✔ **Specify the size of all dimensions when you create a multidimensional array.** (You can get away with specifying the size of only *n* - 1 dimensions for an *n*-dimensional array, but it's usually safer to specify the sizes of all dimensions.)

✔ **The computer doesn't care which dimension you use to represent a particular property.** For example, if you're using a two-dimensional array (with an X axis and a Y axis) to represent two-dimensional space, you can use the first index as x and the second as y, or vice versa. Just be consistent throughout your code.

✔ **The index for each dimension must be listed in its own separate set of square brackets.** That is, [1][7] is not the same as [1,7]. [1][7] accesses an element in a two-dimensional array. [1,7] is the same as [7].

✔ **The compiler doesn't check whether the index you give it is larger than the size of the array.** So, if you have an array with 20 elements and set the value of the 500th element, the compiler generates code that gleefully trashes memory. Make sure that your indices stay in the correct range.

✔ **The compiler also doesn't care if you treat a two-dimensional array as a one-dimensional array.** It just uses the indices to determine a pointer. You can use this fact to play some interesting tricks and to create faster code. You can use this fact also to confuse the heck out of yourself — that's why it's easier and better to continue using the dimensions you defined when you created the array.

And putting stuff in an `ArrayList` is just as easy:

```
//Add a string
poArray->Add(S"A string");
//Add a pointlist object
poArray->Add(poFirst);
```

If you want to get or set the item at a particular index, you can do this too:

```
Console::WriteLine(poArray->get_Item(0));
poArray->set_Item(0, S"Hello");
```

Make sure that you don't get or set an index beyond the end of the array.

You can even do really fancy stuff. For example, you can find which item in the array has a particular value:

```
Console::WriteLine(poArray->IndexOf(S"A string"));
```

Now, the only hard part about using an ArrayList (and a Stack, which you encounter shortly) is iterating through each of the items in it. Suppose an ArrayList has five items and you want to start at the beginning of the array and move through it. You could loop through using the get_Item method. Or, you can do something a bit more complex but that works equally well with all .NET structure classes, including the ultrafancy ones you won't read about in this book. The more complex thing is to create an enumerator, which is a high-fallutin' way of saying "a special thing that lets you go through every item in a structure in an orderly fashion."

Here's how you create an enumerator (is it just me, or do you want to say this really slowly too, imitating Steve Martin?):

```
IEnumerator *poEnumerator = poArray->GetEnumerator();
```

After you have the enumerator, you can use any of the methods from Table 14-1. For example, if you want to loop through and print all items in an ArrayList, you could use code such as this:

```
IEnumerator *poEnumerator = poArray->GetEnumerator();
while ( poEnumerator->MoveNext() )
Console::WriteLine( poEnumerator->Current );
```

This code first creates an enumerator, and then moves through it one element at a time until there are no more items. Note that you need to call MoveNext the very first time through.

Table 14-1		Stuff to Do with IEnumerator
Operator	*Usage*	*Meaning*
Current	poE->Current	Indicates the current item being looked at by the enumerator.
MoveNext	poE->MoveNext()	Advances the enumerator to the next item in the structure. Returns false when there are no more items.
Reset	poE->Reset()	Moves back to the first item in the structure.

Pop Pop, Fizz Fizz

Another cool data structure class that comes with .NET is Stack. Although it sounds like something you'd get at a pancake house, a Stack is a lot more like the way programmers dress. You wear a T-shirt. You spill some food on it, so you throw it on a pile on the floor. You throw some other shirt on top. Maybe you add another one that you actually washed, again by chucking it on the top. When it's time to get dressed, you pull off the T-shirt on the top of the pile and put it on. Maybe you grab the top pair of sweats from the sweatpants pile too.

The method is simple. The thing you grab first is the thing you most recently put on the Stack. Putting something on the Stack is called *pushing*. Taking something off the Stack is called *popping*. Like the ArrayList, you can put any garbage-collected item you want on the Stack.

To create a Stack, use code like this:

```
Stack *poStack = new Stack();
```

To push an item on the Stack, do this:

```
poStack->Push(S"A string");
```

And to remove an item from the Stack, do this:

```
poStack->Pop();
```

You can iterate through the items on the Stack just as you did those in the ArrayList, using code such as this:

```
poEnumerator = poStack->GetEnumerator();
while ( poEnumerator->MoveNext() )
Console::WriteLine( poEnumerator->Current );
```

Enum and Enummer

You've just found out how to use enumerators to walk through items in an ArrayList or a Stack. But you need to know about another enumerator term too: enumeration types. Enumeration types are useful when you have a set of options, but instead of giving them numeric constants, you want to use easy-to-read constants. For example, maybe you want to indicate that a T-shirt can be small, medium, or large. You could say 0 means small, 1 means medium, and 2 means large. Or you could create an enumeration type.

For example, instead of having this in your program:

```
const int smallShirt = 0;
const int mediumShirt = 1;
const int largeShirt = 2;
```

you could have this:

```
enum {smallShirt, mediumShirt, largeShirt};
```

Any of the words used in this enum (smallShirt, mediumShirt, and largeShirt) can be used throughout the program — they'll be treated just like constants.

Safety in enumbers

If you want to be safety conscious, you can also specify that the set of enums represents a specific type. This prevents you from accidentally using one enum constant (say, for song titles) where it isn't expected (say, in an enum for types of motor oil).

For example, you could specify that the various shirt sizes are of type ShirtSizes:

```
enum ShirtSizes {smallShirt, mediumShirt, largeShirt};
```

If you do this, the compiler makes sure that you use these names only with variables that are of type ShirtSizes. Here's a quick example:

```
enum Shapes
{
    Circle,
    Square
};

//Use the enum as a data type
Shapes oMyShape;

//Set the object to an enum value
//Note that oMyShape = Oval would cause a syntax error
oMyShape = Circle;
```

Whenever possible, assign a type for enumeration types. That way, if you try to use an enumerated constant with the wrong type of information, the compiler will generate a warning. The program will still work, but the warning message will help you track down what's going wrong.

A cin of omission

Before you add types to all your enums, however, note that cin knows how to read in information only for the predefined data types. If you try to use cin to prompt the user for an enumeration constant with a specified type, you get a compiler error.

For example, the following code results in a compiler error of no operator defined which takes a right-hand operand of type 'enum Songs' (and a few warnings as well):

```
//Create an enum list
enum Songs {LittleWing, LittleEarthquakes, LittleBrownJug };
//foo is of type Songs
Songs foo;
//Read in what foo the user wants
cin >> foo;
```

And a Sample

If you want to check out any of the techniques discussed in this chapter, look in the DataStructures directory on the accompanying CD. It has short examples of using arrays, enums, ArrayLists, and Stacks. You see ArrayList in use throughout many more sample programs in the book. In fact, in Chapter 17, you use an ArrayList to store information about lines to draw in an update to the drawing program.

Chapter 15

And You Thought Scope Was Just a Mouthwash

. . . .

In This Chapter

▶ Finding out about scope

▶ Examining global and local variables

▶ Discovering why you can have lots of variables with the same names in your program

. . . .

*Y*ou store data inside variables. Variables appear throughout programs. In this chapter, you find out about *scope,* which is the set of rules describing what parts of a program have access to a particular variable.

The Scoop on Scope

As programs get larger and larger, the number of functions and variables they contain increases. Many of these variables are used temporarily. For example, variables are frequently used only to help with loops in a small function or to temporarily hold what the user typed. Fortunately, you don't need to give such variables unique names every time you need them. Otherwise, you'd need to come up with thousands and thousands of unique variable names.

You can create several variables that have the same name. As long as the variables are created in different functions, they won't conflict. For example, you can define a variable named k in a function named foo. And you can define a variable named k in a function named baz. Although they have the same name, they're different variables — one is used only in foo, and the other is used only in baz.

The two variables are different because they have different scope. A variable's *scope* is the place in the program where a variable can be used. For example, the k that was defined in foo has scope foo. That means it can be used inside foo, but it is undefined outside of foo.

You can use two types of variables: global and local. *Global variables* are accessible from any function (including main) in an application. They're defined outside any function body. They're useful if you have some values that you want to be accessible no matter what routine you're in. No two global variables can have the same name.

Local variables are temporary variables used only within one particular function. A local variable is created when the function begins, is used throughout the function, and is destroyed when the function stops. This is known as *going out of scope* for that function and all its variables. You can have only one variable of that name inside that particular function, but you can use the same name inside a different function. (Changing one of these variables has no effect on the other variable.)

The rules are a little more complex than this. A variable is scoped within the { } where it is defined. So if you have a variable named nBob declared in a function named silent, and silent calls a function named righteous, nBob isn't available within righteous. (Unless you pass it in.) Likewise, if you declare a variable named fYou within an if block, such as in:

```
if (nBob > 10) {
  bool fYou = true;
}
```

fYou is available only within those braces.

This is good. Why? Well, suppose that you have a function called CountUp that prints the numbers from 1 to 10. You can use a loop to do this. This loop might use a variable named i for the loop counter. If you have another function called CountDown that prints the numbers from 10 to 1, you can also use a variable for the loop counter. Because they're local variables, you could name both loop counters i. This means you don't have to come up with a unique name each time you write a loop. If you had lots and lots of different functions in your program, some of which were written by other people, you wouldn't have to shout across the room, "Hey, did anyone use sdbsdbsdb-sdb3 for a loop-variable name yet?"

Anytime you define a variable within a function, the variable is *local* to that function. In other words, its scope is that function. You can use it in the function, and you can pass it to anything the function calls. But when the function is finished, the variable disappears. The names used for arguments in a function are also local to the function.

Why Bother Talking about This?

Scope may not sound like something worth worrying about. In a way, it isn't, because you rarely think about it when you program. But scope can be confusing to people new to programming. And when you understand the scoping rules, you can avoid some hard-to-find logic errors.

Consider the following small program:

```
int x;

void ZeroIt(int x)
{
    x = 0;
}

int main(void)
{
    x = 1;
    ZeroIt(x);
    Console::WriteLine(x);
}
```

What happens if you run this program? At first, the global variable x is set to 1. Then the ZeroIt function is called, which sets x to 0. When you get to Console::WriteLine, what will the value of x be? It will be 1.

Why is it 1? The variable x within ZeroIt is local to ZeroIt, so it's created when ZeroIt is called. It's assigned the value passed in, which in this case is 1. It's then given the value 0. Then the function is finished, so the variable x (which has a value of 0 and is local to ZeroIt) is destroyed. Kaput. Now you return to main and do the Console::WriteLine. That's a different x. That's the x with global scope. (After all, if you declare a variable outside any functions, the variable has global scope.)

Likewise, you get the same results with the following program. Again, changes to the variable x within ZeroIt don't affect the value of the global x used in main. That's because the variable x used within ZeroIt is defined inside ZeroIt, so it's local to ZeroIt. And therefore, that x goes away when ZeroIt finishes:

```
int x;

void ZeroIt()
{
    int x;
    x = 0;
}

int main(void)
{
```

```
    x = 1;
    ZeroIt();
    Console::WriteLine(x);
}
```

In contrast, consider this program:

```
int x;

void ZeroIt(int y)
{
    y = 7;
    x = 0;
}

int main(void)
{
    x = 1;
    ZeroIt(x);
    Console::WriteLine(x);
}
```

If you run this program, `Console::WriteLine` prints 0.

Why is it 0 now? Well, this time the argument to `ZeroIt` is called `y`. So when you pass in `x` to `ZeroIt`, the value of `x` (the global `x`, which happens to be the only `x` this time) is assigned to the variable `y`. `y` is given the value 7. Then `x` is given the value 0. Because you have no `x` local to `ZeroIt`, this is the global `x` that is given the value 0. When `ZeroIt` is finished, `y` disappears. Because `x` isn't local to `ZeroIt`, `x` isn't destroyed. And the global `x` is changed.

This example also illustrates a bad coding style. Because `ZeroIt` changes a value that wasn't passed into it, if you didn't read through the entire program, you might not expect `x` to change when `ZeroIt` is called. That means when you run the program, you probably won't get the results you think you will. In general, you shouldn't change variables that aren't passed in by reference or pointers. Change variables only if they're local to the function.

Coping with scoping

Here are some suggestions that will make your programs easier to read and keep scope from getting confusing:

✔ When you define a function, pass in any information that it needs to process as an argument.

✔ Avoid global variables. Use them only for constants.

✔ Don't change stuff out of your scope. If you change only local variables and reference arguments, things won't get too hairy.

Scoping Rules: When Is ARose Not ARose?

Fortunately, the C++ scoping rules are fairly straightforward:

- ✔ **Any variables defined in a function are local to that function.** If you define a variable in a function, that variable is created when the function is called, used throughout the function, and destroyed when the function is finished.

- ✔ **Any variables defined in a block are local to that block.** Variables defined in blocks — such as { } in an if statement — are local to that block.

- ✔ **Any arguments for a function are local to that function.** For example, if you indicate that a function takes a parameter named ARose, ARose is local to that function, just as if you had defined ARose within the function. The name of whatever you passed into the function doesn't matter. The name of the argument does.

- ✔ **When you're in a function, variables local to that function are used instead of global variables of the same name.** For example, suppose that you define an integer named ARose in a function named foo, but a global variable of type float is also named ARose. If you use the variable ARose within foo, you use the integer that's local to foo. You will not use (or be able to access without deviating slightly from your normal path by prepending the variable name with ::) the global variable named ARose that's a float. That is, the local ARose is not the same as the global ARose. They are two different variables that happen to have the same name and are used in different places in the program.

- ✔ **Changes made to a local variable don't affect variables of the same name that aren't local.** For example, if you have a local variable named ARose and set it to 0, that doesn't change a thing in a global variable that also happens to be named ARose.

- ✔ **If you use a variable inside a function that isn't local to the function, the compiler will try to find a global variable with the same name.** For example, suppose that you use a variable named ARose in a function named foo. But ARose isn't the name of one of the arguments passed to foo, and ARose isn't defined in foo. How does the compiler find a variable named ARose to use in foo? It looks for a global variable named ARose. If it can't find a global variable named ARose, it prints an error message.

- ✔ **If you want to access a global variable from a function that has a local variable with the same name as the global variable, precede the variable name with :: (the *scope resolution operator*).** For example, if you have a global variable named ARose and you're in a function that contains a local variable named ARose, ::ARose refers to the global variable, and ARose refers to the local variable.

Chapter 16

Lots of Bugs and Kisses

. . . .

. . . .

You're walking down a maze of twisty passages that are all alike. Your flashlight batteries are running low. And all you hear is "click, click, click." That's when you look down and see that you're knee deep in a nest of menacing, giant cockroaches. Aggghhh!

That may sound like Kafka meets Zork or Stephen King does virtual reality, but when you've been up all night programming, it's amazing how quickly your code can become filled with nasty bugs. And then when you try out your program the next morning, blam! Nothing works.

At this point, you have four choices:

▸ You can give up. (Wimp.)

▸ You can get a really slow computer in the hopes that you'll be able to see what's going wrong. (Bad idea.)

▸ You can fill your program with `print` statements so that something prints after every line that's executed, and you can figure out what's going on. (Works, but is a real pain.)

▸ You can use a debugger. (Works, and isn't as much of a pain.)

A *debugger* is a tool that lets you execute your program line by line. This makes it easier for you to look at the logic in a program and figure out how it operates, pinpoint what's going wrong, and then correct the mistakes.

In this chapter, you use the Visual C++ .NET debugger to find and correct problems in programs.

Syntax Errors versus Bugs

As we describe in Chapter 6, a syntax error occurs when you write something that the compiler doesn't understand. Usually, you've just spelled something wrong, left out a portion of a command, or incorrectly used a variable or a class. You can't run a program when it has syntax errors because the program can't be compiled.

A *bug*, on the other hand, is an error in logic. The program is written in perfect C++, but what it's doing, or what you want it to do, doesn't make sense. Or perhaps it just doesn't do what you wanted it to do.

Flamotherapy 101

If you're using commercial software and run across a bug, it's a good idea to report the problem to the vendor. That way, the vendor can try to correct the problem in the next version of the software.

To report the bug, you can call or e-mail the vendor, send a letter, or post a message on an NNTP newsgroup. Most vendors maintain Web sites, newsgroups, or message forums on the Internet so that you can send bug reports and — if you're lucky — get a work-around sent to you electronically.

Hidden behind the anonymity of an electronic account, bug reports occasionally become pretty nasty. Nasty e-mail pieces are known as flames. They're designed to get a lot of attention by resorting to hyperbole. For example, I've seen plenty of mail messages saying things such as, "Whatever marketing weasels designed this utter piece of garbage deserve to be strung up by their toenails."

In real life, the person who wrote this message is probably a nice person. The person may even be the grandmother who lives next door. But behind the disguise of an e-mail account, the person becomes a flamer.

When a lot of flamers get together and things get very toasty, it's called a flame fest. Some people practice flaming. These people become flame meisters. Watch out for them.

On the one hand, flames can reduce a programmer's stress. (This is called flamotherapy.) On the other hand, more and more people, many of whom don't appreciate flaming, are using message forums.

What's more, it's not exactly a good idea (or very nice) to insult a person who's trying to help you. The people who staff technical-support lines often endure lots of flaming and rude calls, and can become pretty battle hardened as a result. (They're said to have asbestos underwear.)

In general, when you post messages, avoid flames. Usually, a polite request gets you as much attention as a big flame — and you won't need asbestos underwear to avoid the heat of people flaming you back.

For example, consider the following instructions for baking a potato:

1. Take potato.
2. Wrap in aluminum foil.
3. Microwave for three hours.

This is a perfectly understandable set of instructions. There are no syntax errors. On the other hand, if you did what it said, you'd blow up your microwave (not to mention the potato). That wouldn't be the desired result.

To correct the problem, you need to analyze the various steps to see what doesn't make sense. That's what *debugging* is all about: Looking at a problematic piece of code line-by-line until you see what isn't working right.

When programs get large, removing all their bugs is hard. That's because some bugs occur only under strange circumstances. That's where users come in. If you have a lot of people using your program, they'll undoubtedly find bugs in it. And they'll undoubtedly let you know about them.

An Overview of the Debugging Process

The debugging process basically consists of figuring out where bugs occur. The goal is to isolate each problem to a particular area and then examine exactly how the program operates in that area. For example, if you know you have a bug in a particular routine, you can have the program stop whenever that routine starts. Then you can step through the routine one line at a time, so that you can see exactly what's happening. You may find out that something that you intended to happen just isn't happening correctly. You can then change the code, recompile, and try again.

You can use a number of tools in the debugger during this process:

- **Breakpoints:** Tell the debugger to stop when a particular line is reached. Use them when you want to run a program uninterrupted but still want to be able to stop whenever you reach a particular section that you need to examine in detail.

- **Step Into and Step Over:** Run a program one line at a time. Use these features to determine the results of every minute action that occurs, so that you can see exactly when something incorrect happens.

- **Watches:** Display the value of variables while the program is operating. You can use watches to get a live view of a variable as it changes. You can also watch expressions so that you can see how a particular expression changes when variables change.

What's Your Name? Who's Your Debugger? Does It Look Like Me?

Editor windows double as debugger windows. In other words, when you want to perform a debugging action such as setting a breakpoint or examining the value of a variable, you do so directly from an editor window.

The editor and debugger are tightly linked. This makes great sense. After all, when you debug a program, you need to examine the source code to see what's happening. Because Visual C++ combines the editor and debugger, you can use any editor features (such as scrolling, window splitting, and searching) to look through your program as you debug. Heck, you can even type corrections when you find the mistakes in your code.

Not all information shows up in the editor window itself. Many debugging activities cause debugger-specific windows to appear. For example, if you set a watch, the Watch window appears. (You do this a little bit later in this chapter.)

Stop, in the Name of Bugs

Use breakpoints when you want to stop at a particular line. For example, suppose that you have a routine that returns the factorial of a number. For some reason, though, it always returns 0. To figure out why this is happening, you can set a breakpoint at the beginning of the routine. Then, when you run the program, the program stops when the factorial routine is called, and you are placed inside the debugger. You can then use the power of the debugger to figure out what's going wrong. Toward the end of this chapter, you use the debugger to solve a problem like this.

Setting a breakpoint is easy. In the editor window, right-click where you want to set a breakpoint and choose Insert Breakpoint. A stop sign icon appears in the left margin of the line. Okay, it's actually a red circle, not a hexagon, but you get the general idea.

If you don't see a stop sign icon in the left margin when you set the breakpoint, you probably have the selection margin feature turned off. Choose Tools⇨Options to display the Options dialog box. Under the Text Editor/General category, choose General, and then choose Selection Margin. Click OK and you have your stop sign! Plus, you can just click in the selection margin to toggle a breakpoint on that line.

Clearing a breakpoint is just as easy. In the editor window, right-click the line that contains the breakpoint, and then choose Remove Breakpoint. The stop sign icon disappears.

Breakpoints are saved between development sessions. So, if you set a break-point but don't clear it, and then load the project later, the breakpoint is still set. This is great because if you're in the middle of debugging and decide to take a break and do something else — such as eat, sleep, or surf the Web — you don't have to reestablish all your breakpoints from scratch. On the other hand, if you forget that you have breakpoints in your code, you may get some surprises. (Your program will unexpectedly stop while you're running it.) If you're not sure whether you've left some breakpoints in your program, choose <u>D</u>ebug⇨<u>W</u>indows⇨<u>B</u>reakpoints. This displays a window that shows any active breakpoints.

Stepping into and over a Pile of Shaving Cream

After you've reached a breakpoint, you may want to examine how each line of code operates. You can do this by running the program one line at a time. This is called *stepping* through an application.

The two types of stepping are Step Into and Step Over. When functions are called while you're using Step Into, the debugger stops at the first line. When functions are called during Step Over, the functions are executed but the debugger doesn't stop inside them.

You use Step Into when you know something's broken but aren't sure if that something is in the routine you're debugging or one of the functions that's called by the function you're debugging. You use Step Over when you want to look at each line in a function as a single unit.

For example, suppose that you have this program:

```
foo = MySquareRoot(x);
foo = foo + 1;
```

If you know that MySquareRoot is correct, and you just aren't sure whether foo + 1 should be performed, you should use Step Over. Execute the first line — including any lines that are part of MySquareRoot — and then stop before getting to the foo = foo + 1 line.

If you suspect that MySquareRoot could be the source of your problems, you should use Step Into. That way, when you trace the first line, you stop at the first line inside MySquareRoot. You can then see all the different things that MySquareRoot does and, if you're lucky, find out what's going wrong.

When you step through a program, the line that's about to run has a yellow arrow in the left margin. If you set a breakpoint on that line, the yellow arrow appears on top of the breakpoint stop sign.

If you don't see a yellow arrow in the left margin when you step through a program, you probably have the selection margin feature turned off. Choose Tools➪Options to display the Options dialog box. Under the Text Editor/General category, choose General, and then choose Selection margin. Click OK, and the yellow arrow shows up.

To step over, press F10 or click the Step Over button, shown in Figure 16-1. To step into, press F11 or click the Step Into button.

Figure 16-1:
The Debug toolbar contains buttons for running your program.

Note that you don't need to set breakpoints to use Step Over and Step Into. If you want, you can step as the first action you make, instead of running a program. This action stops you on the very first line in the program.

Watching Out for Blunder One

When you're debugging, it's important to be able to see whether the result of a formula is correct, or what's stored in some variable, or the values in an array. Visual C++ provides several ways to check variable values and expressions:

The *Autos window* automatically appears when you start debugging a program (see Figure 16-2). It displays the names and values of variables used in the current statement and the preceding statement. You don't need to type the variable names; they appear automatically as you step through your code.

Figure 16-2:
The Autos
window
shows
values for
variables in
the current
and
preceding
statements.

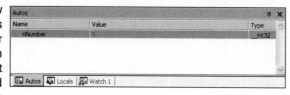

The *Locals window* also appears automatically when you're debugging (see Figure 16-3). Like the Autos window, it automatically displays variables and their values. The Locals window displays all local variables — variables that you define inside a function — for the function you're currently debugging.

Figure 16-3:
The Locals
window
shows
values for
all local
variables.

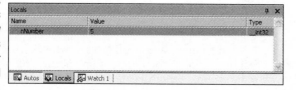

The Autos and Locals windows are convenient, but because they choose which variables to display, sometimes you don't have as much control as you'd like. Don't worry, Visual C++ has got you covered. The Watch windows let you pick the variables you want to watch. There are four Watch windows, numbered Watch1 to Watch4, in case you have *lots* of variables or expressions you want to watch.

To watch the value of an object using a Watch window, follow these steps:

1. **In a Watch window, click a blank line under the Name column.**

2. **Type the name of the object you want to watch.**

3. **Press Enter.**

Any time the object changes, the Watch window is updated. For example, Figure 16-4 illustrates the process of watching three integers. Whenever the value of nNumber, nResult, or i changes, the Watch window is updated.

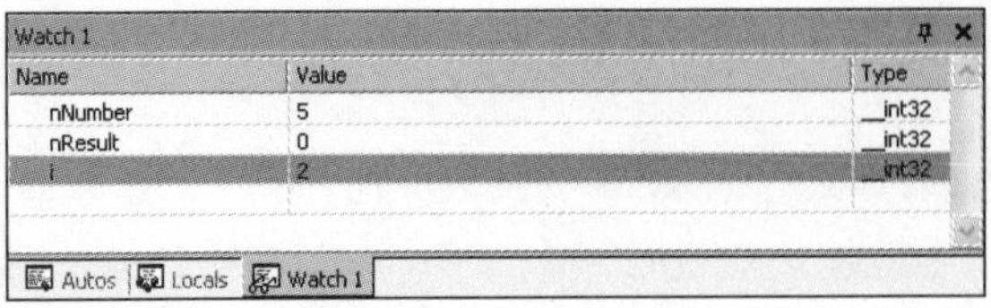

Figure 16-4:
Watches let
you see
variable
values as a
program
runs.

You gotta change your evil values, baby

If you want to, you can even change the value of a variable when you watch it. Just follow these steps:

1. **Select the variable whose value you want to change.**

2. **Select the variable's value.**

3. **Type the new value.**

4. **Press Enter.**

This is useful when you want to make a quick fix to see whether the rest of the program works when the value is correct. At some point, you need to go back to the program to determine why the value was wrong in the first place.

In a hurry? No problem!

Visual C++ also lets you look at variables and expressions without adding them to the Watch window, by using QuickWatch.

To watch the value of an object using QuickWatch, do the following in the editor window: Right-click the name of the object and choose QuickWatch. The QuickWatch dialog box appears, as shown in Figure 16-5. If you decide that you want to add the object you're QuickWatching to the Watch window, just click the Add Watch button.

In an even bigger hurry?

Watches and QuickWatches are convenient, but you have to click the mouse button — sometimes two or three times! Visual C++ has a neat feature called DataTips that lets you see the value of a variable without a single mouse click.

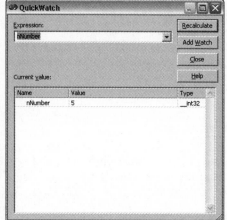

Figure 16-5:
You can see
the values
of variables
without
adding them
to the
Watch
window.

To watch the value of an object using DataTips, follow these steps:

1. **In the editor window, position the mouse cursor over the object whose value you want to see.**

2. **Wait half a second.**

   The DataTip appears. It's like a tooltip but it contains the value of the object, as shown in Figure 16-6.

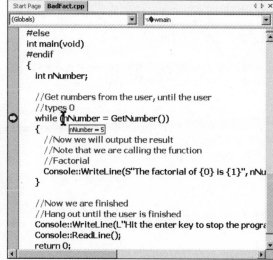

Figure 16-6:
DataTips
show the
values of
variables
without a
single click.

Wash That Bug Right Out of Your Life

Want to see how you can use debugging in real life? In this section, you walk through the various techniques you can use to examine a program, determine where the bugs are, and then correct them.

Begin the buguine

Begin by creating a new managed C++ application project and typing the following C++ code. This is a program for displaying the factorial of a number:

```
#include "stdafx.h"
#using <mscorlib.dll>
using namespace System;

//Computes and returns the factorial of a number
int Factorial(int nNumber)
{
    int nResult = nNumber;
    int i;    //Loop variable

    //Now loop through. Each time through the loop,
    //multiply the result by i.
    for (i = 0; i <= nNumber; i++)
    {
        nResult *= i;
    }

    //Now return the result
    return nResult;
}
//This routine prompts the user for a number
//It returns the value of the number
int GetNumber()
{
    int nNumber;

    Console::WriteLine(S"What is the number?");
    nNumber = Int32::Parse(Console::ReadLine());
    return nNumber;
}

// This is the entry point for this application
#ifdef _UNICODE
```

```
int wmain(void)
#else
int main(void)
#endif
{
    int nNumber;

    //Get numbers from the user, until the user
    //types 0
    while (nNumber = GetNumber())
    {
        //Now we will output the result
        //Note that we are calling the function
        //Factorial
        Console::WriteLine(S"The factorial of {0} is {1}",
            nNumber.ToString(),
            Factorial(nNumber).ToString());
    }

    //Now we are finished
    //Hang out until the user is finished
    Console::WriteLine(L"Press the Enter key to stop the
            program");
    Console::ReadLine();
    return 0;
}
```

If you need help creating a managed C++ project, check out Chapter 3.

This program is located in the BadFact directory on the CD accompanying this book. You can open it by loading the BadFact project.

Now run this program a few times:

1. **Click the Start button.**

   Or choose Debug⇔Start.

2. **Type a value, and then press Enter.**

3. **Examine the result.**

4. **Press any key to close the BadFact program.**

5. **To repeat the process, go back to Step 1.**

You find that no matter what value you type, the result is always 0. Hey, that doesn't seem right!

Stop, programmer, what's that sound? Everybody look, there's a bug around

You can figure out what's broken. Well, the input and output lines look pretty simple:

```
Console::WriteLine(S"What is the number?");
nNumber = Int32::Parse(Console::ReadLine());
return nNumber;
```

You probably don't need to step through these. Instead, concentrate on what happens in the `Factorial` function.

How do you know to concentrate there? Because it's the only function that does anything that might be considered difficult. In a more complex program, you would debug small pieces — functions or objects — one at a time. After you know how the small pieces work, you make sure that the code that puts them together works. That way, you're always debugging small, easy-to-understand parts. This is sometimes called *structured testing*.

You can begin by setting a breakpoint at the beginning of this function:

1. **Scroll in the editor window until you get to the beginning of the** `Factorial` **function.**

   The function is near the top.

2. **Right-click the int Factorial (int** `nNumber`) **line and choose Insert Breakpoint.**

   A breakpoint appears on the line, as shown in Figure 16-7.

Now run the program:

1. **Click the Start button.**

   The program runs and asks you for a number.

2. **Type a number.**

   At this point, the program calls the `Factorial` function. This causes your breakpoint to be reached and the debugger to appear. The line that's about to run is highlighted by a yellow arrow (see Figure 16-8).

Now you can step through the `Factorial` routine one line at a time so that you can see what's going wrong. Because you know that the result returned by the routine is bad, and you know that the result is stored in the variable called `nResult`, you need to see the value of `nResult`. Watching how the value of `nResult` changes as the program runs will, with any luck, help you zero in on what is causing the problem. You can use the Locals window or a DataTip to see the value. You can also use the Watch window, as follows:

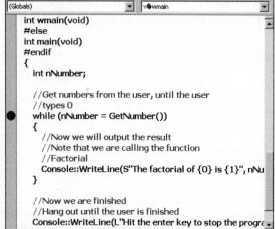

Figure 16-7:
A break-
point is
indicated by
a red circle
icon in the
editor
window.

```
int wmain(void)
#else
int main(void)
#endif
{
    int nNumber;

    //Get numbers from the user, until the user
    //types 0
    while (nNumber = GetNumber())
    {
        //Now we will output the result
        //Note that we are calling the function
        //Factorial
        Console::WriteLine(S"The factorial of {0} is {1}", nNu
    }

    //Now we are finished
    //Hang out until the user is finished
    Console::WriteLine(L"Hit the enter key to stop the progra
```

Figure 16-8:
When you
step through
a program,
the line that
is about to
execute
gets a
yellow
arrow.

```
    nNumber = Int32::Parse(Console::ReadLine());
    return nNumber;
}

// This is the entry point for this application
#ifdef _UNICODE
int wmain(void)
#else
int main(void)
#endif
{
    int nNumber;

    //Get numbers from the user, until the user
    //types 0
    while (nNumber = GetNumber())
    {
        //Now we will output the result
        //Note that we are calling the function
        //Factorial
        Console::WriteLine(S"The factorial of {0} is {1}", nNu
```

1. **In the Watch window, select an empty line in the Name column.**

2. **Type** nResult.

3. **Press Enter.**

You can also use QuickWatch:

1. **In the editor window, right-click the name nResult and choose QuickWatch.**

2. **Click Add Watch.**

   You end up with a screen that looks similar to the one in Figure 16-9.

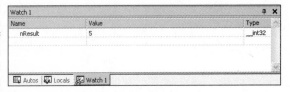

3. **Step through the program one line at a time by clicking the Step Over button several times.**

   The value of nResult is displayed in the Watch window and is updated any time it changes.

You quickly see that after you run the following line, nResult becomes 0, which is hardly what you expected:

```
nResult *= i;
```

Worse, as you continue to run the program, the value of nResult never changes from 0. How do you know that nResult became 0? Simple — the Watch window (or Locals window or QuickWatch or a DataTip) told you so. Your screen should look like the one shown in Figure 16-10.

Figure 16-10:
nResult is 0, which isn't the expected value.

Watch 1 ⊞ ✕
Name	Value	Type
nResult	0	__int32

Autos | Locals | Watch 1

Because nResult is being set to a bad value inside the for loop, you know that something is wrong inside the loop. So, it makes sense to look at the loop closely. Because the first (and only) line in the loop multiplies nResult by i, maybe something is wrong with i. If you look at the beginning of the for loop, you can see that i starts at 0 and goes to 1 less than n:

```
for (i = 0; i < nNumber; i++)
```

This means the first time through the loop, i is 0. So nResult *= i; sets nResult to 0 (because 0 times anything is always 0). No wonder there are problems!

Are we there yet?

The program has a bad for loop. You found the problem by stepping through the program a line at a time, examining the value of the nResult variable, and analyzing the code after you found that the value was set incorrectly. You figured out that instead of going from 0 to n, the loop should go from 1 to n.

Now change the code directly in the editor:

1. **Click the editor window.**

   This brings the window up front.

2. **Move the cursor to the following line:**
   ```
   for (i = 0; i <= nNumber; i++)
   ```

3. **Change the line so that it looks like this:**
   ```
   for (i = 1; i <= nNumber; i++)
   ```
   Now that you changed the line, you need to run the program again to make sure that your change corrected the problem.

4. **Choose Debug⇨Stop Debugging.**

   The program ends. (It was still in the middle of working because you set a breakpoint.)

5. **Click the Build button.**

   The program is compiled.

6. **Click the Start button.**

   The program runs again.

Note that instead of *stopping* the program as you did in Step 4, you can also just click the Build button. The debugger knows that the program has changed, so it asks whether you want to stop debugging. You do want to build so that your correction can take effect, so answer Yes. The debugger then terminates the program and rebuilds it. You can then click the Start button to run it again.

Now that your program is running again, step through it several times to see whether it's working correctly by entering a value of 5. The value of nResult is no longer 0 — so it looks like you've corrected the problem.

There are still bugs

But wait a minute. As you continue to step through the program, you see that something is still wrong. The nResult value is becoming enormous very quickly.

Again, things go badly the first time you run the loop. The first time you step through the loop in Factorial, nResult starts at 5. The next time through the loop, it changes to 10, and then to 20, and so on. By looking at the value of nResult in the Watch window, you can clearly see that you need to examine again how nResult is being set and changed.

Why does nResult start with the value 5? Once more, you need to think about how your program is supposed to work and compare that to what is actually happening. (That is, compare what you want the program to do with what you told it to do.) To compute a factorial, you want to start nResult with the value 1, and then multiply it by 2, and then multiply it by 3, and so on. Is that what happens in the program?

When you look over the code, you see that nResult is initially set to n:

```
//Initialize the result
int nResult = nNumber;
```

Why does this cause a problem? Well, look at what happens if you try to compute 5! (factorial). The program starts by setting nResult to 5. It then multiplies this by 2, and then by 3, and so on. So, you get 5×2×3×4×5 rather than 1×2×3×4×5. What you really want is for nResult to start with the value 1.

Once more, for the Gipper

To make nResult start with the value 1, make a simple correction to the program, as follows:

1. **Click the editor window.**

   This brings the window up front.

2. **Scroll until you find the following line:**
   ```
   int nResult = nNumber;
   ```

3. **Change it to this instead:**

```
int nResult = 1;
```

4. **Click the Build button.**

5. **Answer Yes to stop debugging.**

   The program is compiled.

6. **Click the Start button.**

   The program runs again.

Your debugging session has been quite valuable because now the correct result is returned. For example, if you type the number 6, the program runs correctly, as shown in Figure 16-11.

Figure 16-11:
The program is finally correct.

One breakpoint, one watch, and we're clear

Now you need to remove the breakpoint you set and the watch, if you set one. To remove the breakpoint. follow these steps:

1. **Choose Debug⇨Windows⇨Breakpoints.**

   A list of the breakpoints you set appears, as shown in Figure 16-12.

Figure 16-12:
These are the breakpoints in your application.

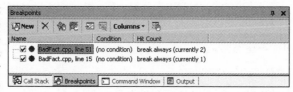

2. **Select the breakpoint you want to clear.**

3. **Click the Delete button.**

   Your breakpoint goes away. (When you want to delete all breakpoints, click Clear All Breakpoints instead.)

Getting rid of the watch is a bit harder because Visual C++ doesn't let you see the Watch window unless you're in the middle of debugging your program:

1. **Click the Step Into button or press the F11 key.**

   Your program starts and the debug windows — including the reluctant Watch window — appear.

2. **In the Watch window, right-click the watch you want to delete and choose Delete Watch.**

3. **Choose Debug➪Stop Debugging to end your program.**

Now when you run the program, it runs to completion without stopping at any breakpoints. (If you don't believe me, try it.)

As you can see, debugging a program isn't hard. But it does take some practice and experience to see why a program isn't working correctly. The more you program, the easier this process will be.

You can do many more things with the debugger. For example, you can view the values of CPU registers, look at the assembly code created by the compiler, and set conditional breakpoints. To find out more about the debugger, experiment with some of the features in the Debug menu or read the debugging sections of the online documentation.

Part III

And Now for Something Completely Object Oriented

In this part . . .

By now, you've discovered quite a bit about C++. But we've only scratched the surface of object-oriented programming (OOP). In Part III, you find out about encapsulating things from the real world into objects, inheriting functionality from other objects, and so on. OOP helps you create programs that are easier to write, understand, test, and expand.

If you skipped Part II, here's a quick review of programming fundamentals for you:

- ✔ Pizza is good — especially for breakfast.
- ✔ Sugar is good — especially for dinner.
- ✔ Coffee is good — especially with breakfast, lunch, dinner, and between-meal snacks.
- ✔ Science fiction is good.
- ✔ Loud music is good.
- ✔ Good music is loud.

Chapter 17

Through the Looking Class

*W*e have some good news and some not-so-good news. The good news is that the overall concepts presented in this chapter are easy: You'll be able to create classes in no time. The better news is that every time you've used a .NET function in a program, you've actually been using classes. So not only are the concepts simple, but you're used to them. The not-so-good news is that figuring out how to create well-designed classes can take a long time. That's why most people end up redesigning their first object-oriented programs several times.

Welcome to Classroom 101

Classes are the fundamental organizing unit of object-oriented programming (called *OOP* for short). A *class* is a structure that contains some data and some routines to process that data. When people talk about designing objects, they're talking about designing classes. Classes help you model the way real-life things behave. They make it easier for you to test complex programs. And they provide the backbone for inheritance, which helps you reuse code (and reusing code is very cool, as well as a great time-saver).

Because the data and the functions are in one spot in a class, figuring out how to use a particular object is easy — or at least easier than if you had to look in multiple places for data and functions. You don't have to worry about which library to use to move a picture on the screen or how to find an employee's home phone number. It's all contained in the object. In fact, the object should contain all the functions needed to interact with it.

For example, suppose that you have a `LineObject` class, and you want to set the coordinates for a line or draw the line. Both functions will be built into the class — you won't need to look at the internal structures of the `LineObject` class to figure out the data you need to look at and the algorithms you need to write.

Not only that, but the only way to change the behavior or data of a class is through the items in the class itself. This avoids confusing situations in which a global variable changes an entire program. You can always control the side effects of changing a value.

Finally, a well-designed class hides the complexity of underlying structures from the user. The user of the class doesn't need to know what types of data structures or algorithms make the class work. You just need some high-level calls that manipulate the object. For example, with the `LineObject` class, you might have a high-level function called `Initialize`. The user of the class calls this function instead of having to know that the coordinates for the line are stored in particular variables or are read using `Console` functions.

A Quick Kick in the Class

Surprise! If you've been reading the book in order, you've already created lots of classes. That's because creating a class is basically the same as creating a structure (and you did that a number of times already). In fact, the only difference between a class and a structure is that you add functions to classes.

In this section, you check out everything you need to know about putting together classes. You find out about class data members and member functions, how to declare a class, and how to restrict access to portions of a class by using the `private` keyword. You also discover how to define member functions.

Data members

Variables that are part of a class are officially called *data members.* (Visual C++ sometimes calls them *member variables,* which means the same thing.) When you analyze a real-world problem and come up with descriptions of an object, the descriptive items turn into data members.

For example, color, size, cost, shape, weight, name, artist, and playing time are all things that could describe an object. They're all things that you might save in variables and use for data members in a class.

Member functions

Member functions are stored in and used for manipulating a class. When you analyze a real-world problem and come up with actions to manipulate an object, those actions turn into member functions.

For example, actions that act on or control an object include setting a color, computing a size, adding parts to find the total cost, or printing a song name and artist. These are the kinds of activities for which you would write member functions.

Declaring a class

You use the class keyword to declare a class, as shown here:

```
class ClassName
{
public:
  public data members and member functions listed here
};
```

Suppose that you want to make a LineObject class. You could start with a structure similar to the PointList structure (used in other chapters) and add functions and some more variables:

```
//Stores line information
__gc class LineObject
{
public:
    void Initialize();
    void Draw(Graphics *poG);
private:
    int m_nXFrom;
    int m_nYFrom;
    int m_nXTo;
    int m_nYTo;
};
```

You would then define what the member functions Initialize and Draw do.

Note that we have made this `LineObject` class garbage collected. That carries with it the advantages discussed in Chapter 16 and is also required by Visual C++ .NET (as you can tell by an error message the compiler gives you if you don't make it garbage collected).

Restricting access

You can prevent inadvertent access to data members by making them private. Private data members are accessible only from member functions that are part of the class.

With the `LineObject` class, only the member functions (in this case `Initialize` and Draw) know about m_nXFrom, m_nYFrom, m_nXTo, and m_nYTo. Users of the `LineObject` class can't alter them. Only member functions of `LineObject` have that right.

As you can see in the `LineObject` declaration, making a data member private is easy. After you've listed the public data members and member functions (which are marked by the `public` keyword), type the `private` keyword followed by a colon. Then list the private data members. (You can have private member functions, too. Private member functions are callable only by member functions in the class. They're helper functions that are useful for making public member functions work, but they aren't so important that they need to be exposed to the outside world through the public interface.)

If you follow the naming convention used in this book, you'll name private and protected data members by starting them with m_, which stands for member. (You might think it's a reference to a Peter Lorre film, but it isn't.)

Protected access

So far, you've found out about two keywords for controlling access rights: `public` and `private`. Public data members and member functions are accessible from outside the class. They provide the public interface to the class. The public interfaces are the ones you call when you use a class.

Private data members and member functions are for internal use by the class; only member functions of the class can use them. Private member functions can't be called from outside the class. Private data members can't be read or changed from outside the class.

By creating private data members and member functions, you can have a complex class with a simple public interface — all the internal complexities are shielded from the user of the class because the internal items are private.

One more access keyword is called `protected`. Protected items in a class can be used only by member functions in that class (just like private items) or by member functions of classes *derived* from that class (like public items but unlike private items).

Defining member functions

After you declare what goes in a class, you define what the member functions do. Defining member functions is almost the same as defining functions (discussed in Chapter 12). But because member functions are part of a particular class, you need to specify the name of the class as well as the name of the function. (After all, several different classes could have, for example, an `Initialize` function.)

To define a member function, list the class name, followed by `::` (two colons), followed by the member function name. The official name for the two colons is the scope resolution operator. (Try saying that quickly 100 times.) The *scope resolution operator* indicates that a particular member function (or data member) is part of a particular class. For example, `LineObject::Draw` refers to the `Draw` member function of the `LineObject` class, and `LineObject::m_nXFrom` means the `m_nXFrom` data member of the `LineObject` class.

The following example defines the `Draw` member function for the `LineObject` class. This function draws a line on the screen:

```
void LineObject::Draw(Graphics *poG)
{
    //Create a pen with which to draw
    Pen *poPen = new Pen(Color::Red);
    //Draw the line
    poG->DrawLine(poPen, m_nXFrom, m_nYFrom, m_nXTo, m_nYTo);
}
```

Note that you don't need to say `LineObject::m_nXFrom` in the `DrawLine` call. That's because within a member function, you don't need to put `::` before the data member names. The items in class scope are automatically used. So when you use the `m_nXFrom` value within `LineObject::Draw`, you automatically are using the value of `SongList::m_nXFrom`. Also note that because `Draw` is a member function of the `LineObject` class, it can access the private data members. (But a routine inside another class, such as `TriangleMan::Draw`, wouldn't be able to directly access the private data members of `LineObject`.)

How Do I Put These Classes to Use?

After you've declared a class and defined its functions, you can use the class in your program. Just as with structures, classes can be created statically or dynamically:

```
//Create a class statically
LineObject oFoo;
//Create a class dynamically
LineObject *poBar = new SongList;
```

Typically, however, you create classes dynamically. You always create .NET CLR classes dynamically.

The same rules and concepts that apply to static and dynamic variables apply to static and dynamic classes. Creating a class is called *creating an instance* or *instantiating a class.*

Accessing class members

Classes are just like any other data structure. If you want to refer to a data member, just use . (period). Note that you can do the same thing to refer to a member function of a class:

```
//Call the Draw method on a LineObject
LineObject oFirst;
oFirst.Draw();
```

If you have a pointer to a class, use pointer notation instead:

```
LineObject *poFirst = new LineObject();
poFirst->Draw();
```

Just like variables, classes have names (when they are instantiated) and types.

At first, beginning programmers often confuse variable names and class names. If you want to access the Draw member function of object oFirst, which is a LineObject class, do this:

```
oFirst.Draw()
```

Don't do this:

```
LineObject.Draw()
```

In other words, remember to use the variable name, not the class name.

Static casts

As discussed in Chapter 14, you can use the .NET `ArrayList` and `Stack` classes to store any garbage-collected object. So if you create a class and indicate that it is garbage collected, you can use `ArrayList` and `Stack` to store it. This is quite useful if you need to keep track of lists of items, such as a list of lines to draw. (Gee, where did that idea come from?)

For example, you could add a `LineObject` to an `ArrayList` with code such as this:

```
LineObject *poLine = new
    LineObject();
ArrayList *paLines = new
    ArrayList();
//Store the LineObject in the
    structure
paLines->Add(poLine);
```

Things become trickier when you retrieve an object from an `ArrayList`. As far as the `ArrayList` is concerned, everything in it is just a generic object. It doesn't know any of the particulars of the object's capabilities. (You can find out more about this in Chapter 19. Here you're getting a sneak preview of what the big word *polymorphism* means.) If you then want to use the object, you need to tell Visual C++ .NET what the object is.

For example, suppose that you want to call the `Draw` member function on a `LineObject` object that you have stored in an `ArrayList`. If you just get the object and try to call `Draw` with the following code, you'll get an error:

```
(poEnumerator->Current)-
    >Draw(poG);
```

That's because there's no `Draw` member function on a plain-Jane generic object. Instead, you need to indicate what the object is using `static_cast`. `static_cast` has a funky syntax. You use the `static_cast` keyword, followed by the type of object you have in angle brackets. For example, to use the `LineObject` you shoved into the `ArrayList`, you'd use code such as this:

```
static_cast<LineObject*>(poEnum
    erator->Current)-
    >Draw(poG);
```

This code says, "Grab the current object out of the ArrayList, and I'm telling you, the durn thing is a pointer to a LineObject, so let me treat it as such by calling the LineObject member function Draw."

Accessing members from member functions

When you're in a member function, you don't need to use . or -> to access other class member functions or data members. You're in class scope, so it's assumed that if you use the name x and x is a member of the class, that's the x you want to use.

Programming a Line Drive

Now that you know the fundamentals about classes, you can take the line drawing program and make it object oriented. You'll define two classes. The first, LineObject, stores basic information about a line:

```
__gc class LineObject
{
public:
    void Initialize();
    void Draw(Graphics *poG);
private:
    int m_nXFrom;
    int m_nYFrom;
    int m_nXTo;
    int m_nYTo;
};
```

If you've read the book in order, you've already delved into this class a bit already. The second class, DisplayObject, stores information about all the objects to show. In particular, it contains an ArrayList of LineObjects. It also contains member functions for adding new LineObjects and for drawing the set of lines:

```
__gc class DisplayObject
{
public:
    void Add();
    void Draw(Graphics *poG);
    void Initialize();
private:
    ArrayList *m_paLines;
};
```

The most interesting member function of DisplayObject is Draw. Draw enumerates all LineObjects in the DisplayObject list and calls the Draw function on each of these objects. So it uses the LineObject class to do all the hard work:

```
//Draw all the lines
void DisplayObject::Draw(Graphics *poG)
{
    //Go through each line object
    IEnumerator *poEnumerator = m_paLines->GetEnumerator();
    while (poEnumerator->MoveNext())
        {
        //Call the draw method for the object
        static_cast<LineObject*>(poEnumerator->Current)-
            >Draw(poG);
        }
}
```

The main function is simple. It creates a new `DisplayObject` class, initializes it, and calls the `Draw` method. Here's the complete listing:

```
// Draw4
// Introduces class structures


#include "stdafx.h"

#using <mscorlib.dll>
#using <System.dll>
#using <System.Windows.Forms.dll>
#using <System.Drawing.dll>

using namespace System;
using namespace System::Drawing;
using namespace System::Windows::Forms;
using namespace System::Collections;

//Stores line information
__gc class LineObject
{
public:
    void Initialize();
    void Draw(Graphics *poG);
private:
    int m_nXFrom;
    int m_nYFrom;
    int m_nXTo;
    int m_nYTo;
};

//Initialize values for this line object
void LineObject::Initialize()
{
    //Read the x and y positions and store them in the
            structure
    Console::WriteLine(S"What is the starting x position?");
    m_nXFrom = Int32::Parse(Console::ReadLine());
    Console::WriteLine(S"What is the starting y position?");
    m_nYFrom = Int32::Parse(Console::ReadLine());
    Console::WriteLine(S"What is the ending x position?");
    m_nXTo = Int32::Parse(Console::ReadLine());
    Console::WriteLine(S"What is the ending y position?");
    m_nYTo = Int32::Parse(Console::ReadLine());
}

//Draw the line
void LineObject::Draw(Graphics *poG)
{
    //Create a pen with which to draw
    Pen *poPen = new Pen(Color::Red);
    //Draw the line
```

```
      poG->DrawLine(poPen, m_nXFrom, m_nYFrom, m_nXTo, m_nYTo);
}


//Store all the lines to draw
__gc class DisplayObject
{
public:
   void Add();
   void Draw(Graphics *poG);
   void Initialize();
private:
   ArrayList *m_paLines;
};

//Initialize the DisplayObject structures
void DisplayObject::Initialize()
{
   m_paLines = new ArrayList();
}

//Add a new object
void DisplayObject::Add()
{
   bool fFinished = false;
   String *pszMore;

   while (!fFinished)
   {
      //Create a new line object
      LineObject *poLine = new LineObject();
      //Initialize it
      poLine->Initialize();
      //Store it in the structure
      m_paLines->Add(poLine);

      //Should we add another one?
      Console::WriteLine("Press y to enter a new line");
      pszMore = Console::ReadLine();
      if (!pszMore->Equals(S"y"))
      {
         fFinished = true;
      }
   }
}

//Draw all the lines
void DisplayObject::Draw(Graphics *poG)
{
   //Go through each line object
   IEnumerator *poEnumerator = m_paLines->GetEnumerator();
   while (poEnumerator->MoveNext())
   {
```

```
        //Call the draw method for the object
        static_cast<LineObject*>(poEnumerator->Current)-
            >Draw(poG);
    }
}

// This is the entry point for this application
#ifdef _UNICODE
int wmain(void)
#else
int main(void)
#endif
{
    //Structures for drawing graphics
    Form *poForm = new Form();
    Graphics *poGraphics = poForm->CreateGraphics();
    DisplayObject *poDisplay = new DisplayObject();

    //Initialize the display object
    poDisplay->Initialize();

    //Add the lines
    poDisplay->Add();

    //Show the display surface
    poForm->Show();

    //Draw the lines
    poDisplay->Draw(poGraphics);

    //Free up the graphics surface
    poGraphics->Dispose();

    //Hang out until the user closes the form
    Application::Run(poForm);

}
```

You can find this program in the Draw4 directory on the accompanying CD.

Clean Up. Clean Up. Everybody Do Your Share

When you created Draw4, you didn't need to worry about cleaning up the memory used by any of the objects. .NET took care of that for you automatically. If you create a similar program using unmanaged C++, you'll need to take care of cleaning up the memory that you use. One way to do so is to create a `Delete` member function on each class. (You find out about another approach in Chapter 18.)

Also, you'll need to create your own linked-list class for storing objects because you can't use the .NET ArrayList class. Draw5 is an unmanaged version of Draw4. It contains a class called LineObjectContainer that is used for creating a linked list of LineObjects:

```
//Class for constructing a linked list
class LineObjectContainer
{
public:
    LineObject *poLine;
    LineObjectContainer *poNext;
    void Delete();
};
```

Note that this class has a Delete member function on it to clean up memory. The Delete member function must be called after the LineObject list is no longer needed.

Because the LineObjectContainer class is used for storing a linked list, the Delete function goes through and frees the memory associated with each item in the list, as you can see in the following code:

```
//Clean up the list
void LineObjectContainer::Delete()
{
    LineObjectContainer *poCur, *poTemp;

    poCur = this;
    while (poCur)
    {
        poTemp = poCur;
        //Clear out the line object
        delete poCur->poLine;
        poCur = poCur->poNext;
        //Delete the container object
        delete poTemp;
    }
}
```

The one tricky part is that you need to delete both the stored LineObject and LineObjectContainer.

Here's an unmanaged version of the object-oriented drawing program. Because of the memory management and list management, it's a bit more complex than the managed version:

```
// Draw5
// Introduces class structures
// Unmanaged

#include "stdafx.h"
```

```cpp
#include <iostream.h>

//Store line information
class LineObject
{
public:
   void Initialize();
   void Draw();
private:
   int m_nXFrom;
   int m_nYFrom;
   int m_nXTo;
   int m_nYTo;
};

//Initialize values for this line object
void LineObject::Initialize()
{
     //Read the x and y positions and store them in the
          structure
     cout << "What is the starting x position?";
     cin >> m_nXFrom;
     cout << "What is the starting y position?";
     cin >> m_nYFrom;
     cout << "What is the ending x position?";
     cin >> m_nXTo;
     cout << "What is the ending y position?";
     cin >> m_nYTo;
}

//Draw the line. We'll write the contents
void LineObject::Draw()
{
   cout << "From " << m_nXFrom << "," << m_nYFrom << " to "
        << m_nXTo << "," << m_nYTo << endl;
}

//Class for constructing a linked list
class LineObjectContainer
{
public:
   LineObject *poLine;
   LineObjectContainer *poNext;
   void Delete();
};

//Clean up the list
void LineObjectContainer::Delete()
{
```

```
        LineObjectContainer *poCur, *poTemp;

    poCur = this;
    while (poCur)
        {
        poTemp = poCur;
        //Clear out the line object
        delete poCur->poLine;
        poCur = poCur->poNext;
        //Delete the container object
        delete poTemp;
        }
    }

//Store a linked list of objects
class ArrayList
{
public:
        void Add(LineObject *poLine);
    LineObject *MoveNext();
    void Delete();
    void Initialize();
private:
    LineObjectContainer *m_poFirst;
    LineObjectContainer *m_poCur;
    LineObjectContainer *m_poLast;
};


//Initialize the structures
void ArrayList::Initialize()
{
    m_poFirst = 0;
    m_poCur = 0;
    m_poLast = 0;
}

//Add a new object to the list
void ArrayList::Add(LineObject *poLine)
{
    //Create a new container
    LineObjectContainer *poLOC = new LineObjectContainer();
    //Set its value
    poLOC->poLine = poLine;
    poLOC->poNext = 0;

    //Tie it in
    if (!m_poFirst)
    {
        m_poFirst = poLOC;
        m_poCur = m_poFirst;
    }
```

```
      else
         m_poLast->poNext = poLOC;
      //Advance the end pointer
      m_poLast = poLOC;
}

//Return the next LineObject item
LineObject *ArrayList::MoveNext()
{
   LineObject *poNext;

   //If there are no items, just return null
   if (!m_poCur)
      return 0;

   //Find the next line object
   poNext = m_poCur->poLine;
   //Advance the pointer
   m_poCur = m_poCur->poNext;
   return poNext;
}

//Clean up memory
void ArrayList::Delete()
{
   //Delete the list of line objects
   m_poFirst->Delete();
}

//Store all the lines to draw
class DisplayObject
{
public:
   void Add();
   void Draw();
   void Initialize();
   void Delete();
private:
   ArrayList *m_paLines;
};

//Initialize the DisplayObject structures
void DisplayObject::Initialize()
{
   m_paLines = new ArrayList();
   m_paLines->Initialize();
}

//Clean it up
void DisplayObject::Delete()
{
   m_paLines->Delete();
}
```

```cpp
//Add a new object
void DisplayObject::Add()
{
    bool fFinished = false;
    char cMore;

    while (!fFinished)
    {
        //Create a new line object
        LineObject *poLine = new LineObject();
        //Initialize it
        poLine->Initialize();
        //Store it in the structure
        m_paLines->Add(poLine);

        //Should we add another one?
        cout << "Press y to enter a new line" << endl;
        cin >> cMore;
        if (cMore != 'y')
        {
            fFinished = true;
        }
    }
}

//Draw all the lines
void DisplayObject::Draw()
{
    LineObject *poLine;

    //Go through each line object
     while (poLine = m_paLines->MoveNext())
    {
        //Call the draw method for the object
        poLine->Draw();
    }
}


int _tmain(int argc, _TCHAR* argv[])
{
    //Structure for the display
    DisplayObject *poDisplay = new DisplayObject();

    //Initialize the display object
    poDisplay->Initialize();

    //Add the lines
    poDisplay->Add();

    //Draw the lines
```

```
poDisplay->Draw();

//Clean up
poDisplay->Delete();
delete poDisplay;

return 0;
}
```

You can find this program in the Draw5 directory on the accompanying CD.

Be Wise, Accessorize

You've already seen how useful it can be to keep data members private and use special functions to access and change the values of data members. Visual C++ .NET takes this one step further by allowing you to create accessor functions as properties automatically. (An accessor function is a function whose purpose in life is to set and get the value of a particular data member.) Here's how:

```
__property int get_X();
__property void set_X(int i);
```

This says there's a property called X. When you want to get the value of X, you can call the get_X() function or use code such as this:

```
n = foo.X;
```

When you want to set the value of X, you can call set_X or use code such as this:

```
foo.X = n;
```

If you provide only a get, the property is read-only.

Note that to make the properties work, you still need to implement the get and set functions. And to do this, you will likely use some private variables, as you can see in the following code.

You can find this program in the Accessors directory on the accompanying CD.

```
// Accessors
// Provides private access functions

#include "stdafx.h"
```

```
#using <mscorlib.dll>

using namespace System;

//This class uses properties for accessors
__gc class PointObject
{
public:
   __property int get_X();
   __property void set_X(int i);
   __property int get_Y();
   __property void set_Y(int i);
private:
   int m_nX;
   int m_nY;
};

//Here we implement what will occur when a programmer
           references
//the X and Y properties of the object. Note how we use
           private
//members for storing the real values
int PointObject::get_X()
{
   return m_nX;
}

int PointObject::get_Y()
{
   return m_nY;
}

void PointObject::set_X(int i)
{
   m_nX = i;
}

void PointObject::set_Y(int i)
{
   m_nY = i;
}


//Hang out until the user is finished
void HangOut()
{
   Console::WriteLine(L"Press the Enter key to stop the
           program");
```

```
        Console::ReadLine();
}
// This is the entry point for this application
#ifdef _UNICODE
int wmain(void)
#else
int main(void)
#endif
{
    PointObject *poPoint = new PointObject();
    //Set the x and y values
    poPoint->X = 3;
    poPoint->Y = 2;

    //Now spit them back
    Console::WriteLine(S"The point is {0}, {1}", poPoint-
            >X.ToString(), poPoint->Y.ToString());

    HangOut();
    return 0;
}
```

When writing unmanaged code, you can get an effect similar to that of properties by making the data member private and creating a public function to
get and set that private data member. You won't be able to use the property
notation you use in .NET. Instead, you call the get and set member functions
explicitly.

You can also make a variable read-only by only providing a get function.

Here is similar accessor code, but this one is unmanaged:

```
// Accessors2
// Provides private access functions
// Unmanaged

#include "stdafx.h"
#include <iostream.h>

//This class uses properties for accessors
class PointObject
{
public:
    int get_X();
    void set_X(int i);
    int get_Y();
    void set_Y(int i);
```

```
private:
    int m_nX;
    int m_nY;
};

//Here we implement what will occur when a programmer
            references
//the X and Y properties of the object. Note how we use
            private
//members for storing the real values
int PointObject::get_X()
{
    return m_nX;
}

int PointObject::get_Y()
{
    return m_nY;
}

void PointObject::set_X(int i)
{
    m_nX = i;
}

void PointObject::set_Y(int i)
{
    m_nY = i;
}


int _tmain(int argc, _TCHAR* argv[])
{
    PointObject *poPoint = new PointObject();
    //Set the x and y values
    poPoint->set_X(3);
    poPoint->set_Y(2);

    //Now spit them back
    cout << "The point is " << poPoint->get_X() << "," <<
            poPoint->get_Y() << endl;

    return 0;
}
```

You can find this program in the Accessors2 directory on the accompanying CD.

Heading off troubles by using header files

If you have a program that spans more than one source file, you should put class declarations in header files. When you need to use a particular class in a source file, use the #include directive to include the header file that declares the class.

If you add data members or member functions to a class or remove them from a class, make sure that you remember to update the header file. If you forget, you get a message such as 'foo' : is not a member of 'baz'. This translates to, "Hey, you forgot to update the header file to put the foo member function in class baz." Or, "Hey, you typed some parameters incorrectly, so what you listed in the class definition isn't what you used when you implemented the thing."

Go to the Head of the Class

When you create an object-oriented program, you need to think about what's going on in the program. Strive to create objects that model what's being manipulated. (For example, if your object-oriented program handles music for a jukebox, you may want to create an object that represents a jukebox and an object that represents the list of songs in the jukebox.)

Follow these steps to design a class:

1. **Analyze your problem.**

2. **Look at the data you're manipulating.**

   What is the data? How are you manipulating it?

3. **Group data and functions together to define elemental objects.**

4. **Hide the way things work.**

   Provide high-level functions for manipulating the object, so the user doesn't need to know, for example, that names are stored in arrays or that songs are kept in a linked list. Keep the details and helper functions as private data members and member functions.

Here are some things to consider when you start designing classes:

- ✔ **Look at how other people have designed classes.** Examine lots of sample programs.
- ✔ **Start small.**

✔ **Think about how you can reuse your class in other parts of your program and in future programs.** Sometimes, the fewer items in a class, the more reusable it will be. You may want to look at the least common denominator of characteristics to use for a base class. Remember that, with inheritance, you can build significantly upon an existing framework.

✔ **Check whether some items in your application act as stand-alone entities.** In other words, if you weren't using OOP, do certain pieces of data have a lot of routines for processing them? This might be a good place to try to create a class. Suppose that you have a structure for containing information about an employee, and you have various routines that compute the employee's weekly paycheck, update the employee's available vacation time, and so forth. You might combine these into an employee class.

✔ **After you create an object, all routines for manipulating that object should be member functions.** Everything in the object should be self-contained. The object should know everything it needs to know about itself.

✔ **If your object uses a global variable and you keep a pointer to the global variable inside the object, the object will be more self-contained.**

✔ **If your program has certain fundamental things that are repeated over and over with only slightly different variations, make a generic class that represents this.**

✔ **Decide whether users need to understand the internal structure of an object to use it.** The object is better designed if users don't need to know anything about the internals. For example, suppose that you keep an array of playing times inside a `choice` object. The user should be able to find the playing time for a particular choice without having to know that there's an internal playing time array. A member function should take the choice and return the playing time. This practice makes the interface much easier for others to master.

✔ **Remember that it's okay to be confused at first.**

✔ **Don't be afraid to scrap everything and start fresh; everyone does.** It's all just part of the learning process.

Chapter 18

Under Construction

C onstructors and destructors are special functions that help with class initialization and termination. In this chapter, you add them to your programming repertoire.

The Joys of Prepping and Cleaning

It's fun to have people over for dinner, but preparing for it and cleaning up afterward (especially the cleaning up afterward part) can be a real drag. Programming is much the same way: It's lots of fun to design great programs, but the related preparation and cleanup work can seem rather ho-hum in comparison.

But don't let yourself get fooled — preparation and cleanup are important programming tasks. For example, if you forget to initialize a variable (which is a type of preparation task), you may discover that your screen always turns blue or that your program crashes because a pointer is bad. Similarly, if you forget to free memory you used, you may discover that your program gets slower and slower as it runs, until finally it won't run at all.

Fortunately (you knew this had to get better, right?), C++ has two built-in features — constructors and destructors — that help you remember to initialize variables and clean up what you've created. *Constructors* are routines that are called automatically when you create an object (instantiate a class). You can put initialization routines inside constructors to guarantee that things are properly set up when you want to start using an object. You can even have multiple constructors, so that you can initialize objects in different ways.

When you're finished with an object — that is, when the function that created it finishes or when you use `delete` — a function called the *destructor* is called automatically. If you need cleanup code above and beyond what .NET automatically provides, that's where you put it.

To avoid hordes of annoying problems from cropping up in your programs, use constructors and destructors. You'll be glad you did.

A Constructor a Day Keeps the Disk Doctor Away

Constructors are functions that are called every time an object is created. If any data members in the object need initializing when the object is created, put that code inside the constructor.

You should avoid doing complex stuff or stuff that is likely to fail within a constructor. As a general guideline, constructors should be short, sweet, and to the point.

Constructors have the same name as the class name. So, the constructor for `DisplayObject` is named `DisplayObject::DisplayObject`. The constructor for `Bam` is `Bam::Bam`.

Constructors can never return values.

To create a constructor, first declare it within the class. For example, this code declares a constructor for `DisplayObject`:

```
__gc class DisplayObject
{
public:
    void Add();
    void Draw(Graphics *poG);
    DisplayObject();
private:
    ArrayList *m_paLines;
};
```

Next, you need to put in the code for the constructor you declared. The Draw4 `DisplayObject` class had an explicit `Initialize` member function that set up the `ArrayList`. You can perform the same code in the `DisplayObject` constructor:

```
DisplayObject::DisplayObject()
{
    m_paLines = new ArrayList();
}
```

Whenever you create a `DisplayObject` class, the constructor is called automatically. You no longer need to specify explicit initialization functions and hope that everyone remembers to call them. It's a simple thing, but it sure saves a lot of headaches.

To check out constructors in action, take a look at Draw6 on the accompanying CD. It works the same way Draw4 does, but uses a constructor rather than an initialization method for DisplayObject.

You need to add the constructor to the list of member functions in the class definition. Constructors can be `public`, `private`, or `protected`.

Multiply your fun with multiple constructors

Sometimes you might want more control over how an object is created. For example, you might want to be able to pass in an initial shape to a `DisplayObject`, or you might want to create a `DisplayObject` with a limit on the number of shapes it will allow. You can do this by using *multiple constructors*. One constructor takes no parameters and creates a normal `DisplayObject`. Another constructor takes parameters that are then used to initialize or alter the class.

You can have as many constructors as you want. Each different constructor, though, needs a different set of parameters. That is, one constructor can take one integer, another can take two integers, a third can take one `double`, and so on. The computerese way of saying this is that each constructor needs a unique *call signature*.

You can pass in parameters when you create the object. The appropriate constructor is called with the parameters. For example, if you pass in two integers when you create the object, the constructor that takes two integers is called. If you pass in a `double` when you create the object, the constructor that takes a `double` is called. If the compiler can't find a match for the parameters passed in, the compiler generates a syntax error telling you that you messed up.

Using a class with multiple constructors is simple. In fact, you've used such classes over and over in your code. Anytime you used new and passed-in parameters, you were calling a parameterized constructor. For example, here's some code from Draw4 that uses one of the several `Pen` constructors:

```
Pen *poPen = new Pen(Color::Red);
```

Note that when the Pen is created, it is passed in a color. But you could have created the Pen and specified the width at the same time, using code like this:

```
Pen *poPen = new Pen(Color::Red, 5);
```

In this case, you are creating a Pen just as before, but using a different constructor.

Creating a class with multiple constructors is easy too. All you need to do is declare the various constructors and then make sure you write the code for each constructor. For example, here is a version of the DisplayObject class that has two constructors:

```
__gc class DisplayObject
{
public:
    void Add();
    void Draw(Graphics *poG);
    DisplayObject();
    //And now we have a second constructor
    DisplayObject(Color *poInitialColor);
private:
    ArrayList *m_paLines;
    Color *m_poInitialColor;
};

//Default constructor
DisplayObject::DisplayObject()
{
    m_paLines = new ArrayList();
}

//Constructor when a color is passed in
DisplayObject::DisplayObject(Color *poInitialColor)
{
    m_paLines = new ArrayList();
    m_poInitialColor = poInitialColor;
}
```

 Remember that each constructor must have a unique signature. For example, even though the following two constructors might do different things and have arguments with different names, their data types are the same. This results in a syntax error:

```
Window::Window(int Left, int Right);
Window::Window(int Width, int Color);
```

Public and private lives of constructors

One good use for multiple constructors is to create public and private constructors. The public constructors are used when new objects are created by the outside world. The private constructors are used internally as helper functions. For example, if you're constructing a linked list of objects, you might use a private constructor to add a new item to the linked list. (The constructor would be private in this situation because it's being called only by a list member function.)

We Will, We Will Destroy You

The destructor is a member function that is called automatically when an object is destroyed. Objects are destroyed for various reasons. For example, a local object might be destroyed when a particular function finishes. Or an object created with new might have been deleted. Or perhaps the program finished and all static objects were therefore deleted.

The compiler calls the destructor automatically. You never have to call it yourself, and you can't pass parameters to it. The destructor has the same name as the class, but with a ~ (tilde) before it. You can have only one destructor per class, and it must be public.

Here's a quick example:

```
//Class for constructing a linked list
class LineObjectContainer
{
public:
    LineObject *poLine;
    LineObjectContainer *poNext;
    ~LineObjectContainer();
};

//Destructor: Clean up the list
LineObjectContainer::~LineObjectContainer()
{
    //For illustration, we'll write a line to the screen
    cout << "Deleting a LOC\n";

    //Delete the line
    delete poLine;
    //Delete the next one
    if (poNext)
        delete poNext;
}
```

Cleaning up your own mess

When you write a .NET program, .NET automatically cleans up after you, or at least it does when you use garbage-collected objects. So in .NET, destructors aren't always needed. But in unmanaged programs, which don't have garbage collection, destructors are absolutely vital.

Because each class has a destructor, each class is responsible for cleaning up after itself. Therefore, you write cleanup code on a class-by-class basis instead of having to write all the cleanup code at once.

In case you are thinking destructors might not be so useful, take a look back at the code in Draw5. The LineObjectContainer, ArrayList, and DisplayObject classes all have Delete methods for cleaning up memory. Draw5 went to great lengths to make sure that the Delete functions were properly called in order to free the various objects that were created. Using destructors makes this a lot easier. In fact, you can get rid of all the Delete methods and instead replace them with destructors. Not only that, but the Delete methods get easier. Draw5 had a rather awkward looking piece of code in LineObjectContainer::Delete:

```
void LineObjectContainer::Delete()
{
    LineObjectContainer *poCur, *poTemp;

    poCur = this;
    while (poCur)
    {
        poTemp = poCur;
        //Clear out the line object
        delete poCur->poLine;
        poCur = poCur->poNext;
        //Delete the container object
        delete poTemp;
    }
}
```

As you may recall, this method was called when the program ended. It was called on the very first LineObjectContainer in the ArrayList. And this code took care of walking through every stinking object in the ArrayList. (Okay, you probably don't recall this at all. In fact, by the time you hit this section of code in Chapter 17, you were either deeply immersed in the latest *Law & Order* episode or counting sheep.)

With destructors, life gets simpler. When you delete an object, its destructor is called automatically. So in the new and improved world, the LineObjectContainer::Delete method looks like this:

```
//Destructor: Clean up the list
LineObjectContainer::~LineObjectContainer()
{
   //For illustration, we'll write a line to the screen
   cout << "Deleting a LOC\n";

   //Delete the line
   delete poLine;
   //Delete the next one
   if (poNext)
      delete poNext;
}
```

This code is simpler. The first object in the ArrayList frees up its memory and then deletes the next object in the list. The next one in the list is also a LineObjectContainer. So its destructor is automatically called when it is deleted. What does it do? Frees up its memory and nukes the next one.

What causes the first LineObjectContainer's destructor to be called? The ArrayList destructor, shown here:

```
ArrayList::~ArrayList()
{
   //Delete the list of line objects
   //All we need to do is delete the first one
   delete m_poFirst;
}
```

And what makes this destructor go? Well, ArrayList is used inside DisplayObject. So it isn't too surprising that when DisplayObject goes away, its destructor deletes ArrayList:

```
DisplayObject::~DisplayObject()
{
   delete m_paLines;
}
```

Continuing to trace back, what makes DisplayObject go away? This line in the main function, called just before the program ends:

```
delete poDisplay;
```

To check out destructors in action, read through and then run the code in the Draw7 directory on the accompanying CD.

Because destructors work this way, you can write the little bits of cleanup code one piece at a time as you design new objects. You don't have to wait until the end of your application and then try to figure out everything in the world that might have been created and how you can possibly clean everything up.

Writing a destructor is similar to the idea that if you just put something away after you use it, you never have a desk or room or car piled with parking tickets, half-read books, and soda cans. It's easier to put into practice with C++, though.

Remember to clean the dynamic stuff, too

If you've created a class or a variable dynamically — that is, if you've created it with new — you must remember to delete it when you're finished using it. Suppose, for example, that you have a class representing photographs, and that when you created the class, you used new to allocate memory to store the photographs. You need to use delete to free up this memory. Otherwise, it just hangs around. (Of course, the pointer will be gone, so the memory will be orphaned, creating a memory leak.)

Or suppose you have a class that contains a list of songs. When you destroy the class, you need to destroy also the linked list so that you can free the memory that it consumes. You also need to make sure that the appropriate linked-list destructors are called.

The easiest way to do this is to have the destructor of the linked-list class know to destroy the next object in the list. That way, as soon as you delete the first item in the list, the rest of the items in the list will be destroyed as well. This is an easy and convenient way to start a domino chain of destruction. If you pronounce that with a deep, serious voice, you can even use it as a movie title.

But remember, when you are writing managed programs, you usually don't need to bother, because .NET's garbage collector will do it for you.

What Happens If I Have a Class in a Class?

As you spend more and more time programming, you'll undoubtedly find yourself creating lots of classes that contain other classes. For example, you might create a class called BandTypes that describes musical groups; this class in turn might contain a LongHair class.

When a class is created, the first thing that happens is that memory is allocated for all its data members. If the class contains data members that are classes (such as a data member that's a LongHair class), the constructors for these data members are called.

Thus, if a class contains classes within it, the constructors for these classes are called first. That's because they need to be created before the class containing them can be created.

When a class is destroyed, its destructor is called. Then, destructors are called for any data members that are classes. For example, when a BandTypes class is destroyed, its destructor is called. Then the LongHair destructor is called.

This concept is probably best illustrated with a simple program like the one that follows. In this program, the class foo contains another class named bar. When you run this program, you see that first bar's constructor is called, and then foo's constructor is called. And when the program ends, first foo's destructor is called, and then bar's destructor is called:

```
// ConstructorDestructor
// Shows the order of constructor and destructor calls

#include "stdafx.h"

#using <mscorlib.dll>

using namespace System;

//A simple class with a constructor and destructor
class bar
{
public:
    bar();
    ~bar();
};

//Let the world know when bar is created
bar::bar()
{
    Console::WriteLine(S"bar created");
}

//Let the world know when bar is destroyed
bar::~bar()
{
    Console::WriteLine(S"bar destroyed");
}

//Foo is a class that contains another class,
//in this case bar. Because it contains another
//class, creating and destroying foo shows
//the order of constructor and destructor calls
class foo
{
```

```
public:
    bar oTemp;
    foo();
    ~foo();
};

//Let the world know that a foo is born
foo::foo()
{
    Console::WriteLine(S"foo created");
}

//Let the world know that a foo has been destroyed
foo::~foo()
{
    Console::WriteLine("A foo and his memory are soon
            parted");
}


//This is the main function It simply creates an object
//of type foo. When oTemp is created, the constructors
//are automatically called. When the program finishes,
//Temp is automatically destroyed so that you can see
//the order of destructor calls.
#ifdef _UNICODE
int wmain(void)
#else
int main(void)
#endif
{
    foo oTemp;
    return 0;
}
```

This program is in the ConstructorDestructor directory on the CD that comes
with this book.

Reading Object-Oriented Programs

You've seen that object-oriented programs can contain lots of classes. Each
class has a declaration that tells what's in the class, followed by a definition
for each of its member functions. The class declaration is usually concise,
but the member functions can be spread out over a file. Because you need to
read the code in the member functions to understand exactly what they do,
figuring out what a class does can mean looking back and forth over a file.

Here are some tips that can help you figure out what your classes do:

- ✔ **If the file has a `main` function in it, skip to it to see what it does.** Work backward from the highest level classes and member functions to the lowest level ones with the most details.

- ✔ **If the file contains a number of classes, look at the class declarations first.** Read any comments the programmer has kindly provided to get an idea of what the class does. Then quickly glance at what its various public member functions and data members do.

- ✔ **Make sure that you take a quick look to see whether the class provides more than one constructor.** You'll probably see them used in the program.

- ✔ **Ignore private and protected member functions and data members until later.**

- ✔ **For unmanaged programs, you might need to look at a header file to find the class declaration.** Look at the beginning of the source file to determine whether the source file includes any header files. (Look for statements that begin with `#include`.) The class declaration could be inside one of those header files.

- ✔ **Usually the highest level classes are declared last, so it's often a good idea to read through the code backward.** Start with `main`. Go up to find the first class declaration. (Skip over its member functions to get to the declaration.) See what that does. Then skip up again to find the next class declaration. If you get confused, try walking backwards. It won't help, but at least you'll give your co-workers something to laugh about.

Chapter 19

Inherit the Wind

Conventional programming can waste a lot of time. You write a routine but can't use it later because you need to make slight modifications. Or you write a routine that works fine in some cases, but then find you need to modify a few more things. So what do you do? You end up copying the code, pasting it somewhere else, customizing it, and giving the routine a new name. This is called *copy-and-paste* programming. In a way, it lets you reuse code, but it has several problems. Not only do your programs get bigger from all that repeated code, but it's an easy way to reproduce bugs all over the place — if you fix a bug in that copied code, you have to fix the bug manually in every place you copied it.

Object-oriented programming helps you avoid the copy-and-paste syndrome. You can just take an existing piece of code, inherit from it, and make any needed modifications. No copying and pasting — just reusing things that work. This strategy is called *inheritance*.

How Inheritance Works

Inheritance is useful when you build objects. For example, suppose you have a class that represents people. You could inherit from that to create a class representing politicians. And then you could further inherit to create a class for honest politicians. (Okay, you'll probably never use that one, but we are discussing theory here.) Each of these objects would inherit behavior from the previous object and would feature some modifications and added touches.

Also, if you correct a bug in a base class, the correction automatically applies to all derived classes. So if you later discover that your politician class has some problems with basic math, correcting the problems will also correct the same problems in the honest politician class.

To inherit from an object, use : (looks like a colon, but is pronounced as "is based on") when you declare the new object, and then list the thing from which you want to inherit:

```
class DerivedClass : public BaseClass
{
};
```

Any member function of the base class (the parent) is now a member function of the derived class (the child). Any data member of the base class is now a data member of the derived class. You just don't have to retype all of them. If you want to add items to the class, list them in the declaration. These will be the special things that differentiate your class from the base class.

For example, the following puts together a declaration for the Politician class:

```
class Politician
{
public:
    void MakeSomePromises();
    void GrabSomeMoney();
};
```

This class provides the basic capabilities that all politicians need. The rarely encountered HonestPolitician class might look like this:

```
class HonestPolitician : public Politician
{
public:
    void TellTheTruth();
};
```

Because it derives from Politician, the HonestPolitician class has the MakeSomePromises and GrabSomeMoney methods as part of it. It just adds the new TellTheTruth method. Pretty easy, huh?

You aren't restricted to inheriting from classes you've written. You can just as easily inherit from any .NET class. For example, you could write code like this:

```
class FountainPen : public Pen
{
};
```

Design for reusability

To get reusability, you need to *design* for reusability. As mentioned in a previous chapter, this is a skill you develop over time. Here are some tips and suggestions to keep in mind when you're designing object-oriented programs:

✔ **Determine whether you can use variations of the object elsewhere.** For example, if you have a basic employee-information-and-processing object, you can use it as the core from which to create other objects. You can add salary information to create a new payroll object. Or you can add health information to create a new health object.

✔ **Ask yourself whether the specific data really matters.** For example, see whether you have a fundamental concept (such as a list of choices) that you can generalize. You

can always modify your inherited objects later to make them appropriate for specific needs.

✔ **Think about your possible future needs.** You may want to keep an old object around so that you can inherit from it.

✔ **Look at the work of other programmers.**

✔ **Remember that it takes a great deal of practice to become skilled at writing object-oriented programs.** You probably write a program, and then say, "Gosh durn it all, if I had only done this and this and this and this, I could have made a real nice object structure and used inheritance with it instead of having these 14 separate objects." That's okay. It's part of the learning process.

How public, private, and protected keywords affect things

Sooner or later, this public versus private versus protected thing will bite you, so here are the rules:

✔ public items from the base class are fully usable by the derived class and fully usable outside the base class.

✔ private items from the base class are invisible to the derived class and invisible outside the base class.

✔ protected items from the base class are fully usable by the derived class but are invisible to nonderived classes.

(Actually, because this is C++ you're reading about, you should know a few additional rules. You can find them in the "Inheriting with private and protected Items" section later in this chapter.)

Kick it into override

If you want, you can change the behavior of an item that you've inherited. To do so, just give the item the same name as an item in the base class. This is called *overriding*, a powerful and frequently used feature of C++.

For example, suppose you have a class representing shapes. (Sound familiar?) It might look like this:

```
__gc class ShapeObject
{
public:
    void Draw(Graphics *poG) ;
    void PrintStats();
private:
    int     nUseCount;
};
```

If you now want to make a class specifically designed for representing lines, you could derive it from the ShapeObject class, and then override the Draw member function:

```
__gc class LineObject : public ShapeObject
{
public:
    void Draw(Graphics *poG) ;
};
```

The LineObject class has all the characteristics and capabilities of the ShapeObject, but it draws differently.

Pump up the base class

Sometimes when you override a member function, you still need to access the corresponding member function in the base class. (By the way, people often call the base class the *parent*. Maybe next Mother's Day you can try sending your mom a Happy Base Class Day card.) No problem. Just write the base class name, followed by :: and the function name.

For example, suppose the Draw member function in LineObject needs to call the Draw member function from ShapeObject. Do this:

```
void LineObject::Draw(Graphics *poG)
{
    //Call the base class
    ShapeObject::Draw(poG);
    //Now do some specifics for lines
```

```
    Pen *poPen = new Pen(Color::Red);
    //Draw the line
    poG->DrawLine(poPen, m_nXFrom, m_nYFrom, m_nXTo, m_nYTo);
}
```

This is a nice feature because if you need to access the functionality that the parent function provides, you don't need to copy and paste the code from the parent class into the derived class. Instead, you can just call the function in the parent class, and then write additional code for performing additional actions.

An eensie-weensie, teenie-weenie example program

Here's a small example program that illustrates inheritance and changing the behavior of a function. This program has two classes. Use the base class to check out one type of behavior and the derived class to check out the second type of behavior. The derived class also calls the base class:

```
// Inherit
// Illustrates overriding a function through inheritance

#include "stdafx.h"

#using <mscorlib.dll>

using namespace System;

//This is the base class. It contains a price and a
//way to print the price.
class Base
{
public:
    int nPrice;
    void PrintMe();
};

//Print it, letting us know it is the base function
void Base::PrintMe()
{
    Console::WriteLine(S"Base {0}", nPrice.ToString());
}

//Derived is inherited from Base but has a
//different PrintMe() function
```

```
class Derived : public Base
{
public:
    void PrintMe();
};

//Let us know the derived one was called and then
//call the base one.
void Derived::PrintMe() {
    Console::WriteLine(S"Derived");
    //Now call the parent
    Base::PrintMe();
}


//Hang out until the user is finished
void HangOut()
{
    Console::WriteLine(L"Press the enter key to stop the
            program");
    Console::ReadLine();
}

// This is the entry point for this application
#ifdef _UNICODE
int wmain(void)
#else
int main(void)
#endif
{
    Base   oBaseClass;
    Derived  oDerivedClass;

    oBaseClass.nPrice = 1;
    oDerivedClass.nPrice = 7;

    Console::WriteLine(S"Call base class function");
    oBaseClass.PrintMe();

    Console::WriteLine(S"Call derived class function");
    oDerivedClass.PrintMe();
    HangOut();
    return 0;
}
```

You can find the program in the Inherit directory on the CD accompanying this book.

How to tell whether you need to create a default constructor

If you inherit from a class that has a set of specialized constructors, you may need to make sure that the base class has a default constructor. If all the following are true, you need to define a default constructor:

✔ You plan to create derived classes from the class.

✔ The class has some constructors that take arguments.

✔ The class doesn't currently have a default constructor.

✔ You don't plan to explicitly (directly) call one of the specialized constructors from the derived class constructor, as shown in the "Impact of inheritance on constructors and destructors" section.

Impact of inheritance on constructors and destructors

As your programs become complex, you start to create classes that have several constructors. Pay attention to this section to find out how to call such constructors when you inherit, because this is a useful technique that will save you many headaches down the road.

When you create a class that inherits from another class, the constructor for the base class is called. The compiler first looks for the default constructor — that is, it looks for a constructor that takes no parameters.

Sometimes you might want to have specialized constructors. For example, you saw that the Pen class can be constructed with a color or a color and a width. If you derive a new class from Pen, you might want to call one of these parameterized constructors when the derived class is created. You can do this in the constructor for the derived class. Just list the base class constructor that you want to call, followed by any parameters:

```
Derived::Derived() : Base(....) {
}
```

Here's an example of this:

```
FountainPen::FountainPen(int nWidth, int nStyle) :
        Pen(Color::Red, nWidth)
{
}
```

You can see that when the FountainPen(int, int) constructor is called, it calls the base class Pen constructor that takes a color and a width.

When you inherit from a class, the constructors and destructors for the both the base class and the derived class are called. It's important to understand the order in which the constructors and destructors are called. When a derived class is created, first the memory for the class is set aside. Then the base class's constructor is called. Then the derived class's constructor is called. When a derived class is destroyed, first its destructor is called, and then the destructor for the base class is called.

You Derive Me Crazy

If you have a pointer that can point to a base class, you can use that same pointer to point to a derived class. Suppose, for example, that poShape is a pointer that points to a ShapeObject class:

```
ShapeObject *poShape;
```

If some other object is derived from ShapeObject, you can use poShape to point to that, too:

```
poShape = new LineObject();
```

"So what?" you might ask. And we answer, "This is important. It provides you with incredible flexibility because you can use a single pointer type for many different objects. So you don't have to know in advance whether a user of the class will make you create a special, derived object or some other object. You can use the same pointer, and it can deal with the base object as well as derived objects."

For example, suppose you write a program that can draw a set of shapes. Some of the shapes are circles and some are lines. You could create a base class called ShapeObject, and created derived classes LineObject and CircleObject from it. You could then keep an ArrayList of such shapes, and always point to them generically using a ShapeObject pointer.

Later on in the chapter, you do exactly this with the Draw8 program. You'll put LineObject and CircleObject into an ArrayList. And when you want to draw them, you simply do this (okay, maybe *simply* isn't the best word):

```
static_cast<ShapeObject*>(poEnumerator->Current)->Draw(poG);
```

Because the LineObject and CircleObject classes are derived from ShapeObject, and because ShapeObject has a Draw member function, this drawing code will work whether or not the object in the ArrayList is a CircleObject or LineObject.

Why does the thing with pointers and classes work?

Normally, C++ is strict about types. For example, you can't use `int *` to point to a `float`. But things are a bit different with derived classes. When the compiler makes a derived class, it makes sure that what is inherited comes first in the class. For example, if the first four items in the base class are integers, the first four items in the derived class are those same integers.

If the compiler has a pointer to the base class, it knows how to find the various data members and member functions by determining where they're located in the class. If you take the same

pointer and point it to a derived class, all the base class member functions and data members are still easy to find because the derived class looks like a spitting image of the base class but with some lucky extras. That's why you have this flexibility. The compiler always knows the offsets of any functions in the base class, regardless of the derived changes.

So what happens if the derived class overrides one of the functions in the base class? You'll find out starting in a few paragraphs.

Inheriting with private and protected Items

When you inherit from a class, you can specify access rights. So far, you've used the `public` keyword when inheriting. You can also use the `private` and `protected` keywords.

Table 19-1 shows the effects of using `public`, `private`, and `protected` when inheriting.

Table 19-1	The Effect of public, private, and protected on Inheritance	
If You Inherit Using . . .	And the Base Class's Member Is . . .	The Inherited Member Is This in Your Class
public	public	public
	protected	protected
	private	nonaccessible

(continued)

Table 19-1 (continued)

If You Inherit Using . . .	And the Base Class's Member Is . . .	The Inherited Member Is This in Your Class
protected	public	protected
	protected	protected
	private	nonaccessible
private	public	private
	protected	private
	private	nonaccessible

Virtual Insanity

Virtual functions are used when a pointer to an object sometimes points to a base class and other times points to a derived class. Fortunately, the concepts aren't as complex or as hard as this sounds. In the "You Derive Me Crazy" section, you saw some code from the Draw8 program, where you use an ArrayList to store a series of CircleObject and LineObject objects. That's all we're talking about.

Of course, there's a catch. Almost any time you use pointers, some little thing will makes your brain hurt. Suppose that one of the things you did in a derived class was to override the behavior of a member function. For example, suppose that the LineObject class overrides the Draw member function so that it draws lines. And the CircleObject class overrides the Draw member function so that it draws circles. Well, if you use a ShapeObject pointer to point to one of these objects and then call the Draw function, you won't get what you expect. Instead, you end up calling the Draw member function from the base class.

This is a bummer. Here's what's happening: Inheritance gives you a fantastic ability to reuse code, and pointers give you all kinds of flexibility — but when you use them together, blammo! You end up with a problem.

Luckily, *virtual functions* solve this problem. When you use virtual functions, the pointers know that they're supposed to call the member functions that have been overridden by the derived class. When people talk about *polymorphism* being an important feature of object-oriented programming, they're really talking about virtual functions.

If you make Draw a virtual function, the problem we just discussed goes away. If you have a LineObject but point to it with a ShapeObject pointer, calling

Draw will call `LineObject::Draw` instead of `ShapeObject::Draw`. Better yet, nothing gets screwed up. So if you point to `LineObject` with a `LineObject` pointer, calling `Draw` will also call `LineObject::Draw`. In other words, only the right thing happens.

A quick check of your virtue

By answering the following four questions, you can determine whether you should make any particular function a virtual function. If you can answer no to any of these questions, you don't need a virtual function:

- ✔ **Do you inherit from this class?** (Do you think you will in the future?)
- ✔ **Does the function behave differently in the derived class than it does in the base class?** (Do you think it will in the future?)
- ✔ **Do you use pointers to the base class?**
- ✔ **Do you ever need to use these pointers to point to a derived class?** In other words, will you ever mix pointers to base and derived classes?

If *all* your answers are yes, you should use a virtual function.

Declaring your virtuous intentions

You declare a virtual function in the base class, not in the derived class. To declare a virtual function, precede the function name with `virtual`:

```
class Base
{
public:
  int Price;
  virtual void PrintMe();
};
```

Now the `PrintMe` function in the class named `Base` is virtual.

Suppose that you derived a new class from this:

```
class Derived : public Base
{
public:
  virtual void PrintMe();
};
```

The compiler now calls the correct member function if you use pointers to these objects.

TIP

You don't need to include the `virtual` keyword in derived classes when you override functions from the base class that are virtual. It's good to do so, though, because when you read the program, it's a lot clearer that you're using virtual functions.

For example, you can use the following declaration for `Derived`:

```
class Derived : public Base
{
public:
  void PrintMe();
};
```

But this is clearer:

```
class Derived : public Base
{
public:
  virtual void PrintMe();
};
```

Don't believe it until you C++ it

Just in case you're feeling a bit confused about virtual functions, this section provides a simple program that uses both a virtual function and a nonvirtual function. If you run it, you see that the virtual function is needed when pointers are used.

This program has two classes, `Base` and `Derived`. `Base` contains a member function called `PrintMe`, which is not virtual, and a member function called `PrintMeV`, which is virtual:

```
class Base
{
public:
    void PrintMe();
    virtual void PrintMeV();
};
```

`Derived` is inherited from `Base` and overrides both member functions:

```
class Derived : public Base
{
public:
    void PrintMe();
    virtual void PrintMeV();
};
```

The main routine starts by creating a `Base` class. It uses pointers so that it can demonstrate the use of virtual functions:

```
Base  *poBase = new Base();
```

Then it calls the member functions:

```
poBase->PrintMe();
poBase->PrintMeV();
```

Next, a `Derived` class is created. Here, the `Derived` class is pointed to by the base class pointer. This is what makes virtual functions interesting — we're pointing to a derived class using a pointer to the base class:

```
poBase = new Derived();
poBase->PrintMe();
poBase->PrintMeV();
```

When this code executes, the `PrintMe` routine from the `Base` class is called, even though `poBase` points to a `Derived` class. That's because `PrintMe` isn't virtual. But notice that the `PrintMeV` routine from `Derived` is called. That's because `PrintMeV` is virtual. (Figure 19-1 shows the code in action.)

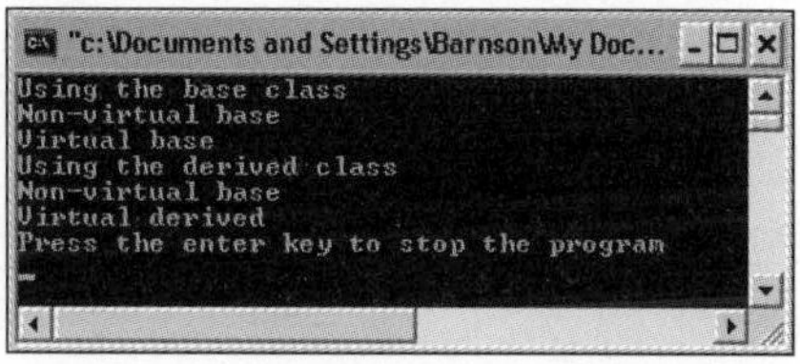

Figure 19-1:
Using virtual functions ensures that the right functions get called.

After you declare that a function is virtual, it remains virtual for all derived classes. For example, `PrintMeV` was declared virtual in the `Base` class. Thus, it is virtual in the `Derived` class. If you were to create a new class (you could call it `DerivedKiddo`) derived from `Derived`, `PrintMeV` would also be virtual in `DerivedKiddo`. No matter how deep the inheritance (and it can go as deep as you want), the compiler determines the correct function to use.

Here's a complete listing of the program:

```
// Inherit2
// Illustrates virtual functions

#include "stdafx.h"

#using <mscorlib.dll>
```

```
using namespace System;

//This is the base class
class Base
{
public:
    void PrintMe();
    virtual void PrintMeV();
};

//Print it, letting us know that it is the base function
void Base::PrintMe()
{
    Console::WriteLine(S"Non-virtual base");
}

void Base::PrintMeV()
{
    Console::WriteLine(S"Virtual base");
}

//Derived is inherited from Base
class Derived : public Base
{
public:
    void PrintMe();
    virtual void PrintMeV();
};

//Let us know the derived one was called
void Derived::PrintMe()
{
    Console::WriteLine(S"Non-virtual derived");
}

void Derived::PrintMeV()
{
    Console::WriteLine(S"Virtual derived");
}


//Hang out until the user is finished
void HangOut()
{
    Console::WriteLine(L"Press the enter key to stop the
            program");
    Console::ReadLine();
}

// This is the entry point for this application
#ifdef _UNICODE
int wmain(void)
#else
```

```
int main(void)
#endif
{
    //Create a base class dynamically
    Base  *poBase = new Base();

    //Call the two functions
    Console::WriteLine(S"Using the base class");
    poBase->PrintMe();
    poBase->PrintMeV();

    delete poBase;

    //Now use the base class pointer to point to the derived
            class
    poBase = new Derived();

    //Call the two functions
    Console::WriteLine(S"Using the derived class");
    poBase->PrintMe();
    poBase->PrintMeV();

    HangOut();
    return 0;
}
```

You can find this program in the Inherit2 directory on the accompanying CD.

Abstraction of Justice

Suppose that you want to create a program to draw shapes. You know that you'll have lots of shapes, such as circles, lines, and squares. You want to store the list of shapes to draw in an `ArrayList`. As a result, you need a base class from which you can derive all these classes. Why? Remember that a pointer to a base class can also point to any derived classes. By having a common base class, you can store all these objects in the `ArrayList`, pull them out as you need them, cast the pointer to the base object, and call the `Draw` member function to draw the shape. By making the `Draw` member function virtual, the right thing will happen. Circles will draw as circles; lines will draw as lines. Thus, you create a `ShapeObject` class that `LineObject`, `CircleObject`, and any other drawing objects derive from.

Note, however, that in this example you never put a true `ShapeObject` into the `ArrayList`. After all, there isn't some generic shape that you will draw. You are always going to draw one of the predefined shapes such as a circle or a line. The `ShapeObject` class just represents the concept of a shape.

Sign up here for parenting classes

Getting ready to inherit? Here's a handy check-list you can use to make sure that your base classes are prepared to have classes derived from them. (Kind of like making sure they're prepared to have children. Is the class's diaper bag ready? And what about a stroller?)

✔ If you plan to use pointers to the class and to classes derived from the class, use virtual functions whenever you override a function.

✔ If you derive from a class with specialized constructors, make sure that the derived class's constructors specifically call one of the specialized constructors, or that the base class also has a default constructor.

✔ If the derived class uses some of the hidden data members and member functions, these items need to be protected rather than private.

✔ If you inherit a lot of money, send some to me.

To communicate this concept and to protect from inadvertently trying to use a ShapeObject directly, you can make it an abstract base class. (Yo, dude, I was like taking bass lessons from my man Bootsy Collins, and like it was so abstract, you know? Whoops, time to leave funk and get back to reality.) An *abstract base class* represents a concept (hence the term *abstract*) but doesn't contain any functionality. You can never create one directly — if you try, the compiler will cuss at you. Instead, you can create only classes that derive from the abstract base class. And the derived classes must define functionality for all the member functions in the abstract base class.

You tell the compiler that a class is an abstract base class by making all its member functions *pure virtual member functions*. Lest you think that I have just joined a monastery, let me explain. A pure virtual function means that the interface is declared but not defined. In particular, you tell the compiler so by using the bizarre syntax of adding an = 0 to the end of the member function declaration:

```
//Store shape information
//An abstract base class
__gc class ShapeObject
{
public:
    virtual void Initialize() = 0;
    virtual void Draw(Graphics *poG) = 0;
};
```

An historic aside: My daughter Gabrielle was born right when I was about to write this paragraph.

After you have done so, you can't actually create the class. That is, you can't create a ShapeObject class with code like this:

```
ShapeObject foo;
```

But that's okay! You never want to create one of these things. You just derive other classes from it. And the derived classes must provide functionality for all the pure virtual functions. Otherwise, the compiler will tell you that you are a goof ball.

Abstract Art

Now that you've found out about virtual functions and abstract base classes, it's time to use those fancy concepts in a program. You'll add functionality to the drawing program so that the user can draw either circles or lines.

How does it work? Well, as before, you use an ArrayList to store a list of shapes to draw. But this time, when you create shape objects to put in the list, you create a LineObject or a CircleObject:

```
Console::WriteLine("Type c to create a circle and l to create
          a line");
pszMore = Console::ReadLine();

if (pszMore->Equals(S"c"))
{
    //Create a circle
    poShape = new CircleObject();
}
else
{
    //Create a line
    poShape = new LineObject();
}
```

Each of these classes is derived from an abstract base class called ShapeObject. And each of these classes uses virtual functions to override how Initialize and Draw work. For LineObject, these members functions grab end coordinates and draw lines. For CircleObject, these member functions grab the radius and the center and draw circles.

As before, when you go to draw all the shapes, you cast the objects in the ArrayList to a particular class. In this case, you cast to ShapeObject and rely on the goodness of virtual functions to do the right thing, depending on whether you have a CircleObject or a LineObject:

```
IEnumerator *poEnumerator = m_paShapes->GetEnumerator();
while (poEnumerator->MoveNext())
{
    //Call the draw method for the object
    static_cast<ShapeObject*>(poEnumerator->Current)-
            >Draw(poG);
}
```

This is really cool functionality. Type this program and try it out, or load it from the Draw8 directory on the accompanying CD:

```cpp
// Draw8
// Uses inheritance and virtual functions


#include "stdafx.h"

#using <mscorlib.dll>
#using <System.dll>
#using <System.Windows.Forms.dll>
#using <System.Drawing.dll>

using namespace System;
using namespace System::Drawing;
using namespace System::Windows::Forms;
using namespace System::Collections;


//Store shape information
//An abstract base class
__gc class ShapeObject
{
public:
    virtual void Initialize() = 0;
    virtual void Draw(Graphics *poG) = 0;
};


//Store line information
__gc class LineObject : public ShapeObject
{
public:
    virtual void Initialize();
    virtual void Draw(Graphics *poG);
private:
    int m_nXFrom;
    int m_nYFrom;
    int m_nXTo;
    int m_nYTo;
};
```

```
//Initialize values for this line object
void LineObject::Initialize()
{
    //Read the x and y positions and store them in the
            structure
    Console::WriteLine(S"What is the starting x position?");
    m_nXFrom = Int32::Parse(Console::ReadLine());
    Console::WriteLine(S"What is the starting y position?");
    m_nYFrom = Int32::Parse(Console::ReadLine());
    Console::WriteLine(S"What is the ending x position?");
    m_nXTo = Int32::Parse(Console::ReadLine());
    Console::WriteLine(S"What is the ending y position?");
    m_nYTo = Int32::Parse(Console::ReadLine());
}


//Draw the line
void LineObject::Draw(Graphics *poG)
{
    //Create a pen to draw with
    Pen *poPen = new Pen(Color::Red);
    //Draw the line
    poG->DrawLine(poPen, m_nXFrom, m_nYFrom, m_nXTo, m_nYTo);
}


//Store circle information
__gc class CircleObject : public ShapeObject
{
public:
    virtual void Initialize();
    virtual void Draw(Graphics *poG);
private:
    int m_nXCenter;
    int m_nYCenter;
    int m_nRadius;
};


//Initialize values for this circle object
void CircleObject::Initialize()
{
    //Read the center position and radius and store them in
            the structure
    Console::WriteLine(S"What is the center x position?");
    m_nXCenter = Int32::Parse(Console::ReadLine());
    Console::WriteLine(S"What is the center y position?");
    m_nYCenter = Int32::Parse(Console::ReadLine());
    Console::WriteLine(S"What is the radius?");
    m_nRadius = Int32::Parse(Console::ReadLine());
}
```

```
//Draw the line
void CircleObject::Draw(Graphics *poG)
{
    //Create a pen to draw with
    Pen *poPen = new Pen(Color::Blue);
    //Draw the line
    poG->DrawEllipse(poPen, m_nXCenter-m_nRadius, m_nYCenter-
            m_nRadius, m_nXCenter+m_nRadius,
            m_nYCenter+m_nRadius);
}


//Store all the lines to draw
__gc class DisplayObject
{
public:
    void Add();
    void Draw(Graphics *poG);
    DisplayObject();
private:
    ArrayList *m_paShapes;
};


//Initialize the DisplayObject structures
DisplayObject::DisplayObject()
{
    m_paShapes = new ArrayList();
}


//Add a new object
void DisplayObject::Add()
{
    bool fFinished = false;
    String *pszMore;
    ShapeObject *poShape;

    while (!fFinished)
    {
        //What shall we create?
        Console::WriteLine("Type c to create a circle and l to
            create a line");
        pszMore = Console::ReadLine();

        if (pszMore->Equals(S"c"))
        {
            //We'll create a circle
            poShape = new CircleObject();
        }
        else
        {
```

```
        //We'll create a line
        poShape = new LineObject();
    }

    //Initialize it
    poShape->Initialize();
    //Store it in the structure
    m_paShapes->Add(poShape);

    //Should we add another one?
    Console::WriteLine("Press y to enter a new shape");
    pszMore = Console::ReadLine();
    if (!pszMore->Equals(S"y"))
    {
        fFinished = true;
    }
  }
}


//Draw all the shapes
void DisplayObject::Draw(Graphics *poG)
{
   //Go through each of shape object
   IEnumerator *poEnumerator = m_paShapes->GetEnumerator();
   while (poEnumerator->MoveNext())
   {
   //Call the draw method for the object
   static_cast<ShapeObject*>(poEnumerator->Current)-
           >Draw(poG);
}
}


// This is the entry point for this application
#ifdef _UNICODE
int wmain(void)
#else
int main(void)
#endif
{
    //Structures for drawing graphics
    Form *poForm = new Form();
    Graphics *poGraphics = poForm->CreateGraphics();
    DisplayObject *poDisplay = new DisplayObject();

    //Add the shapes
    poDisplay->Add();

    //Move the display surface to the far left
    poForm->SetDesktopLocation(0,0);
    //Show the display surface
    poForm->Show();
```

```
    //Draw the shapes
    poDisplay->Draw(poGraphics);

    //Free up the graphics surface
    poGraphics->Dispose();

    //Hang out until the user closes the form
    Application::Run(poForm);
}
```

Chapter 20

Too Hot to Exception Handle

• •

• •

*P*art of the programming process involves testing and debugging your program. But even after your program is bug-free and running fine, it can still have problems. That's because you can't predict what the user is going to do to your program or what conditions your programs will face. The only thing you really can predict is that unexpected things will happen. Murphy's Law was written with computer users in mind.

These unexpected conditions are called *error conditions.* There are lots and lots of reasons why error conditions happen. Maybe the disk is full, or maybe a chad wasn't fully punched, or maybe an input file has bad data, or maybe the user typed "fudge" instead of the radius of a circle.

The point is, *all* these things (and many more besides) can cause bad things to happen in a program. Fortunately, *exception handling* can help you catch and handle errors.

Error Handling the Old Way

So that you can fully appreciate the joys of exception handling, take a look at the old, messy way of handling errors.

Error handling can be divided into two parts: detecting the error and then communicating and handling the error. The first part — detecting the error — isn't usually so bad. Some routine deep in the bowels of the application needs to have some code added to check for errors and to essentially say, "Aha — not enough data. This is an error."

After the error is found, it needs to be communicated and handled. The communication part can be a pain. The item that finds the error might have been called by some function that was called by some function that was called by some function, and so on. All these functions need to be able to see that an error has occurred and then figure out what to do. Usually, some code is checked — if it indicates that there were no problems, the routine keeps going; otherwise, the routine ends early.

In other words, a straightforward set of code such as this:

```
//Call a bunch of functions
ReadSongs();
ReadSizes();
ReadMyLips();
```

would need to turn into this:

```
//Call a bunch of functions. Values
//less than 0 mean errors.
nTemp = ReadSongs();
if (nTemp < 0)
{
  return nTemp;
}
nTemp = ReadSizes();
if (nTemp < 0)
{
  return nTemp;
}
nTemp = ReadMyLips();
if (nTemp < 0)
{
  return nTemp;
}
```

Now imagine doing that after every single function call in every single routine in your program. Yuck.

To make matters worse, suppose that a function is allowed to return a value less than 0. In that case, you'd need another type of error scheme to check after each function is called.

Finally, after going through all this, some function eventually needs to look at the error code and say something like, "Aha, I know how to handle this error." This function needs to be able to differentiate the various types of errors.

In short, it's a pain to do this. You may have to spend far more time writing all this crazy error code than writing the important parts of the program. Plus, this type of error-handling code makes the program ugly and hard to read.

Error Handling the New, Improved Way

With exception handling, all those messy return-code checks after every function call are no longer needed. The unique error codes and problems with function return values disappear.

Exception handling has two parts: One routine throws an exception (it essentially says, "Whoa, error found!"), and a second routine, designated as the handler, takes control when an exception is found.

Another benefit to exception handling is that any objects created locally — that is, any objects created when various functions were called — are automatically destroyed. To illustrate this, suppose that function A creates a local object called ObjectA, and then calls a function called B, which creates a local object called ObjectB, which calls a function that finds an error. ObjectB and ObjectA would be destroyed. So any files, memory, data, and so on that they used would be automatically cleaned up.

To turn on exception checking in a section of code, you put the code inside try {}. This says, "Try out the following routines and see what happens." Following the try{}, you put a catch {}. This says, "If any problems occur, catch them here and handle the errors."

An exceptionally well-handled example

Take a quick look at an example of exception handling in action. (The syntax is discussed in more detail in the section called "Just the Syntax, Ma'am.") The program contains a function that tries to convert a value the user typed into an integer. This code might look familiar. After all, it was swiped from Factorial4:

```
int GetNumber()
{
    int nNumber;

    Console::WriteLine(S"What is the number?");
    nNumber = Int32::Parse(Console::ReadLine());
    return nNumber;
}
```

What happens if the user types something bogus, such as "Whassup"? Because that can't be converted to an integer, a nasty error message appears, and your program ends abruptly. Ouch.

Make way for users!

The great thing about users is that they use your software. This provides you a shot at fame and fortune, or at least means you get to keep your job or pass a class. The bad thing about users is that they often do things with your software that you don't expect. That's why you need to add exception-handling code.

Here are some common error conditions that your program should be able to handle.

✔ **The program runs out of memory.** This can happen for a number of reasons, such as a user who tries to open files much larger than you expect, or a user who doesn't have much memory in his or her machine to begin with.

✔ **The user types a bad filename.** For example, when the program asks the user what file to open, he or she might type "Hey, *@#$, why do you care?" Obviously, that's not a legal filename.

✔ **The user types a number that's outside an acceptable range.** For example, you might want numbers between 0 and 5, but the user types –17.

✔ **A function that the user never gets near gets passed a value out of the expected range.** For example, you can have some internal computation routines that expect numbers in a certain range, and for some reason an invalid number is passed in. Adding error checking makes them safer to use.

✔ **The user loads a file that isn't the correct type.** For example, you might have a program that reads text files, but the user tries to run CMD.EXE through it. This can happen in other parts of your code if you're expecting data structures to be filled with information of a particular format, but for some reason it doesn't come to your function that way.

✔ **Data files are missing.** For example, suppose that your program expects a list of passwords in a file called PASSWD.SCT. But for some reason, the user deleted this file, so now the program can't find the password file.

✔ **The disk is full.** Your program needs to save a file, but no more space is left on the disk.

What is really going on is that .NET throws an exception. If you don't handle it, .NET displays the goofed message and shuts down your program. If you use exception handling, however, you can avoid this. Here's the same function, but this time it checks for errors:

```
int GetNumber()
{
    int nNumber;

    Console::WriteLine(S"What is the number?");
    try
    {
    nNumber = Int32::Parse(Console::ReadLine());
    }
    catch (FormatException *e)
    {
```

```
        Console::WriteLine(e->Message);
        Console::WriteLine("Next time, please enter an integer.
              I'm going to guess you meant 1.");
        nNumber = 1;
        }
        return nNumber;
}
```

If the user types something bogus, a `FormatException` error is thrown. The `catch` code grabs it, displays a friendly error message, and returns a default value.

To see this code in action, load the Factorial6 project on the accompanying CD.

Flexibility: Exception handling's middle name

C++ exception handling provides great flexibility. You can turn error checking on and off selectively by enclosing only certain sections of code within a `try`. You can easily handle different types of errors. And you can process the same error different ways in different parts of the program by having what happens in the `catch` operate differently.

For example, suppose that you call the `AllocateBuf` routine from two different parts in your program. In one part, you're calling it to allocate memory for a file you want to save, and in another part you're using it to allocate memory for a photograph.

You can do the following:

```
i//Try to save the file
try
{
 AllocateBuf();
 SaveFile();
}
catch (Error1 e)
{
 Console::WriteLine(S"Couldn't save file");
}
//Allocate memory for a photograph
try
{
 AllocateBuf();
 ProcessPhoto();
}
```

```
catch (Error1 e)
{
 Console::WriteLine(S"Couldn't process photo");
}
```

The same AllocateBuf is called in each case. And the same type of error occurs if the memory can't be allocated. But the error message that's printed is different in each case.

I Never Forget a Face, but in Your Case I'll Throw an Exception

Groucho Marx wasn't really known for his programming prowess, but if he had been, this is probably how he would describe what functions do when they detect an error condition.

Suppose that a program calls a function named foo. Suppose that foo checks the values inside the buffer passed to it; foo knows that if the first letter is x, an explosion might occur. How would you indicate the presence of an error condition?

Inside a function, you use the throw command if you find an error. This triggers an exception, and the compiler looks for the catch area from the most recent try block.

For example, suppose that you want to calculate the square root of a number. You know that it's illegal to attempt this if the number is less than zero. You could use code such as this:

```
double SquareRoot(int nNumber)
{
    if (nNumber < 0)
    {
        throw new SquareRootException(S"Number must be
            positive");
    }
    return Math::Sqrt(nNumber);
}
```

This code checks to see whether the number is less than zero. If so, it throws an exception. If not, it returns the square root.

You can make as many different types of exceptions as you want. Each throw sends an instance of a data type. You can create whatever data types you want, fill them with data, and use that information to help process the error.

You can even use classes. That way, you can build routines to help process the error right into the error class that's thrown. For example, you can create a new class called MyError. If you run into a problem, you create a MyError variable and then throw that variable.

The catch takes a data type as a parameter. So you can make a ChoiceError class that is caught by one catch and a MyError class that is caught by another.

You can also use inheritance. For example, the MyError class can be derived from the ChoiceError class.

Just the Syntax, Ma'am

Here's the syntax for exception handling:

```
try
{
 //Error handling now on
 statements;
}
catch (error_type_1)
{
 statements to handle this error;
}
catch (error_type_2)
{
 statements to handle this error;
}
 .
 .
 .
```

To trigger the error, you would do this:

```
throw error_type;
```

Note that you can have as many catch blocks as you want. When an exception is caught, the code looks for the first exception where it can find a match, and then executes that block.

All .NET exceptions derive from a class called Exception. So you can always look for it as a catchall catch. The Exception object contains a Message property. You can establish a value for this message when you create the Exception object.

Here's a quick example. The program repeatedly asks the user for a number and prints the square root of the number. If the user types something bogus, the program catches that problem and uses a default number. If the user types a negative number, the program catches that problem and prints an error message.

You can find this code in the SquareRoot directory on the accompanying CD:

```cpp
// SquareRoot
// Exception handling

#include "stdafx.h"

#using <mscorlib.dll>

using namespace System;

__gc class SquareRootException : public Exception
{
public:
    SquareRootException(String *s) : Exception(s) {};
};

//Return the square root
//Throw an exception if there is a range problem
double SquareRoot(int nNumber)
{
    if (nNumber < 0)
    {
        throw new SquareRootException(S"Number must be
            positive");
    }
    return Math::Sqrt(nNumber);
}


//Prompt the user for a number
//Return the value of the number
int GetNumber()
{
    int nNumber;

    Console::WriteLine(S"What is the number?");
    try
    {
    nNumber = Int32::Parse(Console::ReadLine());
    }
    catch (FormatException *e)
    {
    Console::WriteLine(e->Message);
    Console::WriteLine("Next time, please enter an integer.
            I'm going to guess you meant 1.");
```

```
        nNumber = 1;
        }
    return nNumber;
}

// This is the entry point for this application
#ifdef _UNICODE
int wmain(void)
#else
int main(void)
#endif
{
    int nNumber;

    //Get numbers from the user, until the user
    //types 0
    while (nNumber = GetNumber())
    {
        //Output the result
        try
    {
        Console::WriteLine(S"The square root of {0} is {1}",
              nNumber.ToString(),
              SquareRoot(nNumber).ToString());
        }
        catch (Exception *e)
        {
        Console::WriteLine(e->Message);
        }
    }

    //Now we are finished
    Console::WriteLine(S"Bye");
    return 0;
}
```

To read this program, look first at the `try` block, where you see the code to print the square root:

```
try
{
    Console::WriteLine(S"The square root of {0} is {1}",
          nNumber.ToString(),
          SquareRoot(nNumber).ToString());
}
```

If the user passes a negative number to the SquareRoot function, it throws an exception and fills in an error message by passing a String to the SquareRootException constructor:

```
if (nNumber < 0)
{
    throw new SquareRootException(S"Number must be positive");
}
```

A catch area is right after the try block. You can see that there's a catch for anything that throws an exception. The Exception class that's thrown is a real object, so it has a name. The catch routine prints the Message value contained within it:

```
catch (Exception *e)
{
    Console::WriteLine(e->Message);
}
```

So, what happens when this program runs? First, the program enters the loop. At the beginning of the loop, the user is prompted for a number. If the user types a bogus value, GetNumber catches an exception and chastises the user. Within the loop, the program tries to execute the code in the try block, which prints the square root of the number.

If the user enters a number that isn't negative, the SquareRoot function won't throw an exception. In this case, all the code in the try block executes, and the square root of the number is printed. Then, execution jumps back to the beginning of the loop (assuming that the loop isn't over), and the code in the try block is tried again.

If the user types a negative number, the SquareRoot function throws an exception. In this case, the code inside the catch block executes, printing an error message. Then, execution jumps back to the beginning of the loop, and the code in the try block is tried again. When the user types a zero, the program stops.

It looks good, but that type stuff is confusing

Throwing classes solves two problems because you can make as many different types of exceptions as you like, and you can pass a great deal of information about an error and how to process it when a problem occurs.

For example, when a disk error occurs, you might want to indicate the drive that has the problem. And if a file is corrupted, you might want to indicate the filename and the last place in the file that was successfully read. You might even want to have a routine that tries to fix the file.

But when you `throw` a class, how does the compiler know which `catch` to use? That's the great part. The compiler looks at the type of the data you threw and finds the `catch` that knows how to handle those items. So you can make a `FileCorrupt` class, a `DiskError` class, and a `MemoryError` class, with each class containing information describing the problem. Each class can contain completely different types of information.

If you then find a disk error, you do this:

```
DiskError foo;
//In real life, fill foo with info here
throw foo;
```

And if you have a corrupt file, you do this:

```
CorruptFile bar;
//In real life, fill bar with info here
throw bar;
```

Then, the appropriate `catch` is called because `catch` looks to match a data or a class type:

```
//Catch disk errors here
catch (DiskError MyError) { }
//Catch corrupt files here
catch (CorruptFile MyError) { }
```

Using classes is an elegant way to provide great flexibility because you can make whatever error classes you want and store lots of information in them, while making it easy for the compiler to find exactly what exception type was thrown.

If you want, you can use simple data types such as `char *` for exception types. But you're much better off creating exception classes because you can fill each class with a lot of information to describe exactly what went wrong. The routine that finds the error knows all this stuff. The routine that processes the error knows how to use the information to help the user.

Another great thing about designing your own classes is that you can give them member functions. For example, you can build into the class a set of routines to print what error has occurred and to help you process or correct the situation.

Inheriting from error-handling classes

You can derive new error-handling classes from existing ones. This lets you reuse error-handling code quite nicely.

Exception type conversion and catch matching

If an exception type can be easily converted to a type in the catch, it's considered a match.

For example, it's easy to turn a short into an int. So, the catch will be used if you do this:

```
catch (int k) { }
...
throw (short i = 6);
```

Likewise, if you throw class Derived that was derived from class Base, a pointer to the derived class can be easily used as a pointer to the base class:

```
catch (Base foo) { }
...
```

```
Derived foo;
throw foo;
```

In this case, too, the catch will be called. For this reason, you might want to use virtual functions when you create member functions in exception classes.

The compiler calls the first catch that matches the data type. So if you have a bunch of classes derived from a base class, list them first and list the catch for the base class last. That way, the special case (the derived class) catch will be called rather than the base class. Because, after all, the compiler just uses the first one that matches, and both will suffice in this case.

If you're going to create your own exception classes, you may as well derive from Exception. That will give you some nice built-in functionality, and your exceptions will smell like all the other ones in .NET.

When you write unmanaged code, you can't derive from Exception. Instead, make your own classes.

Five Rules for Exceptional Success

Here are five simple rules you can follow when you write exception-handling code:

- ✔ **You should** throw **classes rather than simple data types.** You can provide a lot more information about what went wrong.

- ✔ **You should** throw **classes so that you can add member functions if you need to.**

✔ **Create a different class for each major category of error you expect to encounter.**

✔ **Make sure you match exactly the type of what you** `throw` **with what you** `catch`. For example, if you `throw` a `DiskError *`, make sure that you `catch` a `DiskError *`, not a `DiskError`.

If you mess this up, unexpected things happen. (Note that if the compiler can convert one error type to another type, such as a float to an integer, it will try to do so to find a match for an exception. See the "Exception type conversion and catch matching" sidebar for more information.)

✔ **If no handler is found for the exception, by default the program aborts.** Be prepared for this. Fortunately, because objects on the stack are destroyed, their destructors are called and your application performs cleanup.

Chapter 21

Hot File Stream Sundaes

*O*ne of the fundamental operations of a program is to gather input and store output. The .NET Framework class library includes a set of *stream classes* to manage I/O. (Notice the geek tendency to reduce words to short combinations of letters and symbols. In this case, I/O is shorthand for input/output.) If you want to write unmanaged code, Visual C++ supplies the *iostream* library to do just that.

You can get and save input in lots of different ways. Both the iostream library and the .NET I/O classes handle much of the low-level glad-I-don't-have-to-know-about-them details automatically.

.NET I/O Classes

The .NET Framework System.IO namespace has several classes for reading from and writing to files. You'll look at StreamReader, which lets you read text from a file, and StreamWriter, which lets you write text to a file. The File class is a helper to create the StreamReader and StreamWriter objects. Here's how you open a file stream for writing:

```
StreamWriter *poWStream = File::CreateText(S"test.txt");
```

Writing to the stream is a simple matter of calling the Write method:

```
poWStream->Write(S"Hello this is a test");
```

The `Write` method is overloaded to allow you to write different types of variables, like doubles and ints. You can also call the `WriteLine` method to write a variable with a line-ending character at the end. Remember that the `Write` and `WriteLine` methods have formatting capabilities, so you could write code like this:

```
poWStream->Write(S"Hello {0}, you are {1} and {2}!", sName,
          nAge, sCute);
```

Then close the stream with the (drumroll, please) `Close` method:

```
poWStream->Close();
```

Reading from a file using `StreamReader` is similar:

```
poRStream = File::OpenText(S"test.txt");
Console::WriteLine(poRStream->ReadLine());
poRStream->Close();
```

To get access to the System.IO namespace, use the following declaration:

```
using namespace System::IO;
```

Reading, Writing, and 'Rithmetic

The example in this section writes some numbers and words to files, and then reads them back. You can find it in the File3 directory on the CD accompanying this book.

The following example begins by writing two files. One file contains text, and the other file contains numbers:

```
//Open a stream for writing text into it
StreamWriter *poWStream = File::CreateText(S"text.txt");
//Write out some text
poWStream->WriteLine(S"Hello this is a test");
//Close the stream
poWStream->Close();

//Open a different file and write some numbers
//in it
poWStream = File::CreateText(S"numbers.txt");
poWStream->WriteLine(15);
poWStream->WriteLine(42);
poWStream->WriteLine(1);
poWStream->Close();
```

Next, the `StreamReader` class is used to open a file for reading, and then the `ReadLine` method reads the line of text:

```
//Open the first file for reading, read the line,
//and print it
StreamReader *poRStream = File::OpenText(S"text.txt");
String* pszWords = poRStream->ReadLine();
Console::WriteLine(pszWords);
poRStream->Close();
```

Next, the number file is read. A loop is used to read the entire file, regardless of the number of items in the file. The `ReadLine` method returns 0 when the end of the file is reached, which causes the `while` loop to exit. (See Chapter 11 for a refresher on `while` loops.)

```
//Now we will read through the integers
String* pszLine;
int nTempNum;
poRStream = File::OpenText(S"numbers.txt");

//Read through the file until there is no more
//input
while ((pszLine = poRStream->ReadLine()) != 0)
{
    nTempNum = Int32::Parse(pszLine);
    Console::WriteLine(nTempNum);
}
poRStream->Close();
```

iostream Library Routines

A number of `iostream` library routines can help you read from and write to files. Here's an easy way to open a file for writing:

```
ofstream foo("filename");
```

`ofstream` is a special type of class for sending output to files. (That's what the *o* and the *f* at the beginning of the word stand for: *output* and *files*. The *stream* stands for, well, *stream*, which is the C++ term for the objects used to read and write data, usually to the screen, the keyboard, or a file.) `foo`, in this case, is a stream variable (of type `ofstream`). You can pass a filename to `ofstream`'s constructor, and then use `<<` to write to it:

```
//Write "Hello World" in the file
foo << "Hello world";
```

`ofstream` has a buddy named `ifstream` for getting input from a file. (And yes, the *i* and *f* stand for *input* and *files*.) `ifstream`'s usage is similar:

```
ifstream foo("filename");
//Set up some space to read text into
char buffer[100];
//Read some text from the file
foo >> buffer;
```

If you want to read numbers instead, you can do this:

```
int MyInt;
foo >> MyInt;
```

But wait a minute! Before you use either of these, you need to read in the stream definitions by doing this:

```
#include <fstream.h>
```

Recycling stream variables

When you destroy a stream variable, its file is closed. You can close it before the stream goes away by using the `close` member function:

```
//Close the file used with the stream called foo
foo.close();
```

Typically, you do this when you want to use one stream variable for accessing several files. In this case, you close the first file and then open a different file using the `open` member function:

```
//Now open up "foo.txt"
foo.open("foo.txt");
```

If you want to see whether anything is left in the file, use the `eof` member function, which returns true when the end of the file is reached.

Reading, writing, and 'rithmetic redux

No, you're not imagining things. No, this isn't a reprint. This is the same section from a few pages ago, but written for iostreams, instead of the .NET Framework I/O classes.

The example in this section writes some numbers and words to files, and then reads them back. You can find it in the File2 directory on the CD accompanying this book.

The program begins by writing two files. One file contains text and the other file contains numbers:

```
//Open the new.txt file
ofstream oOutFile("new.txt");

//Write some text to the file
oOutFile << "Row, row, row your boat";

//Now close the file
oOutFile.close();

//Open a different file and write some numbers
//in it. Note that these are separated by
//spaces.
oOutFile.open("numbers.txt");
oOutFile << 15 << " " << 42 << " " << 1;
OutFile.close();
```

Next, the `ifstream` class is used to open a file for reading. This line does not open the file using the constructor for the stream. Rather, the file is opened explicitly using the `open` method. Both approaches work fine, and you can use whichever method you prefer. The program demonstrates both approaches so that you can see how each works:

```
ifstream oInFile;
oInFile.open("new.txt");
```

A buffer is created to store the information read in from the file. In this case, the buffer is made 50 bytes long. You need to make sure that the buffer is larger than the largest item that you read in. If you know what the data is, just make the buffer larger than the largest item. Otherwise, you can control how much information is read in through programming commands.

The file is read into the buffer, and then printed one item at a time:

```
oInFile >> p;
cout << p << endl;
oInFile >> p;
cout << p << endl;
```

Next, the number file is read. A loop is used to read the entire file, regardless of the number of items in the file. The `eof` function indicates when the end of the file is reached. Because the end-of-file character is treated as an integer, a special check is used so that the very last item read from the file (the end-of-file character) isn't printed as one of the numbers:

```
//Read through the file until there is no more
//input
while (!oInFile.eof())
{
    //Read in an integer
    oInFile >> nTempNum;
    //If the end of the file wasn't just reached,
    //print the integer
    if (!oInFile.eof())
        cout << nTempNum << endl;
}
oInFile.close();
```

Finally, the text file is read one word at a time. (By the way, if you stored the words in a linked list of word objects, you'd be well on your way to completing the infamous word-processor homework assignment given in many computer science classes.)

Special things to toss into a stream

Here are some things you can include in a stream to change the way reading and writing is handled. These things (called *stream manipulators*) don't cause anything to be read or written; they just affect the way the following items are read or written:

dec   Read or display the next number as a decimal

hex   Read or display the next number as a hex number

oct   Read or display the next number as an octal number

For example, if you know that the user is going to type a hex number, you can do this:

```
cin >> hex >> TempNum;
```

Or you can use this as an instant hex-to-decimal converter:

```
//Read it in as hex
cin >> hex >> TempNum;
//Print it as decimal
cout << TempNum;
```

Setting the fill and width for integers

By default, numbers are printed using as many characters as it takes to print them. If you need to, though, you can use more spaces. This can be useful when you want to keep things in columns. To do this, use the `width` member function:

```
//Output numbers using 20 spaces
cout.width(20);
```

Or you can put in a fill character instead. For example, you may want to print * in unused spaces so that someone doesn't alter your paychecks:

```
//Use * as the fill character
cout.fill('*');
```

You can set a fill character the same way with file streams.

You can read from and write to the screen and files in hundreds and hundreds of ways. And plenty of extra classes are not covered here. If you want to become an input/output maestro, read through the iostream programming section in the Visual C++ online documentation. In addition to reading the general sections on streams and stream classes, you may want to pay special attention to the sections on formatting methods, format flags, and manipulators.

Five Facts on Files

Here are some handy tips about files:

- ✔ **It's usually best if you don't read from and write to a file at the same time.** It's perfectly legal to do so, but sometimes (especially for beginners) it can be confusing to figure out which part of the file is being read and which part of the file is being written.

- ✔ **When you write numbers to a file using** iostream <<, **the numbers are saved as text, but no spaces are put between them.** So if you want to see

    3.4 5.6 66.28 8

  rather than

    3.45.666.288

  you need to put spaces between the numbers when you write them to a file. For example, you can do this:

```
cout << foo << " ";
```

✔ **A magic character (called the end-of-file character and sometimes written *eof*) is placed at the end of the file to say, "Hey, I'm finished."** When Visual C++ finds this, it knows to say that the end of the file has been reached.

✔ **Strings are read until a delimiter — namely end-of-file or \n — is found.** If the last string in a file doesn't end with \n, the end-of-file is reached immediately after the last string is read.

✔ **When numbers are read in using** iostream >>, **the end-of-file character isn't included when the last number is read.** (This is different from C, for example, which signals that the end-of-file has been reached when you read the last number.) So, if you're not careful, you end up trying to read one more item than is actually in the file and trying to put the end-of-file character into a number. In this case, the >> does nothing, so the number isn't changed.

Chapter 22

You WinForms Some

In This Chapter

▶ Finding out about WinForms
▶ Creating forms and controls
▶ Handling form and control events

Clearly, the smart folks at Microsoft who were designing the .NET Framework wanted to make sure that everyone loved it. .NET supports everything from console programs to Web programs to Web services to visual controls and graphical programs. In this chapter, you develop graphical user interfaces (GUIs) using the .NET Framework GUI classes, which are collectively known as WinForms. (Technically, they're called Windows Forms, but that sounds so formal.)

The WinForms classes in .NET link to the Windows GUI and its windows, dialog boxes, and controls such as buttons, tabs, lists, and trees. The WinForms classes talk directly to the Windows GUI thing that they represent. So, for example, the System.Windows.Forms.CheckBox class looks and acts exactly like any other check box in Windows. This means you can write .NET applications with all the benefits of .NET Framework, Common Language Runtime, and so forth — but have all the capabilities of Windows programs.

No Forms in Triplicate

The WinForms classes cover the user interface part of the Windows Application Programming Interface (API). Other parts of the Windows API are covered by other parts of .NET. For example, the Graphics Device Interface (GDI) is covered by the .NET System.Drawing classes.

Most WinForms classes represent visual controls that are part of Windows. However, some, such as the ContextMenu class, aren't always visible. And some are visible only in a certain way, such as the MainMenu class, which always appears at the top of your program's window.

Table 22-1 contains a list of the WinForms classes you're most likely to use in your day-to-day work.

Table 22-1	WinForms Classes You'll Use All the Time
System.Windows.Form Class	*Description*
Application	Manages your program, including starting and stopping it.
Button	A button control, sometimes called a command button. Buttons invoke actions.
CheckBox	A check box control. Allows several items in a group to be selected at one time (unlike radio buttons).
CheckedListBox	A list of check boxes that can scroll. Provides a lot of check boxes in a small amount of space.
ComboBox	A combo box, a combination (hence their name) of edit controls and list boxes. You can type values or choose them from a list. There are several variations of combo boxes.
ContextMenu	A context menu (that appears when you right-click something). Lets users choose commands and options that apply to a specific thing on the screen.
DataGrid	A grid displaying data from an ADO.NET data source. DataGrids have columns for fields in the data source and rows for records.
FileDialog	A dialog box. Users can browse for files to open and for directories in which to save new files in
Form	The base WinForms class you inherit from for your own forms. Displays both regular windows and dialog boxes.
Label	A text control. Labels other controls. Users can't change this text.
LinkLabel	A label. Displays hyperlinks that users can click to open Web pages or perform other actions.

System.Windows.Form Class	Description
ListBox	A list box. Presents users with a set of options they can choose from.
ListView	A list view. Displays a list of items with an optional icon. List views are used extensively in Windows, and you've probably used them a lot.
MainMenu	A main menu. Appears in a row at the top of your program's window.
PictureBox	A control. Displays a graphic on a form.
ProgressBar	A control. Shows the progress of a long operation.
RadioButton	A radio button control. Allows only one item in a group to be selected at one time.
RichTextBox	A rich text box control. Displays formatted text and lets users type text that your program can use. Formatting can include bold, italic, bullets, and hyperlinks.
Splitter	A splitter control. Allows users to resize controls on a form.
StatusBar	A status bar control, docked at the bottom of a form. Provides information and messages to users.
TabControl	A tab control. Holds multiple pages and lets users move among them by clicking the tab titles.
TextBox	A text box control. Displays text and lets users type text for your program to use. Text boxes can be single-line or multi-line.
ToolBar	A tool bar control. Holds toolbar buttons that users click to perform actions.
TreeView	A tree view control. Displays data in a hierarchy, like the folder tree view in Windows Explorer.

Forms: Make It So

You might be dreading making a WinForms program. If you've tried Windows programming before — or even Windows programming with an application framework such as MFC — you might be worried that you're looking at a similar task to use WinForms. Relax. Microsoft learned from its past and .NET is nicely object-oriented and easy to use.

To create a form, follow these general steps:

1. **Inherit a new class from System.Windows.Forms.Form.**

2. **Set up your form (by adding controls, for example).**

3. **Make your program use the new form.**

Inherit your form

Every form in your program has to inherit from the WinForms Form class. You use inheritance to make each form do and look like what you want it to. Inheriting from the Form class is easy:

```
__gc class MyForm : public Form
{
public:
  MyForm();
};
```

Use __gc to mark your form class as managed.

For MyForm, you're adding a constructor, which is where you'll do all the form setup.

Set it up

One of the most common types of setup you'll do is to add controls to your form. Simply follow these steps:

1. **Create an instance of the control's class:**

```
Button *poOK = new Button();
RichTextBox *poTE = new RichTextBox();
PictureBox *poImg = new PictureBox();
```

Later in this chapter, you make control classes data members of the class. You don't always have to do that. Because .NET automatically manages your program's memory, you don't have to worry about deleting data members, for example. But if you want to be able to manipulate a control in more than one member function, you'll want to make it a data member of the class.

2. Set the control's properties:

```
//Set the button properties
poOK->Text = "OK";
poOK->Left = 280;
poOK->Top = 350;
poOK->BackColor = Color::Blue;
```

3. Add the control to the form's Controls collection:

```
this->Controls->Add(poOK);
this->Controls->Add(poTE);
this->Controls->Add(poImg);
```

The `this->` pointer is assumed whenever you write code in a member function such as a constructor. We use it here so that the syntax coloring of the Visual C++ editor highlights the fact that you're doing something with the form rather than one of its controls.

You can also set properties of the form itself:

```
//Set the size of the form
this->Width = 600;
this->Height = 400;
```

Run with it

After you've created your form and set it up, you still need to tell .NET that you want it to be your program's main form. You do that with another class, the System.Windows.Forms.Application class. Its Run method takes a pointer to a Form that it makes the program's main form. You usually call `Application::Run` from your `main` function:

```
#ifdef _UNICODE
int wmain(void)
#else
int main(void)
#endif
{
  Application::Run(new MyForm());
  return 0;
}
```

You can find the complete program used in this section. Look in the Form folder on the CD accompanying this book.

Handling Events

Programming any kind of GUI means dealing with event-oriented programming. Don't worry, it's not a replacement for object-oriented programming. In fact, objects and events go hand in hand. In Windows and .NET, events happen all the time, usually when the user does something with the program. For example, moving a window, clicking a button, or choosing a menu item all cause events to fire. (Sounds dramatic, doesn't it?)

When you're writing a WinForms program, you get to decide which events you want your program to handle. You don't have to handle all events. In fact, there are thousands of possible events, so if you did handle them all, every program would take several years just to write, much less work out all the bugs.

You can handle events in two ways, depending on whether you want to handle events in an inherited class or whether you want to delegate event handling to another class. For example, in an inherited form class, you can handle that form's events directly as ordinary member functions in that class. However, if you have a button on the form and you want to know when the user clicks it, you don't want to have to inherit a MyButton class just to handle the `click` event, right? So .NET includes the concept of *delegates*, which let you handle the button's `click` event as a member function of the form class where it lives.

That's why I said that event-oriented programming goes hand in hand with object-oriented programming. When you inherit a form class, you're adding all the member functions that make that class work, including delegates to handle the events of the form's controls. Pretty cool, eh?

Back in the saddle again

Control and form classes have built-in member functions for handling a lot of events. They need to handle events to make it possible for programmers like you to handle the events in your own programs. Another benefit is that if you want to change the behavior of a class you're inheriting from, you can do so simply by overriding the appropriate member function. The event-handling member functions all have names that begin with On. For example, the event-handling member function for the MouseMove event is named OnMouseMove. You can find all the names listed in the Visual C++ .NET help under Protected Instance Methods. Because these functions are protected, you can only override and call them from derived classes.

For example, suppose you want a form class that tells the user the X-coordinate of the mouse whenever it passes over the form. You want to override the OnMouseMove member function, but to do that, you need to know the signature of OnMouseMove. (See Chapter 18 for more about member function signatures.) You could look up OnMouseMove in the Visual C++ help system, or you could use the IntelliSense features of the Visual C++ editor. (Try typing On and then pressing Ctrl+Spacebar.) Either way, you'll see that you need to declare an OnMouseMove method like this:

```
void OnMouseMove(MouseEventArgs *e);
```

"What the heck is a MouseEventArgs?," you ask. Well, each event-handling member function needs to know something about the event that happened. Obviously, in the OnMouseMove event handler, you know that the mouse moved, but wouldn't it be nice to also know where it moved *to*? That's what MouseEventArgs provides; it has properties to let you find out the X- and Y-coordinates of the mouse cursor. Different events have different arguments.

Technically, each event-handling member function gets passed a pointer to an instance of a class derived from EventArgs (or to an EventArgs instance itself). There are almost a hundred different EventArg-derived classes.

Now you just have to write the OnMouseMove member function definition. To display the mouse cursor's X-coordinate, make a Label control a data member of the class and set its Text property to the X property of the MouseEventArgs, as shown in the following code:

```
void MyForm::OnMouseMove(MouseEventArgs *e)
{
    //Display the x position
    m_poXPosition->Text = e->X.ToString();
}
```

If you run this program, you'll see that the X-coordinate label is updated only when the mouse passes over a blank part of the form. That's because when the mouse is over one of the controls on the form, that control is getting the MouseMove events, so the form doesn't see them.

Good managers delegate their events

It would get pretty tiring if the only way to handle events was to create a derived class and override member functions. .NET avoids that by making it possible for you to delegate event-handling responsibility to a different class. Delegates work really well for forms and their controls. Generally, you don't need to derive new classes for controls; the built-in functionality works fine. But you do need to handle events to know when a user did something important, such as clicked the Order Pizza button. Delegates make it possible to do that in the class of the form where the button appears.

To add a delegate for a given event, follow these steps:

    1. Declare and define the event-handler member function.

    2. Add the delegate.

Declaring and defining event-handler member functions

Each event has a particular delegate type associated with it. The delegate type decides what your event-handler member function must look like. The Click event, for example, has a delegate type of EventHandler. EventHandler member functions take two arguments:

```
void Change_Clicked(Object *sender, EventArgs *e);
```

The sender argument is the object that generated the event. In the example, it's the button the user clicked. The EventArgs argument would contain information about the event. In the example, all you care about is that the button was clicked, so .NET uses the generic EventArgs, which doesn't have additional information.

.NET doesn't enforce any kind of naming convention for event-handler member functions, but it's a good idea to name yours with some pattern that reminds you of the control and which event the code is handling. For example, Change_Clicked is pretty clearly the Click event handler for the Change button.

The definition of Change_Clicked loads another image into the picture box:

```
void MyForm::Change_Clicked(Object *sender, EventArgs *e)
{
    //Switch the image that is displayed
    m_poImg->Image = Image::FromFile("..\\desert5.jpg");
}
```

Adding delegates

So, having added an event handler, you're finished, right? Nope. You have code that does something, but you haven't told .NET when to do it. You still need to associate the `Click` event with your event-handler delegate.

The process of adding a delegate has four important elements:

- ✔ The control for which you want to handle events
- ✔ The event you want to handle
- ✔ The delegate type for the event
- ✔ The event-handler member function

In the example, the control is the Change button, stored in a data member named `poChange`. The event is `Click`, which has a delegate type of `EventHandler`. The member function is named `Change_Clicked`. So, to add our event handler, use the following code:

```
poChange->Click += new EventHandler(this, Change_Clicked);
```

This approach works for other events too. For example, to handle the `ChangeUICues` event — which fires when the user tabs among controls on a form or clicks a control to give it the focus — you'd look up `ChangeUICues` and find that the delegate type is `UICuesEventHandler`, which requires an event-handler member function with a specific signature:

```
void Change_UICues(Object *sender, UICuesEventArgs *e);
```

Adding the delegate looks like this:

```
poChange->ChangeUICues += new UICuesEventHandler(this,
          Change_UICues);
```

So why do you have to use the += operator to add a delegate? Because .NET supports *multiple* event handlers for events. If you used the = assignment operator, you'd overwrite any other event handlers. Using += lets you *add* yours.

For the complete program used in this section, look in the Events folder on the CD accompanying this book.

Part IV
The Part of Tens

The 5th Wave   By Rich Tennant

"OK, I think I forgot to mention this, but we now have
a Web management function that automatically alerts
us when there's a broken link on The Aquarium's
Web site."

In this part . . .

Part IV presents several lists of tips and ideas that can be invaluable as you go out and start writing your own programs.

The first chapters in Part IV are full of tips that help with some of the common (and annoying) problems that you're likely to run into. Remember, sooner or later, all of us (even computer gurus) run into problems or make silly mistakes. These chapters also tell you why the problems happened, so you can learn from your mistakes.

The last chapter lists the top ten .NET Framework classes. If you find out what some of the common .NET classes do, you'll have an easier time figuring out how the various Microsoft sample programs work their magic.

Chapter 23

Ten Syntax Errors

*A*ll types of things can lead to syntax errors. This chapter describes some of the common mistakes made by C++ programmers, the symptoms you're likely to observe as a result of these mistakes, and solutions to the problems.

If you get a syntax error and you need more help, click the syntax error in the Output window and press the F1 key. The help system will pop up to provide you with a lot more information about what went wrong and how you might correct it.

Using the Wrong Include Paths

Symptom:

```
fatal error C1083: Cannot open include file: 'foo.h': No
such file or directory
```

Using the wrong include path is a common mistake. You know you did this if you get an error message like the preceding one, followed by a million syntax errors about things not being defined.

Make sure the header file you need to load is in the directory in which your source files are located or in the set of include file directories. (Choose Tools⇨Options and select the VC++ Directories category under Projects. In the Show Directories For list, select Include Files.)

The other, less common cause for this problem is that you used ⟨ ⟩ rather than " " to surround a header name. Use " " if the header file is in the same directory as your sources because ⟨ ⟩ searches only the directories specified in the list of include paths.

Missing a Semicolon

Symptoms:

```
error C2628: 'bar' followed by 'int' is illegal (did you
          forget a ';'?)
error C2144: syntax error : 'int' should be preceded by ';'
error C2143: syntax error : missing ';' before '}'
```

Having a missing ; in your code is another common problem. Most often, you receive the three error messages shown here, but you might also receive other errors telling you that a line isn't terminated properly or that lines are really messed up.

Essentially, what's happening is that the compiler doesn't know where to stop, so you usually get the error for the line *after* the one that's missing the semicolon. The solution is simple: Look over your code, starting with the line indicated as having an error and moving upward, to find where you need the semicolon.

One of the most common causes is forgetting to use } ; to end a class definition. (This causes the unexpected 'class' 'foo' error.) If you're not sure about the rules on when to use semicolons, refer to Chapter 12.

Forgetting to Include a Header File

Symptoms:

```
error C2065: 'a' : undeclared identifier
error C2065: 'sin' : undeclared identifier
error C2440: '=' : cannot convert from ''unknown-type'' to
          ''unknown-type''
```

Forgetting to include a header file is another classic mistake. You can find all types of symptoms, usually indicating that a class, a type, or a function isn't defined, or that a return type isn't what was expected.

This problem frequently happens when you use functions from the runtime libraries but forget to include the appropriate header file. For example, if you use `cout`, be sure to include iostream.h; if you use `sqrt`, be sure to include math.h.

Look at the lines where the compiler starts spluttering. If these lines use runtime library functions, make sure that you've included the appropriate library. You can check Help or Books Online if you're not sure what library to include.

If the problem is with a function or class that you've defined, make sure you've included the appropriate header file. If you define a class, function, or variable in one file, you need to use a header file if you want to use that class, function, or variable in another file.

Forgetting to Update the Class Declaration

Symptoms:

```
error C2039: 'g' : is not a member of 'test5'
error LNK2001: unresolved external symbol "?bar@foo@□AEXXZ
(public: void __thiscall foo::bar(void))"
```

Forgetting to update a class declaration is a common mistake, especially for folks who are moving to C++ from C. The symptom is typically something similar, like `baz is not a member of foo` (from the compiler) or an unresolved external symbol message from the linker.

By the way, all that strange gibberish in the unresolved external symbol error message is the mangled name for the symbol. As discussed in Chapter 7, mangling is a way that the compiler manipulates symbol names so that each name is unique. When you call `foo::bar( )`, the compiler translates this to `?bar@foo@□AEXXZ`.

C++ is very strict about data types. If you change the parameters passed to a member function, you need to make sure that you also update the class declaration. If, as is common practice, you have placed the class declaration in a header file, be sure to update the header file. Likewise, if you add new member functions to a class, make sure that you update the class declaration, too.

Using the Class Name Rather Than the Variable Name

Symptoms:

```
warning C4832: token '.' is illegal after UDT 'error7'
error C2275: 'error7' : illegal use of this type as an
              expression
error C2143: syntax error : missing ';' before '.'
```

Using the class name rather than the variable name when accessing an instance of a class is another classic mistake made by C programmers switching to C++. You usually get a syntax error indicating that the type you've used is illegal. You might also get a message saying a period or the -> operator is causing some problem.

Remember that the name of a variable is different from the name of a type of a class. For example, suppose you have the following code:

```
CDialog foo;
```

Here, foo is a variable of class type CDialog. If you want to call the DoModal member function, you must do this:

```
foo.DoModal();
```

not this:

```
CDialog.DoModal();
```

Forgetting the Semicolon after a Class Declaration

Symptoms:

```
error C2146: syntax error : missing ';' before identifier
             'foo'
fatal error C1004: unexpected end of file found
```

If you forget to put ; after a class declaration, you end up with lots of errors. This mistake happens frequently enough to make it worth repeating. Check out the section called "Missing a Semicolon" for more information.

Forgetting to Put public: in a Class Definition

Symptom:

```
error C2248: 'error8a::a' : cannot access private member
              declared in class 'error8a'
```

Forgetting to put public: in a class definition is another common mistake. You get messages such as error C2248: 'bar' : cannot access private member declared in class 'foo'.

By default, any data members or member functions in a class are private. So if you forget to put public: at the beginning of the class definition, you get this message.

For example, if you do the following, you can access bar only from within a member function of foo (so it's illegal):

```
class foo {
 int bar;
};
foo salad;
salad.bar = 1;
```

If you do this, you can access bar from anywhere you're using a foo class:

```
class foo {
public:
 int bar;
};
```

The following will work just fine:

```
foo salad;
salad.bar = 1;
```

Using the Wrong Variable Name

Symptom:

```
error C2065: 'b' : undeclared identifier
```

Using the wrong name for a variable or function falls in the "oh shoot" category. You get messages like 'SongsNum' : undeclared identifier. This mistake usually happens when you're so busy programming that you forget whether you called a variable NumSongs or SongsNum. If you guess incorrectly and use the wrong name in your program, you get a nasty message. Take a deep breath and make sure you spelled your variable names correctly. You get similar problems if you misspell the names of classes or functions.

Using -> When You Meant . and Vice Versa

Symptoms:

```
error C2819: type 'error6' does not have an overloaded member
             'operator ->'
error C2227: left of '->f' must point to class/struct/union
error C2143: syntax error : missing ';' before '.'
```

You might accidentally use -> rather than . (period) if you forget that you have a reference to a class, not a pointer to a class. You start doing this after you get addicted to pointers and hope that everything is a pointer. As a result, you get a message such as error C2231: '.foo::bar' : left operand points to 'class', use '->'.

For example, the following code causes this problem:

```
CDialog foo;
foo->DoModal();
```

This doesn't work because foo is a CDialog, not a pointer to a CDialog. Use this instead:

```
foo.DoModal();
```

Another common mistake when dealing with classes and structures is to use . (period) when you really needed ->. Here, you think you have a reference, but you actually have a pointer. You get a message such as error C2227: left of '->bar' must point to class/struct/union. For example, the following code causes this problem:

```
CDialog *foo;
foo.DoModal();
```

This doesn't work because foo is a pointer to a CDialog, not a CDialog. Use this instead:

```
foo->DoModal();
```

Missing a }

Symptom:

```
fatal error C1004: unexpected end of file found
```

Forgetting to put an ending } is a bit more excusable than forgetting a semicolon. This usually happens when you have lots of nested if statements or other blocks in a function. Generally, you just forgot where you needed to end things. You can get a variety of nasty messages, such as the fatal error shown here, which means the compiler went right up to the end of the file looking for the missing }.

You need to go through your code to make sure that all opening braces have matching closing braces. You can use the editor to help find matches.

Chapter 24

Ten More Syntax Errors

● ●

In This Chapter

▶ Using constructors that take no arguments

▶ Forgetting to end a comment

▶ Using the wrong type for a variable

▶ The program worked as a C program, but now it won't compile

▶ Using nothing rather than a void

▶ Forgetting to use #using

▶ Not using a public constructor when you need one

▶ Putting a semicolon at the end of a #define

▶ You're out of disk space

▶ Things are really messed up

● ●

*H*ey, did you really think there were only ten common syntax errors? Of course not. You're a C++ programmer. And real programmers like syntax errors. Heck, when I was a kid, we had 200 common syntax errors. And we liked it. Now wait a minute, where was I?

Using Constructors That Take No Arguments

Symptom:

```
error C2228: left of '.getFrobozz' must have
            class/struct/union type
```

If you have a class with a constructor that takes no arguments, like this:

```
class Doohickey
{
public:
  Doohickey();
  int getFrobozz();
};
```

you might think you could create an instance of the class, like this:

```
Doohickey myDoohickey();
```

After all, that's how the constructor is written, and indeed the compiler won't complain if you do so. However, the first time you try to use the instance of the class, you'll get an error. The compiler thinks that you declaring a function — remember, they take parentheses too — that returns a Doohickey object.

The right way to create an instance of a class using a parameter-less constructor is to just leave off the parentheses:

```
Doohickey myDoohickey;
```

Forgetting to End a Comment

Symptoms:

> All types of strange errors can occur.

Forgetting to end a comment is much more common with C programmers who use /* and */ for comments than with C++ programmers who use //. That's because the C-style comments can extend across several lines, so it's easy to forget to end them. The result is unpredictable. You get a variety of weird error messages that make no sense.

If you're using the Visual C++ .NET editor with syntax coloring turned on (the default), you know when you have this problem because a bunch of your code is in the wrong color. That is, lots of your code is in the comment color (the default is green) when you really don't want it to be.

You need to look through your code to find where you forgot to put the */.

Using the Wrong Type for a Variable

Symptoms:

```
error C2664: 'error11f' : cannot convert parameter 1 from
              'char *' to 'int'
warning C4244: '=' : conversion from 'float' to 'char',
               possible loss of data
```

Using the wrong type for a variable is usually the result of sloppy programming. You get messages such as C2664 and C4244. This happens when you try to assign to a variable of one type some value that is incompatible. For example, you get it from code such as this:

```
int i;
char* p = "Hello";
i = p;
```

Take a look at the line that has the problem and make sure that you used the correct types. Usually, you just forgot to access a member function or are somehow confused.

In rare cases, this type of error occurs when you have an out-of-date or missing header file.

Note that this problem is common when you take a bunch of C code and compile it with a C++ compiler. That's because C is lax about type checking. C++ is strict and discovers all types of potential problems you never knew existed.

As a last resort, use a typecast to resolve the problem.

You get similar messages if you pass the wrong type into a function. What happens here is that you call some function and pass in an argument that's the wrong type. You get a message such as error C2664: 'bar' : cannot convert parameter 1 from 'char*' to 'int'. Look back over your code. Make sure that you passed in parameters of the correct type. It usually helps to look at the function definitions at the same time you look at where you call them.

It Worked Fine as a C Program, but Now It Won't Compile

Symptom:

The program won't compile as a C++ program.

If your program compiled fine when it was a C program but generates errors when you compile it as a C++ program, you're probably using an incorrect type. C++ is much stricter about type checking than C. Nine times out of ten, the mistake is one of the problems discussed in the section "Using the Wrong Type for a Variable."

Using Nothing Rather Than a Void

Symptoms:

```
error C2556: 'int error12::b(void)' : overloaded function
            differs only by return type from 'void
            error12::b(void)'
error C2371: 'error12::b' : redefinition; different basic
            types
```

Declaring a member function as `void` but defining it without using `void` as the return type generates an error. This mostly bites C programmers. If you've declared that a function is a `void` function in a class but you didn't specify `void` when you defined the function, you get a message such as `error C2556: 'bar' : overloaded functions only differ by return type`.

For example, the following code causes this problem:

```
class foo {
void Bummer();
};
foo::Bummer() {
}
```

In the declaration, `Bummer` is a `void`, but in the definition, no return type is specified (so the computer assumes that `Bummer` returns an int). Returning a `void` is different than returning nothing. You need to do this instead:

```
void
foo::Bummer() {
}
```

Forgetting to Use #using

Symptom:

```
error C2871: 'System' : does not exist or is not a namespace
```

Whenever you write a .NET program, you need to remember to use #using to load any universal runtime library functions that you need. Otherwise, you'll get all types of fun errors indicating that something you know exists can't be found.

Not Using a Public Constructor When You Need One

Symptom:

```
error C2512: 'error13b' : no appropriate default constructor
            available
```

Not creating a public constructor when you need one or not explicitly calling a base class constructor leads to errors. This situation is rare, but it's confusing when you hit it. This problem happens only when you have derived some class from another class; call it foo. The constructor from the derived class tries to call the constructor for a foo but can't find it. That's probably because you haven't defined a default constructor for foo. Or perhaps all the constructors for foo take arguments, and you haven't explicitly called one of these constructors.

Check out Chapter 18 for more information on initializing constructors and creating default constructors.

Putting a Semicolon at the End of a #define

Symptoms:

All types of strange errors.

Putting ; (semicolon) at the end of #define will lead to all types of problems. This is one of those royally vexing mistakes. You get some very strange syntax error somewhere in the middle of your code, but the code looks just fine. If you notice that you happen to be using a macro (bad thing!) somewhere around where the problem occurred, it's quite possible that you have a bad macro. Look for the macro definition and make sure that it's correct and that it doesn't end with a semicolon.

In general, using #define to create macros is a bad idea because, as just mentioned, macros are bad things. That's why this book doesn't explain them.

You're Out of Disk Space

Symptoms:

```
fatal error C1088: Cannot flush precompiled header file:
'WinDebug/NOHANDS.pch': No space left on device
fatal error C1088: Cannot flush compiler
intermediate file: '': No space left on device
fatal error C1033: cannot open program database
           'd:\project\debug\vc70.pdb'
error LNK1104: cannot open file "FOO.exe"
```

It's rare to run out of disk space, but when you do, you get an error message. When you get messages such as these that just don't make sense, make sure that you still have some free disk space. If you don't, erase files that aren't important until you do have some free space. Or visit your local computer store for a little 40GB drive — they're cheap these days.

Things Are Really Messed Up

Symptom:

Error-free code suddenly generates syntax errors.

Sometimes key Visual C++ .NET files become corrupted, leading to strange syntax errors. For example, maybe you come back to your computer after a quick game of Frisbee golf and nothing compiles any more. And maybe some really simple programs give you errors such as `missing ; in stdio.h`. And you know darn well that you never touched stdio.h (or windows.h, or some other file that isn't part of your source code).

This usually means that some Visual C++ information file has become corrupted. Go to Explorer (or the DOS prompt or whatever), and erase the *.PCH files in your directory. If that still doesn't correct the problem, erase the *.SUO file (which is hidden), .VCPROJ file, or *.SLN file. You need to re-create your project, but the problem will most likely go away. You can also try rebuilding all source files one at a time, starting with the lowest CPP source file and working your way back to the main one.

Chapter 25

Top Ten .NET Functions

*I*f Calvin and Hobbes created a common runtime library, they would probably call it GROSS (Get Rid Of Slimy classeS). And it would have only two member functions (whose names should be obvious), mostly designed to throw water balloons. Although .NET has more than two member functions, it doesn't have any for throwing water balloons. At least not yet.

In the meantime, here are the ten most important .NET functions; you'll use them all the time. Functions listed by class::function are typically called directly, whereas those listed with pointer notation are typically called from a pointer to the class.

Console::WriteLine

The `Console::WriteLine` function writes output to the screen.

```
Console::WriteLine(S"What is the starting x position?");
```

Console::ReadLine

You use `Console::ReadLine` to read input from the user. Note that if you want to turn the result into a numeric value, you need to call one of the `Parse` functions.

```
m_nXFrom = Int32::Parse(Console::ReadLine());
```

Int32::Parse

The `Int32::Parse` function converts strings to integers and is quite useful when processing data entered by a user.

```
m_nXFrom = Int32::Parse(Console::ReadLine());
```

Application::Run

The `Application::Run` function runs a form as the `main` application window.

```
#ifdef _UNICODE
int wmain(void)
#else
int main(void)
#endif
{
   Application::Run(new MyForm());
   return 0;
```

Graphics->DrawLine

The `Graphics->DrawLine` function draws a line.

```
void LineObject::Draw(Graphics *poG)
{
    //Create a pen with which to draw
    Pen *poPen = new Pen(Color::Red);
    //Draw the line
    poG->DrawLine(poPen, m_nXFrom, m_nYFrom, m_nXTo, m_nYTo);
}
```

Color::FromArgb

`Color::FromArgb` creates a color object given a set of color values.

```
void LineObject::Draw(Graphics *poG)
{
   //Create a pen with which to draw
   Pen *poPen = new Pen(Color::FromArgb( 128, 0, 128));
   //Draw the line
   poG->DrawLine(poPen, m_nXFrom, m_nYFrom, m_nXTo, m_nYTo);
}
```

Graphics->DrawString

`Graphics->DrawString` draws text in a graphics window.

```
void Factorial::UpdateDisplay(Graphics *g)
{
   Brush *poBrush = new SolidBrush(Color::Black);
   g->Clear(Color::AntiqueWhite);
   g->DrawString(fltResult.ToString(), DefaultFont, poBrush,
         0, 0);
}
```

Image::FromFile

The `Image::FromFile` function loads an image from disk.

```
poImg = new PictureBox();

//Set the image properties
poImg->Width = 160;
poImg->Height = 120;
poImg->Image = Image::FromFile("..\\desert4.jpg");
poImg->SizeMode = PictureBoxSizeMode::StretchImage;
```

Form::OnMouseMove

`Form::OnMouseMove` handles mouse movements on a form.

```
//Handle mouse movements on the form
void MyForm::OnMouseMove(MouseEventArgs *e)
{
   //Display the x position
   poXPosition->Text = e->X.ToString();
}
```

Controls->Add

The Controls->Add function adds a control to a form.

```
this->Controls->Add(poOK);
this->Controls->Add(poTE);
```

Appendix

About the CD

On the CD-ROM:

▶ All the sample code in the book — to save typing time

▶ Some extra code not appearing in the book

System Requirements

Make sure your computer meets the minimum system requirements listed next. Otherwise, you may have problems using the contents of the CD. Note that these requirements are the same as those for Visual Studio .NET — so if you can run Visual Studio .NET, you can run the sample code on the CD.

- PC with a Pentium II-class processor, 450 MHz; Pentium III-class processor, 600-MHz recommended

- Microsoft Windows NT 4.0, 2000 Professional or Server, or XP Professional — note that Windows 95, 98, and Me are *not* supported

- 96MB RAM for Windows 2000 Professional; 128MB recommended. 192MB RAM for Windows 2000 Server; 256MB recommended.

- At least 10MB of hard drive space available to install all the sample code from this CD. Additional space is required to compile the code.

- A CD-ROM drive

- A monitor capable of displaying at least 256 colors or grayscale.

- Microsoft mouse or compatible pointing device

Using the CD

If you are running Windows NT or 2000, follow these steps to get to the items on the CD:

1. **Insert the CD into your computer's CD-ROM drive.**

   Give your computer a moment to take a look at the CD.

2. **When the light on your CD-ROM drive goes out, double-click the My Computer icon (It's probably in the top-left corner of your desktop.)**

   This action opens the My Computer window, which shows you all the drives attached to your computer, the Control Panel, and a few other handy things.

3. **Double-click the icon for your CD-ROM drive.**

   Another window opens, showing you all the folders and files on the CD.

If you are running Windows XP, follow these steps to get to the items on the CD:

1. **Insert the CD into your computer's CD-ROM drive.**

   Give your computer a moment to take a look at the CD.

2. **When the light on your CD-ROM drive goes out, choose the Open Folder to View Files Using Windows Explorer option, and then click OK.**

   This action opens a Windows Explorer window for the CD. The window shows you all the folders and files on the CD.

To use the CD in Windows NT, 2000, or XP, follow these steps:

1. **Double-click the file named License.txt.**

   This file contains the end-user license that you agree to by using the CD.

2. **When you've finished reading the license, close the program that displayed the file.**

3. **Double-click the file named ReadMe.txt.**

   This file contains instructions about installing the code from the CD. You might find it helpful to leave this text file open while you're using the CD.

4. **Copy the Code folder to somewhere on your computer. (The easiest way to do this is to drag the Code folder to your desktop.)**

   You won't be able to open and build the sample solution files because Visual C++ can't write the output files to the CD. (The CD is a read-only disc.) That's why you need to copy the code to your computer's hard drive, where Visual C++ can write new files.

5. **Remove the read-only setting from the files in the Code folder and subfolders.**

   When Windows copies files from a CD, it marks them with the read-only attribute because the files were read-only when they were on the CD. This is kind of annoying for our purposes, because Visual C++ wants to be able to write any changes you make to the solution and project files. If you don't perform this step, Visual C++ will tell you every time you open a solution that it won't be able to save changes to it.

   To remove the read-only setting, follow these steps:

   a. **Right-click the Code folder on your desktop (or wherever you copied it) and choose Properties.**

   b. **Clear the Read-only check box, and then click Apply.**

      Windows asks whether you want to apply this change only to the Code folder or to all subfolders and files too.

   c. **Make sure the Apply Changes to This Folder, Subfolders, and Files option is selected, and then click OK.**

What You'll Find

Throughout the book, the icon on the left appears to let you know the name of the folder where the code appears. Subfolders for each sample project are in the Code folder. Follow the instructions in the "Using the CD" section and you'll be able to open the sample solutions in Visual C++ .NET, build them, run them, modify them — whatever you want.

Following are the folder names on the CD and the chapter where the project is described:

Folder name	Chapter	Folder name	Chapter
Accessors	17	ßConstructorDestructor	18
Accessors2	17	DataStructures	14
BadFact	16	Draw	13
CircleArea	7	Draw2	13
CircleArea2	7	Draw3	13
CircleArea3	9	Draw4	17
CircleArea4	10	Draw5	17
CircleArea5	10	Draw6	18

Folder name	Chapter	Folder name	Chapter
Draw7	18	Graphics	13
Draw8	19	HelloWorld	3
Events	22	HelloWorld2	3
Factorial	11	HelloWorld3	3
Factorial2	11	HelloWorld4	12
Factorial3	12	Inherit	19
Factorial4	12	Inherit2	19
Factorial5	12	Point	13
File	21	Point2	13
File2	21	SquareArea	2
File3	21	SquareRoot	20
Form	22	Strings101	7

If You Have Problems of the CD Kind

We tried our best to compile programs that work on most computers with the minimum system requirements. Alas, your computer may differ, and some programs may not work properly for some reason.

The two likeliest problems are that you don't have enough memory (RAM) for the programs you want to use, or another program is affecting the installation or running of the programs. If you get error messages such as Not enough memory or Setup cannot continue, try one or more of these methods and then try using the software again:

- ✔ **Turn off any antivirus software that you have on your computer.** Installers sometimes mimic virus activity and may make your computer incorrectly believe that a virus is infecting it.

- ✔ **Close all running programs.** The more programs you're running, the less memory is available to other programs. Installers also typically update files and programs. So if you keep other programs running, installation may not work properly.

- ✔ **Have your local computer store add more RAM to your computer.** This is, admittedly, a drastic and somewhat expensive step.

If you still have trouble with installing the items from the CD, please call the Hungry Minds Customer Service phone number: 800-762-2974 ((toll call outside the United States: 317-572-3994).

Index

Notes

Notes

Installation Instructions

To install the CD in Windows NT or 2000, follow these steps:

1. **Insert the CD into your computer's CD-ROM drive.**
2. **When the light on your CD-ROM drive goes out, double-click the My Computer icon.**
3. **Double-click the icon for your CD-ROM drive.**

   Another window opens, showing you all the folders and files on the CD.

To install the CD in Windows XP, follow these steps:

1. **Insert the CD into your computer's CD-ROM drive.**
2. **Choose the Open Folder to View Files Using Windows Explorer option, and then click OK.**

   This action opens a Windows Explorer window for the CD. The window shows you all the folders and files on the CD.

To install the CD in Windows NT, 2000, or XP, follow these steps:

1. **Double-click the file named License.txt.**
2. **When you've finished reading the license, close the program that displayed the file.**
3. **Double-click the file named ReadMe.txt.**
4. **Copy the Code folder to somewhere on your computer.**
5. **Remove the read-only setting from the files in the Code folder and subfolders by doing the following:**
   a. **Right-click the Code folder on your desktop (or wherever you copied it) and choose Properties.**
   b. **Clear the Read-only check box, and then click Apply.**
   c. **Make sure the Apply Changes to This Folder, Subfolders, and Files option is selected, and then click OK.**

Hungry Minds, Inc.
End-User License Agreement

READ THIS. You should carefully read these terms and conditions before opening the software packet(s) included with this book ("Book"). This is a license agreement ("Agreement") between you and Hungry Minds, Inc. ("HMI"). By opening the accompanying software packet(s), you acknowledge that you have read and accept the following terms and conditions. If you do not agree and do not want to be bound by such terms and conditions, promptly return the Book and the unopened software packet(s) to the place you obtained them for a full refund.

1. **License Grant.** HMI grants to you (either an individual or entity) a nonexclusive license to use one copy of the enclosed software program(s) (collectively, the "Software") solely for your own personal or business purposes on a single computer (whether a standard computer or a workstation component of a multi-user network). The Software is in use on a computer when it is loaded into temporary memory (RAM) or installed into permanent memory (hard disk, CD-ROM, or other storage device). HMI reserves all rights not expressly granted herein.

2. **Ownership.** HMI is the owner of all right, title, and interest, including copyright, in and to the compilation of the Software recorded on the disk(s) or CD-ROM ("Software Media"). Copyright to the individual programs recorded on the Software Media is owned by the author or other authorized copyright owner of each program. Ownership of the Software and all proprietary rights relating thereto remain with HMI and its licensers.

3. **Restrictions On Use and Transfer.**

   (a) You may only (i) make one copy of the Software for backup or archival purposes, or (ii) transfer the Software to a single hard disk, provided that you keep the original for backup or archival purposes. You may not (i) rent or lease the Software, (ii) copy or reproduce the Software through a LAN or other network system or through any computer subscriber system or bulletin-board system, or (iii) modify, adapt, or create derivative works based on the Software.

   (b) You may not reverse engineer, decompile, or disassemble the Software. You may transfer the Software and user documentation on a permanent basis, provided that the transferee agrees to accept the terms and conditions of this Agreement and you retain no copies. If the Software is an update or has been updated, any transfer must include the most recent update and all prior versions.

4. **Restrictions on Use of Individual Programs.** You must follow the individual requirements and restrictions detailed for each individual program in the "About the CD-ROM" appendix of this Book. These limitations are also contained in the individual license agreements recorded on the Software Media. These limitations may include a requirement that after using the program for a specified period of time, the user must pay a registration fee or discontinue use. By opening the Software packet(s), you will be agreeing to abide by the licenses and restrictions for these individual programs that are detailed in the "About the CD-ROM" appendix and on the Software Media. None of the material on this Software Media or listed in this Book may ever be redistributed, in original or modified form, for commercial purposes.

5. **Limited Warranty.**

   (a) HMI warrants that the Software and Software Media are free from defects in materials and workmanship under normal use for a period of sixty (60) days from the date of purchase of this Book. If HMI receives notification within the warranty period of defects in materials or workmanship, HMI will replace the defective Software Media.

   (b) **HMI AND THE AUTHOR OF THE BOOK DISCLAIM ALL OTHER WARRANTIES, EXPRESS OR IMPLIED, INCLUDING WITHOUT LIMITATION IMPLIED WARRANTIES OF MERCHANTABILITY AND FITNESS FOR A PARTICULAR PURPOSE, WITH RESPECT TO THE SOFTWARE, THE PROGRAMS, THE SOURCE CODE CONTAINED THEREIN, AND/OR THE TECHNIQUES DESCRIBED IN THIS BOOK. HMI DOES NOT WARRANT THAT THE FUNCTIONS CONTAINED IN THE SOFTWARE WILL MEET YOUR REQUIRE-MENTS OR THAT THE OPERATION OF THE SOFTWARE WILL BE ERROR FREE.**

   (c) This limited warranty gives you specific legal rights, and you may have other rights that vary from jurisdiction to jurisdiction.

6. **Remedies.**

   (a) HMI's entire liability and your exclusive remedy for defects in materials and workman-ship shall be limited to replacement of the Software Media, which may be returned to HMI with a copy of your receipt at the following address: Software Media Fulfillment Department, Attn.: *Visual C++ .NET For Dummies*, Hungry Minds, Inc., 10475 Crosspoint Blvd., Indianapolis, IN 46256, or call 1-800-762-2974. Please allow four to six weeks for delivery. This Limited Warranty is void if failure of the Software Media has resulted from accident, abuse, or misapplication. Any replacement Software Media will be warranted for the remainder of the original warranty period or thirty (30) days, whichever is longer.

   (b) In no event shall HMI or the author be liable for any damages whatsoever (including without limitation damages for loss of business profits, business interruption, loss of business information, or any other pecuniary loss) arising from the use of or inability to use the Book or the Software, even if HMI has been advised of the possibility of such damages.

   (c) Because some jurisdictions do not allow the exclusion or limitation of liability for consequential or incidental damages, the above limitation or exclusion may not apply to you.

7. **U.S. Government Restricted Rights.** Use, duplication, or disclosure of the Software for or on behalf of the United States of America, its agencies and/or instrumentalities (the "U.S. Government") is subject to restrictions as stated in paragraph (c)(1)(ii) of the Rights in Technical Data and Computer Software clause of DFARS 252.227-7013, or subparagraphs (c)(1) and (2) of the Commercial Computer Software - Restricted Rights clause at FAR 52.227-19, and in similar clauses in the NASA FAR supplement, as applicable.

8. **General.** This Agreement constitutes the entire understanding of the parties and revokes and supersedes all prior agreements, oral or written, between them and may not be modified or amended except in a writing signed by both parties hereto that specifically refers to this Agreement. This Agreement shall take precedence over any other documents that may be in conflict herewith. If any one or more provisions contained in this Agreement are held by any court or tribunal to be invalid, illegal, or otherwise unenforceable, each and every other provision shall remain in full force and effect.